The COUNTERWEIGHT HANDBOOK

The

COUNTERWEIGHT

HANDBOOK

*Principled Strategies for Surviving
and Defeating Critical Social Justice
—at Work, in Schools, and Beyond*

HELEN PLUCKROSE

PITCHSTONE PUBLISHING
DURHAM, NORTH CAROLINA

Pitchstone Publishing
Durham, North Carolina
www.pitchstonebooks.com

Library of Congress Cataloging-in-Publication Data

Names: Pluckrose, Helen, author.
Title: The counterweight handbook : principled strategies for surviving and
  defeating critical social justice - at work, in schools, and beyond /
  Helen Pluckrose.
Description: Durham, North Carolina : Pitchstone Publishing, [2023] |
  Includes bibliographical references and index. | Summary: "Over the last
  several years, organizations and institutions throughout the West have
  adopted comprehensive diversity, equity, and inclusion policies and
  mandated new forms of employee and student training on antiracism,
  unconscious bias, gender diversity, cultural sensitivity, and related
  topics. The stated goals of these programs are often reasonable if not
  noble—to create a more welcoming space and inclusive environment for
  all. But such training, when based on the activist ideology known as
  Critical Social Justice, crosses an illiberal line when participants are
  required to affirm beliefs they do not hold. Indeed, the mildest
  questions about or objections to common teachings in these
  sessions—that all white people are racists, that all underrepresented
  minorities are oppressed or useful tools of the majority, that sex and
  gender differences have no biological basis—are regularly met with pat
  commands: "Educate yourself," "Do the work," "Listen and learn." At
  work, raises, promotions, and even future employment may well depend on
  one's nodding approval during such training. At school, grades,
  nominations, and awards may be contingent upon one's active agreement
  with these ideological beliefs. When faced with such a
  predicament—between silent submission and risky if ethical
  opposition—what is a person to do? The Counterweight Handbook provides
  individuals with a practical and easily navigable guide to understanding
  and addressing the issues that are likely to arise when this activist
  ideology is implemented in their organization or institution. It also
  teaches them what to do when they are asked to affirm their commitment
  to beliefs they simply do not hold, undergo training in an ideology they
  cannot support, or submit themselves to antiscientific testing and
  retraining of their "unconscious" minds. It is for everyone who wishes
  to push back against the hostile work and educational environments such
  training inevitably creates—or who fears being fired, censored, or
  cancelled for their sincere beliefs and principled convictions"—
  Provided by publisher.
Identifiers: LCCN 2022054260 | ISBN 9781634312288 (cloth) | ISBN
  9781634312295 (ebook)
Subjects: LCSH: Control (Psychology) | Cancel culture. | Opposition
  (Political science)
Classification: LCC BF632.5 .P583 2023 | DDC 158.1—dc23/eng/20230222
LC record available at https://lccn.loc.gov/2022054260

Contents

Acknowledgments

My most profound thanks must always be to Carrie Clark, the reason Counterweight existed at all, and it wasn't just me pouring everybody into a Discord server and triaging emergencies extremely inefficiently. Thank you for your amazing logistical brain that manages to somehow keep up with everything and everyone, produce briefings on them all at the drop of a hat, and plan out and oversee a dozen projects all at once. You exhaust me, woman. I am always indebted to Kevin Lowe, whose immense, systemizing, analytical brain is equally sharp at detecting flaws and inconsistencies in ethical arguments and at solving tech problems. Thank you for being our Head Vulcan. (Yes, that is a perfectly appropriate job title). Thank you to Harriet Terrill, our first successful client, then media manager, then CEO, for her astonishing versatility, creativity, patience, persistence, organization, and positivity and to Isobel Marston, her right-hand woman who managed to fly in and produce things of greatness in between changing the grading curve of various philosophy departments and caring for people overcoming addiction. The two of you not only made Counterweight work, but restored my faith in humanity when I was at risk of losing it. I am extremely grateful for the input of Laura Walker-Beavan, a deeply knowledgeable critic of postmodern thought and Critical Social Justice theories from a consistently principled and scrupulously honest liberal position.

Special thanks must go to Mike Burke and Elizabeth Spievak, the heart of the Counterweight academic team, who kept its vision alive and its resources intact and have done great things since, even while facing intense and unjust cancellation attempts themselves. Mike, you are the perfect liberal conservative foil to my liberal leftism (but do stop trying to steal my 'walking British stereotype" crown. You will fail). Elizabeth, the way you have powered through everything with grace, fairness, and compassion intact is awe-inspiring. I am deeply grateful to Jennifer Richmond, who has been astonishingly productive and ever-engaged in a dozen different projects and bringing everybody together despite a truly hellish few years. Thank you, my friend. Thanks too to Jennifer Friend, whose dedication to preserving the therapeutic profession and supporting those struggling in authoritarian Critical Social Justice environments almost makes up for her tutworthy sense of humor and tea-heresy. I owe much to Trish Nayna Schwerdtle, defender of rigorous scholarship in medicine and humanitarian aid, a woman of such steely determination that whenever she says "I will make time," I imagine her literally altering the laws of physics, and to Laura Kennedy whose immensely powerful brain is surpassed only by her ability to verbally eviscerate the rude, the presumptuous and the authoritarian in a softly spoken sentence. Thanks to Neil Thin, whose endless calm, kindness, balance, and reasonableness make him an invaluable asset to any project and to James Petts, whose precision in reasoning and ethical consistency can be eye-watering but valuable and somewhat softened by his ability to make excellent cakes. I appreciate all the prominent public figures who made Counterweight a well-known resource and the truly liberal organizations in our orbit who remain steadfastly principled despite great pressure to buckle one way or the other, particularly, the Institute of Liberal Values, Free Black Thought, and Queer Majority.

The COUNTERWEIGHT HANDBOOK

Introduction: The Problem of Critical Social Justice at Work and in Schools

If you work or study in the United States, the United Kingdom, or any number of other Western countries, you are probably familiar with the words diversity, equity, and inclusion (DEI) and many of the policies and programs that come with it, such as antiracist or unconscious bias training. Today, almost all major corporations and universities have offices committed to DEI, with many having vast bureaucracies tasked with advancing and promoting DEI agendas.[1] Just over half of workers in the United States have DEI trainings or meetings at work,[2] and it is not uncommon for schools—from universities to preschools—to ask prospective faculty, students, or families how they will contribute to a culture of diversity and inclusion. Such requests seem benign to the uninitiated. Surely all people of goodwill want to be inclusive of a diverse range of people? Companies, universities, and schools have a legal responsibility to comply with antidiscrimination law and a moral responsibility to oppose discrimination against people on the grounds of their race, sex, sexuality, etc. Isn't DEI just a natural extension of that obligation? It should come as no surprise to anyone reading this book that the answer is no. In practice, diversity, equity, and inclusion are inextricably connected with an illiberal, authoritarian ideology.[3]

This reality is becoming increasingly clear to increasing numbers of people. Those who were hitherto only vaguely aware of this ideology as something that belongs to an academic activist culture or that only mattered in the online culture wars have suddenly found themselves confronted with it and been told to "educate themselves," "do the work," or otherwise commit to affirming their belief in the tenets of this ideology. It is no longer something that one can avoid by simply avoiding academics, activists, or the parts of the Internet that are bathed in the culture wars. Indeed, today it is actively being promoted by otherwise liberal democratic governments and is coming into places people have to go and cannot simply avoid, such as work or school or even the doctor's office.[4] This ideology, with its authoritarian prescriptions and coercive policies, represents a belief system that is sometimes referred to as "wokeism" or "cancel culture." But it can more precisely be referred to as "Critical Social Justice," an approach to social justice activism that has a basis in neo-Marxist concepts of "critical consciousness"—being aware of oppressive power systems that most people cannot see—but derives more from postmodern concepts of knowledge as a construct of power operating in the service of the powerful and perpetuated by language.

This book is intended to be a resource for people who are suffering from the imposition of Critical Social Justice ideology on them at their place of work, in their university or school, or in their wider community, and who object to it and wish to combat it based on liberal principles. Although I explain Critical Social Justice in greater depth elsewhere in the book, I first must make one thing plain: Critical Social Justice is not synonymous with "social justice"—the aim for a just society—which can be approached using any number of frameworks, even if many Critical Social Justice proponents believe and act as though their approach is the one and only form of social justice. While some might approach social justice from a Critical Social Justice perspective or a religious perspective or a socialist perspective, I approach social justice issues from a liberal humanist perspective and will use the word "liberal" quite frequently in this book. If you Google my name or read an article about me, you will most likely find me described as an "anti-woke campaigner" or a "critic of wokeness,"[5] but only because this is less of a mouthful than "advocate of liberal approaches to social justice and critic of Critical approaches to social justice who nevertheless wants everyone to be free to hold and express whatever views they have (including woke ones) provided they don't impose them on anybody else."

It is important to understand that this term, liberal, when used in its philosophical sense, does not refer to and should not be read as a synonym for the political left, a conflation often made in the United States. Rather, it refers to a broad set of values that seeks to defend every person's freedom of belief and speech, support viewpoint diversity, and recognize and value our shared humanity. With this comes the moral responsibility to defend the same rights, freedoms, and responsibilities for everybody. Under this definition, which is the one that defines liberal democracies, liberalism can be found on both the political left and political right. American readers might be most familiar with it as the principle that all people should be considered equally deserving of the right to life, liberty, and the pursuit of happiness. While liberals on either side of the political spectrum may disagree about economic issues and other issues of policy, they are united in their support for individual liberty, common humanity, freedom of belief and speech, the value of viewpoint diversity, and the need for consistent principles in which the same rules and freedoms apply to everyone. This is where "liberals," in the broadest sense of the word, often find their own principles of social justice at odds with those of "Critical Social Justice" and, increasingly, find themselves in need of defending not only their rights but also their principles.

In *Cynical Theories*, published in the summer of 2020,[6] James Lindsay and I presented a genealogy of Critical Social Justice ideas and made the case for liberal principles in the face of them. We described the problem of (Critical) Social Justice as "reified postmodernism" and argued that it had solidified into its current form in academia around 2010. This more easily graspable and dogmatic form of earlier theories thoroughly crossed the barrier of academia to become a significant cultural force in mainstream society across the Anglosphere by around 2015,[7] and it continued to escalate with each passing year. Until the summer of 2020, Critical Social Justice activism had manifested mostly as small eruptions, like bubbles surfacing out of agitated lava, often on the very university campuses on which the ideology had been cultivated and refined.[8] For example, the academic couple Nicholas and Erika Christakis aroused angry student protests at Yale University for suggesting students should be able to choose their own Halloween costumes; psychologist Jordan Peterson faced wrath at the University of Toronto for challenging the compelled use of preferred pronouns; biology professor Bret Weinstein was chased off the campus of Evergreen State College after he objected to white people being asked to remain home for a ceremonial "Day of Absence"; social critic Camille Paglia caused outrage by criticizing aspects of the #MeToo movement at the University of the Arts; and law professor Ronald Sullivan's appointment as a faculty dean at Harvard University was not renewed after he joined disgraced Hollywood producer Harvey Weinstein's legal defense team.[9]

The same type of phenomenon was occurring in other tightly knit, highly competitive fields and industries populated with graduates of elite universities, such as Hollywood: talk show host Ellen DeGeneres was condemned for posting a picture of herself riding the back of black Olympic athlete Usain Bolt; actor Matt Damon was pilloried for suggesting some forms of sexual assault were more serious than others; comedian Kevin Hart was uninvited from hosting the Oscars for past use of homophobic slurs; and J. K. Rowling was threatened for defending the concept of "women" as a biological sex category.[10] Explosions occurred in other enclosed communities as well, ranging from knitting to young adult publishing,[11] that did not always gain nearly as much national or even international attention but that all had the same ideological imprint and exhibited the same dogmatic fervor. To many of us addressing the issue of authoritarian Critical Social Justice and hearing from people regularly, it seemed clear that these visible explosions occurring mostly in intense enclosed communities signaled a vast ideological pressure below the surface that would lead to a much larger culture-wide explosion.

The trigger for that explosion finally occurred in the late spring of 2020. In a period of lockdowns and in a culture of fear over a virus that was not yet fully understood, an unarmed black man suspected of a petty crime died at the knee of a police officer with a reputation for using excessive force. The death of George Floyd energized the already active and influential Critical Social Justice antiracist movement and ignited mass protests under the banner of Black Lives Matter that raged across the United States, much of the Anglosphere, and parts of Europe throughout the summer. Politicians, celebrities, and businesses large and small immediately pledged their allegiance and commitment to the cause—or at least to its slogans. Seemingly overnight, Critical Social Justice ideas were mainlined directly into many of our most important institutions and informed many of their most important policies and programs, while mainstream media played the role of cheerleader and social media companies played the role of enforcer, suppressing or outright banning certain contrarian or dissenting views. This led people to organize into self-selected echo chambers, further creating a false sense of consensus around Critical Social Justice, even as it encouraged a culture of fear, grievance, hostility, and polarization. In the face of this dogmatic and authoritarian ideological movement that had suddenly engulfed not only places of work but also society at large, those who objected to it or even had basic questions about it often either kept their heads down and quietly submitted to training or reeducation of one kind or another, or were outright bullied into compliance for fear of being canceled, mobbed, or fired.

For every cancellation or public outrage that had made headlines, there were countless people quietly being fired or disciplined or having it made very clear to them what they were or were not allowed to believe with a short email of termination or a curt meeting with a human resources officer. Vast numbers of people whose lives or work were adversely affected simply weren't notable enough to have their more routine dismissal or demotion tried in the court of public opinion. Everyday people caught up in this cauldron that was not of their making and from which they wished to escape searched for some kind of resolution. In the vast majority of cases, they did not understand why their place of work or their place of education had suddenly adopted an authoritarian ideology that demanded their compliance, and they sought ways to make sense of it and to find a way out without risking their employment or education.

As someone whose work criticizing Critical Social Justice and highlighting its excesses had made international headlines in recent years—and who had just cowritten a best-selling book on the subject—many of those same people began reaching out to me. Hundreds of emails began pouring into my inbox and the inboxes of many of my colleagues and collaborators each day from people seeking help with the new illiberal and dogmatic policies and training programs rooted in Critical Social Justice at their workplace, university, or school. In this context of unprecedented demand and acute need, I cofounded Counterweight, an organization aimed at helping those faced with coercive Critical Social Justice practices in just about any and every conceivable type of setting, including corporations, universities, schools, hospitals, nonprofits, engineering firms, tech firms, emergency services, publishing companies, art studios, museums, professional societies, social clubs, and so on. With every message my colleagues and I received, it became ever clearer that people in all walks of life and all spheres of society were experiencing different manifestations of the same problem.[12]

We heard from people who were concerned that their place of work had implemented Critical Social Justice–based policies and training programs that required white employees to affirm themselves as racists and non-white employees to affirm their adherence to Critical Social Justice concepts of antiracism. None of them appreciated being told what values they held, and all complained that being told they must hold particular values because of their race felt pretty racist.

We heard from parents who were alarmed that their local schools had begun to teach Critical Social Justice beliefs about racism. White parents were concerned that their children were being required to pretend to have been socialized into racist beliefs that actually ran counter to the values they had been taught at home, while non-white parents were afraid of the impact a belief in invisible racial power systems would have on the ability of their children to be confident in the world and succeed.[13]

We heard from volunteers and workers at nonprofits and humanitarian aid groups who were horrified that their organizations had been so deeply infected by the ideology that it undermined the vital services being provided to the most vulnerable people in desperate need of them.[14] As one such individual (who is not white) said to me, "Money going into training humanitarian aid workers about the problems of 'white saviorism' is needed for laboring women and malnourished children fleeing warzones."

We heard from academics who were concerned that Critical Social Justice ideology had begun to enter all academic disciplines and thus made rigorous scholarship and pursuit of knowledge even more difficult. In some cases, they were directly told that Critical Social Justice causes, including DEI initiatives, trump academic freedom,[15] and in others, they faced having to compromise their principles when required to write a DEI statement for a job application, a promotion package, or a grant or to simply accept that they would not get the job, promotion, or award.

We heard from parents whose children were being introduced to Critical Social Justice ideas about race and gender in kindergarten and early elementary classrooms, with teachers using illustrated books and cartoons based on these ideas. In some cases, kids as young as four and five were asked to identify their skin color and the skin color of their classmates and then told that only white people can be racist and only people of color can experience racism.[16] In other cases, teachers encouraged children to think about their sexual orientation and gender identity using the so-called gender unicorn or genderbread person.[17]

We heard from therapists and professionals in the medical field who were concerned that they were being expected to affirm a Critical Social Justice version of gender identity ideology even if they or their patients had ethical objections to the concept of gender or did not believe they had a gender identity or even if their patients were simply experiencing difficulties that had other underlying causes in need of investigation and treatment.

We heard from people who were more broadly concerned about the negative social effects of Critical Social Justice ideology. They ranged from people who had suffered social media dogpiles for expressing a non–Critical Social Justice view to those whose families and friendship groups had become divided over political issues.[18] Navigating these issues was particularly difficult for some of our clients who were neurologically atypical or suffered from anxiety disorders. Many of them reported struggling with increased anxiety and fears that they might accidentally say something that could be interpreted as racist or otherwise problematic, even though they opposed racism and other bigotries. This, they told us, had caused them to become even more anxious in social interactions and even more likely to avoid them, and this was a particular problem for many of them who already faced significant challenges in this area and now felt even more isolated and lonely.[19]

We heard from teachers, parents, academics, students, emergency services personnel, medical practitioners, psychologists, engineers, blue-collar workers, businesspeople, charity workers, and more. Their particular situations were different, but in every case, the cause of their distress was the imposition of the same set of ideas: Critical Social Justice.

Although I eventually had to step away from the heavy demands of Counterweight to recover my health, I have continued to provide assistance to people in trouble, whether they are in positions of power in major institutions seeking help to hold back the Critical Social Justice tide in their organizations or on the lowest rung of their vocational ladder being asked to affirm beliefs they do not hold and morally object to if they want to continue to be able to feed and house their families. Indeed, since the release of *Cynical Theories*, not a day has gone by in which I haven't been contacted by someone in need of assistance or advice because of a new illiberal program, policy, or protocol at their place of work or at their school or in their nonprofit or in their hospital or in their social club. While I and many of my colleagues have done much to help people behind the scenes, the demand for such assistance far outweighs what any one individual or organization can realistically supply. It quickly became clear that an accessible, practical, and user-friendly guide to understanding the problem is much needed—especially one that provides the tools for people to push back against this once insurgent but now increasingly entrenched ideology themselves.

Written with this goal in mind, *The Counterweight Handbook* has been designed to help you, the employee, volunteer, student, concerned parent, or even employer, not just understand the problem but also assess the problem and respond to the problem. The ideas and recommendations I present in this book stem not only from the many years I have spent reading, thinking, and writing about Critical Social Justice ideology but also from my own work directly helping people push back against it. It explains how proponents of Critical Social Justice see the world as structured into invisible systems of power and privilege that everybody has been socialized into and how they propose to fix it using the policies and training programs that you and so many others are today being subjected to. It provides practical advice on what you can do when you are told to affirm your commitment to beliefs you do not hold, undergo training in an ideology you cannot support, or submit to antiscientific testing and retraining of your "unconscious" mind. Consequently, much of the book deals with the basics: what is Critical Social Justice exactly, and how do you determine whether your organization is adopting the ideology in its practices and policies and to what extent? If you establish that it is, the book provides the information you need before you start trying to address it and discusses what mindset and attitude is most helpful to take when trying to raise your concerns. Where possible, we advise people to take a calm, persistent, and polite but firm approach to addressing problems as they arise and to network with others to form communities of resistance and initiate grassroots activism.

Because people so often feel that their options are either to keep their heads down and submit to the ideology or to throw themselves on the grenade to fight it, the book outlines the various ways you can address Critical Social Justice problems depending on the severity of the problem, your own personal circumstances, and your personality and skill set. It also looks specifically at unconscious bias testing and training, explaining how these tools are supposed to work and why they actually don't work and can even be counterproductive and detrimental to an organization. Because it is nearly always most effective to put your concerns and objections in writing, the book includes writing templates that you can adapt to your own needs and a glossary that explains the terms you are most likely to hear or encounter and might need to draw on. The handbook also provides a breakdown of the common talking points you are likely to face and need to respond to when addressing Critical Social Justice problems and includes anonymized case studies to show what doing that looks like in practice. It concludes by discussing why Critical Social Justice must eventually fall and how to prepare for replacing it with an approach to social justice that is compatible with individual freedom of belief, liberalism, and viewpoint diversity.

A growing number of organizations and individuals take a big-picture approach to the problem of Critical Social Justice in the workplace, in schools, and even in government. They aim to attack it from the top down, with the idea that putting legal or financial pressure on companies, universities, and other organizations, lobbying and fundraising for "anti-woke" politicians, and changing incentive structures is the best way to combat Critical Social Justice. Any and all approaches to stopping the influence of Critical Social Justice that are ethical and legal, that will benefit individuals, and that do not themselves lead to the authoritarian or illiberal are worthwhile, but *The Counterweight Handbook* takes a decidedly different approach. It works from the bottom up and is written for individuals who want to combat Critical Social Justice policies and programs in their daily lives and has been developed to help them address the problem they face in the most ethical and effective way possible and with the minimum personal risk. Although this book is aimed primarily at those facing Critical Social Justice at work or in school or university, the book contains useful information for all readers affected by Critical Social Justice, and all users of the handbook should be able to easily dip into the book and find relevant information and advice. No matter your specific needs or aims, however, I strongly recommend that you read the book first, familiarize yourself with its contents, and only then refer back to the various tools and templates if you find yourself needing to take action.

Although there is growing awareness of the problems with Critical Social Justice and its demonstrably negative impacts on the institutions that it dominates, it continues to be a primary driver of society-wide polarization and hostility. It continues to surface in troubling but predictable ways and to pose a significant threat to liberal democracies alongside a rising authoritarian reactionary backlash. Thus, it is essential that concerned individuals take principled action when they encounter authoritarian Critical Social Justice, whether this is by making an issue public, taking legal action, issuing a direct and uncompromising challenge, questioning the materials and supplying counterviews, feeling out support within an organization, or simply declining to contribute to the false impression that there is a consensus in favor of it. Critical Social Justice is too unstable, incoherent, contradictory, cannibalistic, and divorced from reality—and it alienates far too many people, including those it claims to represent—to survive forever, but the longer it retains its power, the more damage it will do to individual people and to society. If liberal-minded people keep their heads down and go along with it, only voicing their opposition behind closed doors or via anonymous social media accounts, it will continue to push into our lives and our institutions, damaging both. If our first goal is to survive Critical Social Justice, our second goal is to defeat it. To do so, we need the positive action of individuals like you who are willing to stand against it on all levels and in all spheres of life, not only for your rights and interests but also our common rights and interests. We, as individuals, need to fight back against this coercive, divisive, and authoritarian ideology wherever we find it and reaffirm our collective commitment to freedom of belief, expression, and conscience.

We are the counterweight that is so greatly needed.

1 Understanding the Theories behind Critical Social Justice: Key Tenets

If you are somebody who has decided to read this book, you will almost certainly already have some idea of the problem that is commonly referred to as "wokeism" or "cancel culture." Because these terms are so slippery, it can be very hard to define them in a universally accepted way and thus to criticize them in a knowledgeable and principled way. This is made especially hard when advocates of the theories behind this particular form of activism insist that the word "woke" is a pejorative used by right-wing bigots to prevent people from talking about important issues of social justice or maintain that cancel culture is a myth created to shield those with privilege from accountability and to delegitimize the marginalized who call out bigotry.[1] Nevertheless, "wokeism" refers to a real phenomenon with identifiable characteristics that is not simply about opposition to racism or other bigotries.[2] After all, opposition to prejudice and discrimination is central to all ethical frameworks that seek a more just society where nobody is disadvantaged due to their immutable characteristics. Equally, cancel culture refers to a real phenomenon that operates much more broadly than by moralizing scorn aimed at celebrities and other high-profile people on social media for something they've said, done, or believe. It affects many more average people who have been bullied, pilloried, shamed, or fired simply for expressing an unpopular idea or for asking the wrong question,[3] and we see manifestations of it daily that threaten fundamental rights and inhibit democratic processes.[4] Rather than use these two separate but interrelated terms that are often inadequately defined and overly charged, however, I will refer to this overall phenomenon as "Critical Social Justice" to be precise in my meanings, definitions, and prescriptions.[5]

The core tenets of Critical Social Justice are easily recognizable and distinguishable from other ethical frameworks. Central to this is a belief in largely invisible systems of power that into which everybody has been socialized. This simplistic belief rejects both the complexity of social reality, which does not break down so neatly into identity-based power structures, and the individual's agency to accept or reject bigoted ideas. This makes it different from most other ethical frameworks that oppose prejudice and discrimination. Critical Social Justice theorists and activists apply their "Critical" methods to analyze systems, language, and interactions in society to "uncover" these power systems and make them visible to the rest of us. In their framework, these systems include "whiteness," "patriarchy," "colonialism," "heteronormativity," "cisnormativity," "transphobia," "ableism," "fatphobia," etc., and are believed to infect all aspects of society and even the most benign everyday interactions. The belief that people are unable to avoid being racist, sexist, or transphobic because they have absorbed bigoted discourses from wider society is a tenet of faith that bears testament to its origins in postmodern thought, particularly that of Michel Foucault.[6]

Following on from its focus on invisible systems of oppressive power and how language often serves those systems, Critical Social Justice demands enforcement of the right ways of thinking and punishment of the wrong ways of thinking. When teachers are fired for including black intellectuals like Glenn Loury in Black History Month; when firefighters face disciplinary action for saying they do not care what race or gender identity an individual has when saving their lives; when African Muslim immigrants are barred access to jobs for saying they have *not* experienced any racism or Islamophobia in their new country; and when graduate students are at risk of not being allowed to finish their PhDs for the crime of referring to people who give birth as "mothers," we can safely say that we are living in a culture in which people are removed from earned positions for thinking the wrong way.[7]

Critical Social Justice is, at root, based on two core premises: (1) invisible power systems like white supremacy, patriarchy, and heteronormativity permeate all of society, and (2) most people cannot see them because these systems just seem normal to us and, for the majority and the powerful, it is more convenient that we not see them.

Therefore, Critical Social Justice focuses primarily on oppressive attitudes, beliefs, biases, and narratives assumed to exist in society and be perpetuated primarily by the groups in society seen as dominant—the white, the male, the straight—but which can also be upheld by groups seen as marginalized. Just as dominant groups may knowingly uphold things like "white supremacy" to maintain their power or because they are ignorant or indifferent, marginalized groups may knowingly uphold "white supremacy" to curry favor with the dominant groups or because they have internalized the narratives underlying them. According to Critical Social Justice ideology, the way to dismantle these invisible power structures is to address the attitudes, beliefs, and biases people are assumed to have using specific "Critical" methods that center on scrutinizing and policing the use of language in society.

To be "woke," as popularly understood, is to have become aware of these alleged invisible power systems and to want to act to dismantle them. This involves "awakening" others to the Critical Social Justice view of the world and getting them to take on the same assumptions and policing of themselves and others. The symbolism of being "woke" reflects the belief that a specific process is needed to arouse people from their stupor and get them into a state of awareness. This heightened awareness and intentional engagement can be understood as a variation on "critical consciousness" as developed by Paulo Freire writing in the neo-Marxist tradition.[8]

Of course, beliefs that one's ideological group has developed a consciousness of oppressive power dynamics that broader society largely accepts uncritically is a trait of overly certain ideologues rather than of the left. We might think of the concept of being "red-pilled," which references the film *The Matrix,* to describe having been suddenly awakened to a social reality that one had previously been asleep to, and which is associated mostly with the right-wing "anti-woke."[9] Humans are highly prone to believing that they have "seen the light" and have a responsibility to make others see it, too. Those on both left and right who favor the "marketplace of ideas" approach to evaluating ideas on their merits while mitigating one's own bias as much as possible via evidence, reason, and viewpoint diversity generally reject any way of determining what is true that relies on believing one's own ideological group to be awake and all others asleep.

Within Critical Social Justice, the word "consciousness" is used in the usual sense to indicate being awake and aware of a certain reality. However, within academic theory, the term "critical" holds a different meaning from its everyday usage. In common usage, to be critical can mean to think negatively of something, or it can be related to what we'd usually think of as "critical thinking," where we attempt to step back from an issue and survey it as rationally and objectively as possible with the purpose of establishing whether it is true or ethically sound. Critical theorists, however, draw a sharp distinction between the everyday meaning of "critical" and their meaning of "critical." Alison Bailey, a Critical Social Justice theorist in education, makes this distinction explicit. She begins by describing what is meant by "critical thinking":

> The critical-thinking tradition is concerned primarily with epis-
> temic adequacy. . . . To be critical is to show good judgment in
> recognizing when arguments are faulty, assertions lack evidence, truth
> claims appeal to unreliable sources, or concepts are sloppily crafted
> and applied. For critical thinkers, the problem is that people fail to
> "examine the assumptions, commitments, and logic of daily life . . .
> the basic problem is irrational, illogical, and unexamined living." . . .
> In this tradition sloppy claims can be identified and fixed by learning
> to apply the tools of formal and informal logic correctly.[10]

Here, Bailey provides an accurate understanding of what is generally meant by critical thinking. Humans are not perfectly rational, objective, and logical beings; we get at truth best by evaluating arguments
and truth claims on the grounds of the soundness of their reasoning and
the strength of their evidence. To work properly and minimize confirmation bias (only looking at the evidence that confirms what one already
believes) and motivated reasoning (using rationalizations for what one
already believes), this evaluation needs to be done with other people with
different views. Other people are likely to be equally biased but will be
more likely than us to see the flaws in our arguments, point out the problems with our evidence, and offer counterarguments and disconfirming
evidence for us to consider. If an expectation exists that viewpoint diversity, reason, evidence, and civil and honest debate govern these discussions, we are far more likely to arrive at a greater approximation of truth
and find more productive solutions to our problems than if we did not
undertake such an endeavor. This is not a perfect system, but science has
advanced significantly, and human rights and equality have improved
dramatically in societies where this process has been allowed.

As Bailey makes clear, however, this is not how the word "critical"
is used within Critical Social Justice theories. Rather, the word "critical"
in this narrower context refers to the application of a certain theoretical framework to any analysis of society. Because Critical Social Justice

emerged from both neo-Marxist and postmodern thought, the word "critical" refers to criticizing power structures that are believed to exist according to the ideology—and not to seeking truth. For Bailey and other theorists, then, critical thinking, which she accurately describes, is something quite different from things like, say, "critical pedagogy," an approach to teaching methods that uses "critical" theories. She explains,

> Critical pedagogy begins from a different set of assumptions rooted in the neoMarxian literature on critical theory commonly associated with the Frankfurt School. Here, the critical learner is someone who is empowered and motivated to seek justice and emancipation. Critical pedagogy regards the claims that students make in response to social-justice issues not as propositions to be assessed for their truth value, but as expressions of power that function to re-inscribe and perpetuate social inequalities.[11]

Although such ideas might have originated in neo-Marxist thought, Critical Social Justice theorists and activists are less interested in class and socioeconomic status and more interested in race, gender, sexuality, and other identity-based groupings. They begin by assuming an oppressive power imbalance exists and then apply their critical methods to find it. This is how critical theorists Kiaras Gharabaghi and Ben Anderson-Nathe describe it in "The Need for Critical Scholarship," saying, "Critical scholarship is less an approach and more an invitation; it is a way of thinking about research as a form of resistance." They invite scholars "to submit your scholarship that is critical not in its conclusions but in its starting points" and sum up their approach like this: "Critical research is not out to create truth; it aims to consider the moment and looks forward to a way of seeing that moment in ways we could not have imagined. Finally, it invites into the research process an active identification of and engagement with power, with the social systems and structures, ideologies and paradigms that uphold the status quo."[12] This is an explicit statement that "critical" scholarship is not about truth but about criticizing things via a specific theoretical framework that begins with set assumptions about power dynamics and identity.[13]

I have traced the complicated evolution of this scholarship elsewhere,[14] but the assumptions and doctrines that are foundational to Critical Social Justice ideology are rather simple. The core tenets are as follows:

1. *Knowledge is a social construct created by groups in society. These groups are determined by their identity in terms of race, gender, sexuality, and more and are deemed to have either dominant or marginalized positions in society.*

2. *The dominant groups—white, wealthy, straight, Western men—get to decide which knowledges are legitimate and which are not. They choose the ones that serve their own interests.*

3. *These legitimized knowledges then become dominant discourses in society and simply the way to speak about things. Everybody is unavoidably socialized into them and cannot escape being so.*

4. *People at all levels of society then speak in these ways, thereby creating and perpetuating systems of oppressive power like white supremacy, patriarchy, and cisnormativity.*

5. *Most people cannot see the systems of oppressive power that they are complicit in because they have been socialized into having those very specific biases and thus unconsciously act on this socialization.*

6. *Therefore, the systems of oppressive power are largely invisible and their existence and means of operation need to be theorized by Critical Social Justice scholar-activists.*

7. *Only those who have studied Critical Social Justice theories—particularly the marginalized groups who subscribe to them—are fully able to see the invisible power systems and must convey them to everybody else.*

8. *Social justice (as defined by Critical Social Justice theories) can only be achieved by making everybody believe in these theories. This entails seeing and affirming these invisible power systems and their own complicity in them, as well as committing to dismantling them.*

9. *Any disagreement with or resistance to affirming Critical Social Justice beliefs is evidence of either ignorance or selfish unwillingness to accept one's complicity in the oppressive power systems. Thus, any disagreement or resistance is automatically invalid.*

10. *Therefore, the liberal belief in the individual's agency to evaluate a range of ideas and accept or reject them is a self-serving myth, and liberalism, above nearly all other ideologies, is a major impediment to achieving (critical) social justice.*

These ideas were once contained in the somewhat fringe academic departments in which they were developed. Only after they escaped the bounds of the academy and were applied to and acted upon in the world—namely, in the form of Critical Social Justice—did people more broadly begin to take notice of the damage and problems they inevitably cause in practice. A primary reason that an illiberal, authoritarian ideology that spreads by rejecting the marketplace of ideas and individual autonomy, demanding religious-like adherence to its tenets, and taking advantage of people's basic sense of justice and empathy has been able to become culturally powerful is that no one of goodwill wants to stand against social justice. No one ever says, "There's too much justice in this society. We'll need to reduce that," do they? It is, in fact, rather presumptuous for the Critical Social Justice movement to appropriate for itself the title "social justice" and act as though it owns the term—as though the rest of the politically engaged world is seeking something else. Different political factions primarily disagree on the fine details of what a fair and just society should look like and how to achieve that in relation to things like taxes and welfare programs. Nevertheless, there is a general consensus that a just society is one in which everybody is equal under the law and no group is denied access to any rights, freedoms, or opportunities given to others. That is, the mainstream view of social justice is that society should be fair to everyone, from which the view of Critical Social Justice advocates differs profoundly.

People who express concerns about Critical Social Justice are often asked how they can be against social justice, so it is important to know and be able to say that the scholars are using their own *theoretical* definition that differs significantly from other aims to make society more just. Another way of expressing this is to say that "woke" simply means being kind or empathetic and caring about social injustice, a claim often made by well-intentioned people who have mistaken Critical Social Justice for something much more universalist and liberal than it really is. Activists within the field have refuted the claim that "woke" simply means "being kind." They maintain that this definition amounts to a "whitewashing" (repurposing in the interests of white people) of the term because it fails to acknowledge the Black Radical Tradition from which it originates.[15] Similarly, academics have taken pains to inform people that Critical Social Justice is not simply the aim to create a just society and, in fact, stands against many approaches to doing so, especially those based on empirical evidence that focus on the individuality of all people and our common humanity. As education professors Özlem Sensoy and Robin DiAngelo write in their book *Is Everyone Really Equal?*, "Most people have a working definition of social justice; it is commonly understood as the principles of 'fairness' and 'equality' for all people and respect for their basic human rights. Most people would say that they value these principles."[16] They then go on to explain how their own approach differs from this:

> While some scholars and activists prefer to use the term *social justice* in order to reclaim its true commitments, in this book we prefer the term *critical social justice*. We do so in order to distinguish our standpoint on social justice from mainstream standpoints. A critical approach to social justice refers to specific theoretical perspectives that recognize

that society is stratified (i.e., divided and unequal) in significant and far-reaching ways along social group lines that include race, class, gender, sexuality, and ability. Critical social justice recognizes inequality as deeply embedded in the fabric of society (i.e., as structural), and actively seeks to change this.[17]

As this passage indicates, other approaches to social justice may not hold that society is stratified so simply along identity markers or that these stratifications permeate everything all the time. Indeed, people who care about a just society but are not convinced that the "critical" method will help to achieve one can take a variety of approaches to measuring and addressing inequalities, prejudice, and discrimination.[18] Yet, these once-fringe "critical" theories have, by design and intention, entered the mainstream, and its adherents, as taught and trained, are actively seeking to change the inequalities that they believe are "deeply embedded in the fabric of society." They act accordingly wherever and whenever they can, whether in government, the judicial system, corporations, educational institutions, religious congregations, or even hobbyist groups.

The idea that we have all been socialized into horrible bigoted beliefs like white supremacy and patriarchy and that even those of us who think we abhor them have them lurking deeply in our unconscious has been affecting everyday people for some time now in places they simply have to go and cannot avoid. In all kinds of places of work or study and in many vital institutions, people find themselves obligated to allow specialist trainers to dig these unconscious bigoted beliefs out for us, tell us what they are, have us affirm them, and commit to dismantling them via approved processes and re-education materials. Further, these ideas have been adopted and integrated across a wide range of academic and professional fields. Because we, as a society, still need scholarship and expertise that is not influenced or corrupted by ideology, this is a matter of urgent concern.

Critical Social Justice is a worldview that aims to make everything into a zero-sum political struggle around identity and the power dynamics, experiences, and knowledges believed to be tied to them. Critical Social Justice texts—forming a kind of Gospel of Social Justice—express, with absolute certainty, that all white people are racist,[19] that being nonracist isn't possible,[20] that masculinity is pathological,[21] that sex is not biological and exists on a spectrum,[22] that disbelief in the concept of gender identity is killing people,[23] that language is literally violence,[24] and that everything needs to be decolonized.[25] In a matter of a few years, these ideas went from being discussed in obscure academic departments and journals to enjoying significant social prestige and political capital and having immense influence on mainstream media, major corporations, institutions of higher education, and the policies and proposals of major political parties. The dominance of these ideas needs to be challenged more assertively and more unapologetically from a basis of knowledge and consistent principles if we genuinely want to create a better society for everyone.

2 Analyzing the Core Claims
of Critical Social Justice: Simple Resources

The core claims of Critical Social Justice are all intertwined because they stem from the same cluster of beliefs that make up the Critical Social Justice concept of the world and ethical framework. The underlying worldview may seem quite complicated and often baffling, but it is actually very simplistic—not just in theory but also in practice. This base assumption that knowledge is a construct of power created by dominant groups to oppress and marginalize nondominant groups and operating through language inevitably leads to crude truth claims. Although many of the core tenets of Critical Social Justice outlined in the last chapter might seem unfamiliar, you will almost certainly be aware of many of the core claims that flow from those tenets. The base assumption produces far too many simplistic claims to address in any one book, so I will focus on the main ones that you are most likely to encounter—the ones that have seemingly overnight come to be accepted as true by many of our most important public and private institutions, including, of course, the places where you might work, volunteer, or go to school.

Because Critical Social Justice rejects on principle any debate or discussion over its core tenets and claims, it can be difficult to change the minds of true Critical Social Justice believers based on appeals to evidence or reason, but most people in your company, school, or organization are not true believers. Most simply recycle these claims or nod along to them because they, like you, are managers, administrators, employees, or students who want to make a living or get an education and are simply trying to get by without getting fired, expelled, or canceled. Many who are skeptical of Critical Social Justice claims are unsure how to say so without being thought racist, sexist, transphobic, or otherwise bigoted. These individuals can potentially be emboldened by appeals to evidence, reason, and liberal principles. For those who are far less easily swayed by such appeals, once you understand the underlying ideology and basic tenets behind these claims, you can often refute these claims on Critical Social Justice's own terms using its own particular language.

Claim 1: All White People Are (and Only White People Can Be) Racist.

In Critical Social Justice approaches to antiracism, such as those popularized by American theorists like Robin DiAngelo and Ibram X, Kendi, the default assumption is that Western society in general and the United States in particular is set up as a white supremacist system. According to this view, the belief that white people are superior and should have more power and rights than everybody else is legitimized by white people and, therefore, becomes common knowledge. This belief is accepted by all white people (and many non-white people) who are born into this society and who inevitably learn this "knowledge." (Interestingly, Kendi stands out among antiracist scholars for refuting the claim that *only* white people can be racist and that *all* white people are racist, but antiracist DEI training typically promotes the more popular Critical Social Justice assertion, as advanced by DiAngelo and others, that all white people are racist and only white people can be racist[1]—even as the DEI trainers and consultants leading such trainings recommend Kendi's books and highlight other elements of his work.) As a result, everyone speaks as though this belief is true without thinking critically about whether it actually is true or ethical. These ways of speaking—dominant discourses—uphold the white supremacy in society on the level of beliefs and attitudes. Even after legal equality was obtained and overt racism became socially unacceptable, these white supremacist ways of thinking and speaking remained all pervasive and deeply internalized. Hence, black people and other underrepresented minorities continue to be disadvantaged today in ways that are less empirically evident.[2]

It is important to note that, from a historical standpoint, this account is true. White supremacy really was baked into the US system during the eras of slavery and Jim Crow. Racist beliefs did not simply disappear when antidiscrimination laws were put into place or once racism came be recognized as stupid and unethical. The truth of an oppressive racist history and the existence of lingering racist attitudes are overwhelmingly acknowledged by people with a variety of political and ideological worldviews. However, Critical Social Justice theorists and activists understand themselves to be the ones who can see the systems of white supremacy that are as strong as ever while the rest of us remain in (willful) ignorance.[3] As they believe, racial progress has *not* been made and white supremacy is *not* being overcome. It has simply changed form, become harder to see and easier to deny, and thus requires critical theoretical interpretation to be made visible. This belief that they alone are alert to oppressive power dynamics is why they are known as the "woke."[4]

People of color who subscribe to Critical Social Justice beliefs and their lived experiences are held up as authoritative, while those who hold different views about race and racism are largely overlooked or explained away. People of color with different beliefs may be dismissed as having internalized white supremacy or as trying to gain personal advantage in a white supremacist society at the expense of other people of color. Because the theorized systems of "whiteness" and "white supremacy" are largely invisible but believed to be everywhere at all times,[5] Critical Social Justice theorists are needed to interpret interactions and utterances through their critical methodology in order to reveal them. Things that have been claimed as evidence of whiteness include science, justice, liberalism, punctuality, hard work, and individualism,[6] even though all of these can be and are valued (or devalued) by people of all races. Actions that have been claimed to be evidence of racism have included disagreeing with people of color,[7] asking people of color for input on racism,[8] not asking people of color for input on racism enough,[9] complimenting people of color, and smiling at people of color.[10]

Critical Social Justice activists and trainers are needed to convey this to the general (white) public. They must do so to convince them that they have been socialized into unconscious racist biases and are complicit in an invisible system of white supremacy. All white people who hear this message then have a moral imperative to affirm their racism and undertake a lifetime of "work" to dismantle it in themselves. Doing so via mandatory or voluntary (but socially pressured) "training" is increasingly common for employees of both public and private institutions today. At the same time, white people are told that only they can be racist. This is due to the most common and popular definition of racism used in Critical Social Justice activism and scholarship: prejudice plus power. The logic here is clear: because we live in a white supremacist world and only white people have power, only white people can be racist—no matter how prejudiced, discriminatory, or bigoted a non-white person might be toward white people, and no matter who that person is or how much economic, social, or political power that person might have. This is the logic that might lead activists to say a black person can't be racist against Jews or Asians, no matter how prejudiced and discriminatory the person might be toward them in word and action.

Any white person who claims themselves not to harbor deeply engrained racist attitudes that affect the way they interact with others is believed to be, at best, ignorant or, at worst, selfishly trying to preserve their own white privilege. The idea that a white person could encounter a black person without immediately and unconsciously attributing all kinds of negative characteristics to them is regarded as impossible. People's individual backgrounds, upbringing, experiences, and actions are not taken into account. Those white people raised to strongly oppose racism and who continue to hold those values are no less racist than those raised by white supremacists who continue to hold white supremacist beliefs. In fact, white liberals are often considered to be even more racially harmful.[11] This is because the liberal belief that society is made up of a variety of discourses that individuals can accept or reject is seen as hopelessly naive or just a way to excuse oneself from complicity in racism. As with much of Critical Social Justice ideology, this charge is, of course, utterly unfalsifiable and leaves only two options: be racist and admit it, or be racist and deny it. The former is considered virtuous and thus creates pressure on white people who don't hold actual racist beliefs to claim to hold racist beliefs because they want to be seen as good people. The latter is considered contemptible and ostracizes white people who genuinely do not hold racist beliefs and who do not think it is right to lie. It is entirely unclear how any of this will reduce racism.

How to Respond to This Claim

Point out that Ibram X. Kendi and Robin DiAngelo, arguably the two most prominent antiracist scholars, do not even agree on this point. Kendi accepts that white people can be genuinely antiracist (which, for him, is the opposite of racist), saying, "To be antiracist is to never conflate racist people with White people, knowing there are antiracist Whites and racist non-Whites."[12] DiAngelo, on the other hand, urges white people to "accept that racism is unavoidable and that it is impossible to completely escape having developed problematic racial assumptions and behaviors."[13] While these two stances can be made compatible by arguing that Kendi does not mean to refute DiAngelo's view that racist socialization is the norm and DiAngelo does not mean to deny that white people can be active in antiracism, there is a fundamental and antithetical difference in their foundational premises. If you read their work carefully, it's clear that Kendi has a much greater belief in the individual's ability to accept or reject racist ideas than DiAngelo, who seems to believe that the best white people can do is become more aware of their own racism and attempt to do less harm with it. This makes Kendi less reliant on Critical Social Justice ideology overall.

Make known that, according to Kendi, the very statement that all white people are racist is itself racist. Here, you might cite him directly: "Whenever someone classifies people of European descent as biologically, culturally, or behaviorally inferior, whenever someone says there is something wrong with White people as a group, someone is articulating a racist idea. The only thing wrong with White people is when they embrace racist ideas and policies and then deny their ideas and policies are racist."[14] Similarly, he bristles at the idea that only white people can be racist because only white people can have power: "Like every other racist idea, the powerless defense underestimates black people and overestimates white people."[15] This idea is damaging to his own form of advocacy because it "shields people of color in positions of power from doing the work of antiracism, since they are apparently powerless, since White people have all the power. This means that people of color are powerless to roll back racist policies and close racial inequities even in their own spheres of influence, the places where they actually do have some power to effect change."[16] On a pragmatic level, it will be very difficult for a Critical Social Justice–minded trainer to argue against the stance of the leading black antiracist scholar using the leading white antiracist scholar given their own identity-based concepts of authentic knowledge about racism. While Kendi has other ideas that are illiberal, I give him credit for this liberal one, which accepts individual agency and rejects collective blame.

Openly state your guiding principles and make clear that Critical Social Justice is not the only framework from which to overcome any ongoing racism or prejudice. For example, if you hold liberal beliefs (in the broadest sense), you might argue that changes in law and rejection of racism across much of society are evidence that liberalism has worked to change minds and erode racism. At the same time, you might argue that it is erroneous and unethical to attempt to overcome remaining racist ideas by continuing to consistently reinforce the idea that people should be evaluated by their race, which is an approach that serves only to fortify or reconstitute racism, and that we should instead treat people as individuals in order to remove all material and social barriers standing in the way of their success. In this way, today's Critical Social Justice scholar-activists should not be seen as ideologically connected to or the natural predecessors of past civil rights movements grounded in a liberal vision of universal rights and individual liberty.[17]

Claim 2: Science Is Oppressive.

Science is generally regarded negatively within Critical Social Justice because it aims to discover objective truth and is regarded (with good reason) as the most authoritative source of knowledge production yet discovered. Because of the postmodern concepts of knowledge as a construct of power that operates in the service of dominant groups that underlie Critical Social Justice, the high prestige of science is regarded with suspicion.[18] Science is considered a dominant discourse that marginalizes "other ways of knowing"—primarily lived experience that complies with Critical Social Justice theories. Because of its postmodern influence, Critical Social Justice is radically skeptical of objective truth in principle, although it increasingly often presents its own ideas—that is, the belief that invisible power systems like "white supremacy" or "whiteness" permeate everything—as objectively true. This perspective is regularly encountered in the "training" that is imposed upon people.

Relatedly, science and STEM, more broadly, are often falsely claimed to be white, Western, masculine, and imperialist ways of knowing despite considerable evidence that Europe was a latecomer to scientific approaches to knowledge production, failing to develop them until the modern period. Although the Scientific Revolution did occur in the West, science, technology, engineering, and mathematics exist everywhere (and are also denied everywhere for a variety of reasons) and do not "belong" to the West.

The idea that science is an oppressive white, Western narrative leads to the largely false claim that science legitimized racism, sexism, and homophobia. In reality, ideas that non-white "races" were inferior to white ones, that women were inferior to men, and that homosexuality is unnatural were not a product of the scientific method. Rather, they were theoretical assumptions made by early social scientists based on prescientific or pseudoscientific ideas and are no more supported by evidence or scientifically grounded than the theoretical assumptions of Critical Social Justice today.

How to Respond to This Claim

Ask people to consider whether the reason that society regards science as a particularly strong producer of knowledge might be because it has shown that it works—the results of this include flight, the mapping of the human genome, and the eradication or cure of numerous diseases that today allows the vast majority of children to survive to adulthood.

Point out that claiming STEM to be a white, Western, masculine way of knowing is profoundly disrespectful of the vast numbers of scientists, doctors, technicians, engineers, and mathematicians who are not white, Western, or male. Furthermore, this claim re-creates old colonial attitudes that the West is rational, scientific, and advanced while the rest of the world is irrational, superstitious, and backward. This is not widely appreciated by non-Westerners, particularly the doctors and engineers recruited from India, Pakistan, and Nigeria by the Western world due to its crisis of interest in STEM. Suggest that the claim itself is colonialist as it appropriates the Arabic numerals and algebra central to STEM for white Westerners. Suggest that if the goal is to "decolonize" "Western ways of knowing," advocates should start by weeding out Critical Social Justice ideology, which is decidedly a product of the West, and not science, which has been a worldwide project for millennia to which Europe was a relative latecomer.

Make people aware that science did not "discover" the inferiority of non-white races and women or the disordered nature of homosexuals, even if some of the people who advanced such ideas claimed to be speaking on behalf of science. Science is a tool that, in the hands of humans, can be misused, but when used as intended, it is the best tool we have for revealing truths about the structure and nature of the physical world. Application of the scientific method to these theories revealed that "race" is largely meaningless as a biological concept, although "populations" (which do not map neatly onto what we understand as race) can share traits that are sometimes useful to be aware of, such as susceptibility to certain genetic diseases. However, such traits do not indicate superiority or inferiority.

Claim 3: Everything Is a Social Construct.

This is a direct correlation between the rejection of objective knowledge and skepticism of science. Appeals to social constructionism and blank slatism are key features of Critical Social Justice theories, particularly with regard to the sexes. It is, therefore, applied mostly to issues of gender or whatever you want to call the cognitive, psychological, and behavioral differences on average between men and women. The fact that men and women generally differ in some ways is dismissed as the result of socialization. Such differences are frequently claimed to be socialized to give men dominance and make women subordinate. These differences include men and women's disparate degrees of interest in working with things or people, their preferences when it comes to work/life balance, their proclivities toward casual sex, their preferred traits in their partners, their differing styles of communication, and their tendency toward verbal or physical expressions of emotion, on average.[19]

However, social constructionism is also applied to many other issues. While our current understanding of race is that it is largely a social construct (with, as noted above, populations being a more accurate biological definition of differences between groups with shared gene pools), sexuality probably isn't. Activism for gay and lesbian rights was historically based in scientifically supported claims that sexual orientation is innate and in liberal ethics, which held that people should not be discriminated against for feeling romantic love and sexual attraction to others of the same sex or for being gender atypical. For liberals, expanding the same rights, freedoms, and dignity to homosexuals as heterosexuals was a straightforward matter of fairness and equality. Equally, bullying people for their same-sex attractions or for their gender presentation—which are not moral issues and harm no one else—is never acceptable. However, some trans activists who work on Critical Social Justice approaches to LGBT rights do attempt to shame people into being attracted to others because of their gender identity rather than their biological sex.[20] In doing so, they may claim or act as though they believe that sexual attraction (or even biological sex) is a social construct and something that can be made to comply with political or ideological beliefs rather than an innate sexuality that is nobody else's business.

We also see a lot of social constructionism in disability and fat studies. It is frequently claimed by fat activists that obesity, being widely regarded as unhealthy and less attractive, is a social construct born of fatphobia. This is regarded as "healthism" and romantic discrimination. Similarly, disability activists have claimed that being able-bodied is itself a social construct and the preference for being able-bodied over being disabled and even attempts to treat, alleviate, or cure disability are evidence of discrimination based on hatred of disabled people and a wish that they did not exist.[21]

How to Respond to This Claim

Show people the mountains of evidence that cognitive, psychological, and behavioral differences on average between men and women are biologically based and rooted in sexual selection and differing levels of estrogen and testosterone. Further, point out that the assumption that accepting that men and women differ innately at all makes women inferior is itself a misogynistic assumption. Many female-dominated fields—education, psychology, healthcare, and publishing—are highly influential on society, dealing, as they do, with how people think and feel. They are also less likely to be made redundant by artificial intelligence.

Argue that it is extremely unlikely that biological sex or psychological differences on average between the sexes or heterosexuality are social constructs because we are as sure as we can be of anything that we are a sexually reproducing species. Further, point out that we do not need to believe sex or gender or sexuality to be social constructs to be accepting of naturally occurring variations within all of those categories and supportive of the rights and dignity of homosexuals, trans people, intersex individuals, or gender atypical people.

Point out that there is much evidence that obesity correlates with poorer health on average and that concern about this does not indicate hatred of fat people. It is also extremely likely that people who are a healthy weight are perceived as more attractive due to sexual selection, as healthier people are more likely to be able to produce and protect offspring. There is also considerable evidence that the human body does have optimal ways of working that are most conducive to full functioning. The preference to be fully able-bodied or for one's child to be able-bodied is almost certainly not a social construct but simply a recognition of the advantages of all one's body parts working optimally. This does not indicate prejudice against the disabled. The leap from "It is better to be able to see" to "People who can see are better people than people who cannot see" is neither a logical conclusion nor a commonly held belief.

Claim 4: Policing Language and Silencing Speech Is Not Only Necessary but Also Good.

Critical Social Justice ideology's intense focus on language stems from its belief in social constructionism. The Critical Social Justice belief that people are inevitably socialized into white supremacist, patriarchal, imperialistic, homophobic, transphobic, ableist, and fatphobic beliefs stems from the belief that all of these ideas are dominant discourses in society. That is, they are just the common way of speaking about things, and they are all so normal to us that we do not notice them. This creates the invisible systems of power that permeate everything and continue to oppress marginalized groups.

If one believes this, it then becomes necessary to scrutinize language very closely and find the inherent oppressive discourses within it, make them visible, and prevent people from saying them. More than this, it becomes a moral imperative to get people to affirm certain statements that counter the oppressive dominant discourses. This is the only way to get at and dismantle them. Resistance to this can only be a way of protecting one's own privilege or, if one is not of a dominant group, currying favor with it.

This results in a number of society-wide phenomena that we have all become familiar with. Cancellation is central to this. Cancellation may take the form of literally succeeding in getting somebody fired from their job and making them unemployable, or it can take the form of attempts to publicly impugn their character. Consider the cancellation attempt against author J. K. Rowling. She is too rich and influential to literally be canceled but because she said that "sex is real" and that she feels kinship with other biological women, she has been widely abused online.[22] Actors in the *Harry Potter* movies have been pressured or felt the need to repudiate her, and bookstores have been pressured to remove her books. Recall how many responses to her lengthy statement explaining her position simply took the form of the mantra "trans women are women" rather than any attempt to engage with any of her arguments.[23] This is because of the belief that she had put out a harmful discourse that influenced society in a way that hurts trans people, and it must be countered with an opposing discourse to try to influence society in the "right" direction again. Fighting discourses with discourses rather than responding to arguments with counterarguments is a hallmark of Critical Social Justice approaches to social justice.

The idea that language has this degree of oppressive power also manifests in other worrying ways. It underlies the practice of unconscious bias training, where people are assumed to have internalized these oppressive beliefs and need to have them dug out of their unconscious minds via specialized programs. It is expected that with training, they will then accept and affirm that they do have these prejudices and commit to dismantling them. It also underlies the concept of microaggressions, which are understood to reveal the internalized prejudices that have led to the production of systems for people to report microaggressions and the formation of "bias response teams" to address them. The idea that language is dangerous also explains the advocacy of no-platforming, trigger warnings, and safe spaces to protect people from ideas they might find upsetting. Words are not just words—they construct realities.

How to Respond to This Claim

It is of primary importance to question the assumption that dominant discourses are white supremacist, patriarchal, imperialistic, homophobic, transphobic, ableist, and fatphobic. While people with these views certainly exist and certainly should still be opposed, are they really widely regarded as socially acceptable? Does it not seem as though Critical Social Justice itself is more of a dominant discourse in current culture? People aren't being canceled for calling out white supremacy or patriarchy, after all.

Where these bigoted ideas do exist, is there any evidence that attempting to silence them is a better way to defeat them than arguing against them? The strongest argument in favor of freedom of belief and speech is that it allows us to expose and defeat bad ideas through argument. It seems to be highly intuitive to humans to try to ban some discourses and coerce affirmations of others, but does history show this to ever have worked out well for minorities or to have advanced knowledge? On the contrary, both scientific knowledge and human rights have progressed fastest when people have been able to argue for a wide range of ideas with an expectation that reasoned and evidenced arguments will be provided.[24]

While people may well hold all sorts of biases, including racist, sexist, and homophobic ones, these are likely to vary considerably by individual. Unconscious bias testing and training are deeply unscientific and have been largely refuted (see chapter 3), but even if they worked, it is profoundly illiberal to give employers and educational institutions the right to access the minds of employees and students for purposes of retraining them, even if we believe individuals do secretly hold ideas we wish they did not. We can only demand certain *behaviors* by law or by employment policy and try to influence people away from horrible ideas with arguments against them and social disapproval. (This includes Critical Social Justice ideas, of course. Any coercive attempt to "train" people out of them would be illiberal. We can only argue against them, try to reduce their social prestige, and require that people do not impose them on others).

There is good reason to believe that the attempts to protect people, particularly young people, from difficult ideas make them less resilient and less able to cope with differences. As Greg Lukianoff and Jonathan Haidt argue in *The Coddling of the American Mind* and as Bradley Campbell and Jason Manning argue in *The Rise of Victimhood Culture*,[25] it is not at all clear that the no-platforming, trigger-warning, safe-space approach to difficult issues is making younger generations any safer. In fact, anxiety, mental illness, and suicide are rising. Worryingly, it may also prevent them from learning to make and evaluate arguments.

Claim 5: The Marginalized Have Access to Special Forms of Knowledge.

Related to the belief that science is a white, Western, and male way of knowing and developing from the social constructionist beliefs of earlier theories is the current Critical Social Justice belief that all ways of knowing are related to identity. In principle, this makes them all equally valid. However, because white, Western, and male ways of knowing are perceived as having been overvalued for centuries and to have created discourses that justified slavery, colonialism, patriarchy, homophobia, and other oppressive systems, these are to be devalued and other ways of knowing and speaking elevated instead. In the scholarship, this is known as "research justice," and it refers to including as research things that are not generally regarded as such—cultural customs, religious beliefs, experiences, feelings, and unverifiable theories.[26]

Critical Social Justice adherents hold that people are given different positions in society according to their identity and that they then see society from that standpoint. It also believes that because society is set up for straight, white, Western men, straight, white, Western men can usually only see the surface of things. Women can see a little more because they have their own ways of knowing *and* have to live in a society built for men, so they have no choice but to see that, too. Black, indigenous, and other people of color can similarly see more of society because they have their own ways of knowing and have to operate in a world set up by white people. When someone has intersecting elements of marginalized identity, they are believed to be able to see much more of society. For example, a fat, black, disabled, trans woman would have multiple forms of knowledge created by being fat, black, disabled, trans, and a woman, while also having to navigate a society set up for thin, white, able-bodied, cisgendered men. This is understood to produce different levels of consciousness and is often referred to as "double consciousness" or even "kaleidoscopic consciousness."[27]

This belief that the marginalized have access to multiple forms of knowledge that the privileged do not have underlie the concept of "positionality." This means that people see things from their own position and that they are seriously limited in seeing things from any other position. Therefore, we will often hear in the scholarship about the need to engage one's positionality. In journal articles, for example, there is often a section where the scholar situates herself within various positions and states in which ways she is privileged and in which ways she is marginalized to set out the limits of what she can know. In everyday activism or training, we are more likely to hear a simpler version of positionality, whereby white people and men are not supposed to speak on certain subjects—whitesplaining and mansplaining—and they are asked to "listen to women of color" or "listen to trans women."

How to Respond to This Claim

This concept of knowledge as being produced by one's position in society is not entirely without foundation, of course. If one asked a slave owner for his views on slavery, he might present ideas quite different from those of an enslaved person. Similarly, we might want to hear from a wheelchair user about how accessible a certain building is rather than an able-bodied person. But these are solid, material positions in relation to structures of society. The claim that identity itself carries with it certain ways of knowing is much more nebulous and theoretical and requires everybody to see themselves as oppressed in specific theoretical ways.

The idea that there are female ways of knowing, black ways of knowing, or trans ways of knowing is simply not supported by the evidence. After all, all of these groups are ideologically diverse. As mentioned above, many women and non-white and non-Western people disagree that science is a white, Western, masculine way of knowing and consequently practice science as their profession without concern or worry that they are unable to access this way of knowing. Similarly, many women do not believe themselves to live in a patriarchal rape culture, and those of us who don't believe this are liable to have our voices considered to be less authentically female than the voices of those who do believe it. Similarly, people of color can hold a variety of views on race and racism, whether and how it affects them and how to address it, but those who do not subscribe to Critical Social Justice versions of antiracism will be considered less authentic than those who hold the "right" view. This has the effect of allowing only some voices to be legitimate and to be heard.

Often, particular vitriol is reserved for trans people who do not believe in Critical Social Justice approaches to trans activism and consider sex to be a biological category and themselves to still be the sex indicated by their biology at birth. They often refer to themselves as "transsexual" rather than "transgender" and may support gender-critical views. Their "position" is not considered legitimate. Also, many gay men and lesbians do not politicize their sexuality, and neither do many disabled or fat people. They may or may not believe themselves to be oppressed, and if they do find they experience prejudice, they may not perceive it in Critical Social Justice terms of invisible systems of oppressive power or believe themselves to be possessors of certain knowledges and insights tied to their sexuality, ability, or weight. In fact, many women, people of color, LGBT people, disabled people, and fat people are liberals or conservatives or Marxists or libertarians or religious believers and consequently have conceptions of how prejudice works and how to address it that are different from the beliefs of Critical Social Justice activists.

It is sometimes necessary to point out to Critical Social Justice activists that significant ideological diversity exists among groups seen as marginalized, so that when they ask us to "believe all women" or "listen to people of color," they are actually just telling us to listen to those who agree with them. There isn't a problem with encouraging people to listen to those whose views you think are well-founded as long as you admit that you are doing just that. A liberal or conservative could certainly point to many black, female, trans, gay, lesbian, disabled, and fat liberal or conservative intellectuals and recommend their arguments to others. However, they would be promoting their work while openly admitting that they were doing so because they think their ideas are sound and not claiming them to be the authentic voice of identity group X, Y, or Z. It is important that we encourage Critical Social Justice activists to admit that people who don't agree with the same thinkers they do aren't necessarily ignoring the "people of color" but are simply more convinced by other "people of color."

Claim 6: The Lived Experience (of Select Groups and Individuals) Is Authoritative.

The belief in lived experience is directly related to the subject of knowledge as tied to identity and perceived position, but only the lived experiences of people who agree with Critical Social Justice ideas are considered authentic. People often ask why the word "lived" needs to be there when surely all experience is lived. The reason is to distinguish the perceptions, experiences, and beliefs gained through everyday living from other kinds of experience, such as that gained by professional expertise. Lived experience, therefore, is a very subjective thing made up of an individual's sorting of their own interpretations of myriad experiences into a pattern. When this pattern matches the worldview of Critical Social Justice theorists and activists, it is considered authentic knowledge and to have been devalued by the privileging of white, male, Western, or cisgendered knowledge (which is understood to include science and reason).

The lived experience (more accurately, perception) of a marginalized person that complies with Critical Social Justice ideology, therefore, trumps any other form of knowledge, including evidence that truth claims made from the lived experience are not actually true. It is considered a privileged denial of lived experience for anyone from a dominant group to ask for evidence of any claim that complies with Critical Social Justice ideology being made by a member of a marginalized group or to point to evidence that counters such claims. If it is someone's perception that unarmed black people are being lynched daily by police officers while going about their business, or that US or UK society is a profoundly misogynistic rape culture, or that trans women are being murdered daily because gender-critical feminists argue that "woman" is a biological category, this is to be respected as true, and action must be taken against anyone who holds a belief to the contrary. It does no good to show evidence against any of these things and is likely to get one accused of being in support of murder and rape.

How to Respond to This Claim

Point out that members of marginalized groups are politically and intellectually diverse and that one cannot claim to be respecting the lived experience of, say, black people, if one considers any member of that group who does not comply with Critical Social Justice ideology to be inauthentic.

Stress the need to separate perceptions and feelings from data and facts and that, as humans, we can actually care about both. If someone feels and perceives things a certain way, we can care about their feelings and perceptions without throwing data and facts out of the window. We normally do this naturally. For example, if someone has suffered a still-birth, her friends and family and various supportive organizations will care about how she is feeling and what they can do to emotionally support her, while other people—doctors and medical researchers—will focus on the data and facts around stillbirths with a view to reducing them.

A good example of a way in which perceptions can be factually incorrect but still revealing of something of social significance is a study which showed that Britons believed (on average) that 1 in 6 Brits were Muslim when the actual number is less than 1 in 20.[28] It would clearly be ludicrous to demand that this misperception be taken as a true lived experience and acted upon in some way—perhaps by requiring Muslim Brits to minimize their visibility? Yet, it is significant that this misperception exists. It is important to know *why* this disparity between perception and reality exists. In order to find out the cause of it and address related social issues effectively, we need to be able to distinguish perceptions (or lived experiences) from facts, care about both of them, and analyze the significance of them, not simply accept the perceptions of certain groups as authoritative.

Point out that being able to make this distinction between perception and fact is vital for actually solving problems like police brutality and the disproportionate number of violent deaths suffered by black men, the existence of sex offenders in society, and violent crime perpetrated against trans women. Only by understanding the problem and being able to look at data and causes in ways other than the lived experiences of an ideological subset of the affected individuals can we hope to actually reduce genuine and serious problems.

Claim 7: Denial of Racism/Homophobia/Transphobia, etc., Is Evidence of Racism/Homophobia/Transphobia, etc.

Within Critical Social Justice ideology, it is taken as fact that people understood to belong to dominant or privileged groups commonly use a number of defensive moves.[29] They do this to avoid having to accept their complicity in oppressive power systems and to provide evidence of their own innocence. This is understood to be because individuals are invested in believing themselves to be good people, and accusations of holding bigoted ideas make them feel as though they are not good people. Within the Critical Social Justice mindset, this is believed to be a form of self-protective denial that gets in the way of dismantling oppressive power systems. This is most strongly theorized, and in the greatest detail, within Critical Social Justice approaches to antiracism. However, the same arguments can be applied to other perceived power systems.

A straight denial of racism is seen as one such defensive move—specifically, white people claiming that they are not racist and that they evaluate people as individuals. A white person might say, "I don't see race," which is understood to be impossible given the assumption of the inevitability of having absorbed the dominant discourses of a white supremacist society, and so such a statement is just interpreted as a way to ignore racism. This is related to the concept of "color-blindness," which Critical Social Justice antiracist theorists tend to take rather literally as a claim not to be able to notice what skin color other people have rather than just not using it to evaluate them on a social and moral level.[30] It is inconceivable to these theorists that anybody could casually notice what skin color someone else has without leaping to a whole load of assumptions about their moral character and social standing. Any attempt to convince them that this is quite possible and, in fact, normal will just be seen as more denial.

Sometimes, white people will provide evidence of their commitment to opposing racism by saying or showing that they have taken part in antiracist activism or raised objections to racism consistently. Within Critical Social Justice ideology, this is seen as a way of claiming oneself to be a "good white" and thus not part of the problem of racism, which is down to other white people who perpetrate or condone racist ideas and actions. Critical Social Justice antiracists seldom accept this as evidence that somebody is not racist and opposes racism. They will usually regard this as more white defensiveness used in the service of failing to take responsibility for one's inevitable complicity in white supremacist society.[31]

Another way that white people are understood to avoid confronting their own racism is by defending themselves when their actions are interpreted as racist when race had not, in fact, been in their mind at all.

Sometimes, white people who are not racist will attempt to evidence this by pointing out that their partner, child, or best friend is black. This always goes down very badly indeed and is considered a common defensive trope known as "proximity to blackness."[32] Often, activists will point out that slave owners were in close proximity to black people they had enslaved, and this didn't stop them from being racist.

In short, any attempts on the part of a white person to argue that they are not racist because they do not hold racist views, have never behaved negatively to anyone for reasons of racism, have consistently opposed racism, and love and respect people of all races have been anticipated and theorized as white defensiveness or fragility. They are consequently interpreted as an attempt to evade inevitable complicity in white supremacy. The same reasoning can also be applied to a man's denial of his sexism, a heterosexual's denial of her homophobia, a cisgendered person's denial of his transphobia, or an able-bodied person's denial of her ableism.

How to Respond to This Claim

It is particularly worrying when Critical Social Justice activists attempt to undermine the perception that being racist or subscribing to other kinds of prejudice makes somebody a bad person.[33] The consensus that racism is morally reprehensible is a positive development. The Critical Social Justice belief that racism is normal and ordinary and that it is virtuous to affirm oneself as a racist if white is alarming—it creates pressure upon white people who want to be seen as good people to pretend to be racist or to convince themselves they are racist. It is quite possible that a sustained pretense of this kind or a sustained attempt to believe oneself to be racist could result in genuinely developing racist beliefs. It is difficult to see how this will help to reduce racism.

The tendency of Critical Social Justice antiracists to take literally the claim "I don't see race" and to conflate "color-blindness"—holding principles against evaluating people by their race—with racism-blindness—declining to notice when racism is occurring—is profoundly unhelpful. A genuine commitment to principles of color-blindness includes noticing when racism occurs and objecting to it. Neither the statement "I don't see race" nor the commitment to color-blindness literally means that someone becomes unable to notice what color somebody else's skin is. It means that it is no more significant to them than what color their hair or eyes are. This is a good thing!

People who reference their non-white loved ones in defense of themselves against false accusations of racism probably should not bother as this will not be accepted, but the claim that this is no defense because of the proximity of white slave owners to slaves is nonsense. This is an entirely different scenario from having a close loving relationship with another human being. While it is possible to sustain the cognitive dissonance of believing one race to be inferior to another while loving and respecting someone of that race, it is surely much harder to sustain that false belief in such a situation. Nevertheless, this claim should not be made as it will only be used as evidence of your naivety and ignorance of how racism works.

It is much better to just assert one's nonracism on the grounds of disbelief in the premises that all white people are inherently racist and one's own knowledge of one's own mind! Liberals and conservatives (who are not mutually exclusive) generally accept that individuals are not simply vessels passively filled up with the ideas theorized to dominate society by any particular group. They believe that individuals have the agency to evaluate, accept, or reject ideas from among the number that circulate throughout society at any time. If you reject racist ideas, just confidently say so. "I do not accept the premise that all white people are racist. I believe that people can and should choose not to hold racist ideas and I do not hold them."

Claim 8: Intentions Do Not Matter—Only Impact Matters.

Within Critical Social Justice, intentions do not matter, only impact does, and the person saying they have been impacted bears no responsibility for their own interpretation of any event. For example, psychology professor Derald Wing Sue, the originator of the concept of microaggressions, gives the example of a white air hostess who asked him and a black colleague to move to balance out the plane. Although she claimed that their race had nothing to do with them being the ones asked to move, Sue argued that her intentions were irrelevant. She had committed a microaggression because of the way her actions impacted him and his colleague.[34] This claim that intentions don't matter and only impact does is profoundly misguided. For example, if someone makes constant fat jokes around me, I can tell them it annoys me and ask them to stop. If someone tells me they think I am wrong about something, I could assume this is because they think women are ignorant or stupid, but they might just think I am wrong about something, and I should assume this first before feeling "impacted" by misogyny.

How to Respond to This Claim

Acknowledge that a speaker does have some responsibility to be thoughtful and aware of statements that might be hurtful, but a listener also has some responsibility for her own interpretations and feelings.

State unequivocally that, of course, intentions matter. Give the following scenario: If your partner elbows you in the face by mistake, they have been careless, and you have the right to be annoyed with them. If they do it on purpose, they are an abuser, and you should leave them.

Argue that the expectation of great tact and sensitivity and knowledge of all the connotations theorized to exist is not realistic for most people and is particularly difficult for older people, recent immigrants, and those who are neurologically atypical.

Claim 9: Anyone Who Does Not Subscribe to Critical Social Justice Ideology Does Not Understand It.

This is a particularly presumptuous trope common among Critical Social Justice advocates. Because they believe so strongly in their own ideas that we are all socialized into internalizing oppressive power systems, we will frequently hear instructions to educate ourselves rather than an argument for their beliefs. It is not considered possible that anybody could have a strong understanding of the Critical Social Justice belief system and still not subscribe to it. This implies that education (i.e., training) is needed until they subscribe to it. This type of posturing is typical of zealots. A certain kind of religious believer is prone to telling people to read their holy texts if they don't share their faith and, upon being told that they have, saying they couldn't possibly have understood them properly if they still don't believe in the faith and must study (or pray) more.

There are variations on the claim that one simply hasn't educated oneself if one still doesn't believe in invisible power systems. The word "learning" is often used when what is meant is "subscribing to Critical Social Justice beliefs." This is used alongside "unlearning" the beliefs one is assumed to hold simply because one is born into a certain identity group within a certain society. To be fair, this isn't applied only to nonbelievers. Robin DiAngelo, the leading scholar asserting the inevitable racism of all white people, describes herself as still engaged in a lifelong battle to unlearn racism and learn antiracism. Similarly, a Twitter thread from the Vagina Museum read: "Instead of 'women's health', say 'reproductive health' or 'gynecological health' (whatever you prefer) Instead of 'women and girls', say 'people who menstruate' or 'people who have periods' . . . Remember it takes practice and it's okay to mess up. Try not to have a knee-jerk reaction when somebody flags this with you. We're all learning as language is evolving!"[35]

There's an absolute certainty in one's own rightness that comes with telling others to "educate yourself" or "learn" the tenets of Critical Social Justice. Sometimes, this is simply referred to as "doing the work," with the implication that anybody who doesn't agree with the ideology simply hasn't worked hard enough at it. This is again related to the assumption of defensiveness, fragility, and people rejecting the ideological assumptions of Critical Social Justice only because they are protecting themselves. Central to "educating oneself," "learning," and "doing the work" is learning to "sit with discomfort." If one is uncomfortable with any aspect of this, it is again seen as their own problem, and the solution is to work harder.

How to Respond to This Claim

Point out the presumptuousness of this claim and resist it. To do so properly, you must have a basic understanding of the fundamental tenets of Critical Social Justice and be able to demonstrate that one's objection is both knowledgeable and principled. (If you've read this far, this should be possible for you.) This won't convince the zealots who will continue to assume that lack of agreement must signify either ignorance or selfish preservation of privilege. However, most people are not zealots, and being able to say, "I understand your conception of the world and ethical framework, but I do not share it," is very important and emboldening to others who are also not on board with the ideology.

I used the example from the Vagina Museum because this is a perfect example of simply refusing to consider that some people may have well-thought-through objections to replacing the words "women and girls" with "people who menstruate." In fact, gender-critical feminists have an entire body of scholarship of their own on this subject and have been developing it for over fifty years. They would object strongly to the idea that their refusal to change their language in the way suggested by Critical Social Justice advocates is a "knee-jerk" reaction or that they are "messing up" because they are still "learning," and they would not be alone. Many women and girls would prefer to be known as women and girls rather than "people who menstruate." The same principle holds for antiracist theories like those advanced by DiAngelo. While she may consider herself to be "unlearning" racism and learning how to be "less white," many other people will consider themselves to legitimately disagree that they have racism to unlearn or that there is benefit in learning (read: accepting) Critical Social Justice concepts of whiteness. This is one of the strongest examples of the Critical Social Justice refusal to accept the validity of differing viewpoints.

DiAngelo often speaks of white people's resistance to her ideas as so predictable that they could all have been learned from the same script.[36] It does not seem to occur to her that when very many people who have never met each other make the same objections repeatedly to her ideas, it could be because there are glaring flaws in them that are clear to large numbers of people. If people are "uncomfortable" with the idea that they are inherently racist, or with any other tenet or claim of Critical Social Justice, they do not necessarily need to "learn to sit with discomfort."[37] They might need to learn this—defensiveness is a real thing, and we would all do well to consider why a certain idea makes us uncomfortable—but more often than not, the Critical Social Justice ideas and prescriptions make liberals uncomfortable because the ideas and prescriptions are illiberal, and we must be able to say so.

Claim 10: Liberalism Is an Oppressive Power Structure.

This brings us to the final big claim of Critical Social Justice, which involves its critique of liberalism. It is not just liberalism that Critical

Social Justice misunderstands. It misunderstands every ideology that disagrees with it as giving people a way to preserve their privilege or to avoid "doing the work," but it is liberalism that it targets specifically. This is because liberalism has been the leading and most successful model for addressing racism, sexism, homophobia, and other forms of prejudice and discrimination in society.

Liberalism has worked by trying to remove social significance from identity categories like race, sex, and sexuality and by appealing to individualism, pluralism, and universalism. That is, liberalism believes that somebody's race, sex, or sexuality should not define or limit them to any particular role in society. Instead, people should be treated as individuals who should be able to pursue their own fulfillment and potential without barriers. Liberals also have a pluralistic concept of society in which it is okay, and even positive, if people differ in all sorts of ways—in which we can coexist and actually benefit from all these different experiences and worldviews without any one worldview or identity needing to be imposed on any group by any other, or by other members of the same group. Liberals also believe in universality, which means that we believe in the common humanity of all people and universal human rights, freedoms, and opportunities.

These are all problems for Critical Social Justice for a number of reasons. Firstly, liberals tend to want to reform liberal systems rather than revolutionize them so that they are more fully open to everyone and, thus, properly liberal. Full suffrage, antidiscrimination laws in employment, and the extension of marriage to same-sex couples are examples of this. Liberal individualism and universalism lead liberals to favor "color-blind" policies in which somebody's race should make no difference to their rights and freedoms. Liberal individualism and pluralism cause liberals to support viewpoint diversity and to believe that individuals can evaluate each other's ideas even if they have different identities. Liberals maintain that there is value in this and in not assuming that people will have certain ideas because they have a certain identity. Liberal pluralism and universalism lead us to the conclusion that while perspectives and experiences may vary and this is valuable, there *is* an objective truth, and there *are* optimum moral values, although we can never be too confident about having found them and will need to keep working on this forever. (Some of you who consider yourselves to be conservative and have not been sure the focus on liberalism in this book applies to you will hopefully be recognizing that it does at this point!)

For Critical Social Justice advocates, this is all hopelessly naive at best and the imposition of white, Western, male ideas on everybody else at worst. They consider what liberals refer to as individualism, pluralism, and universalism as actually just white and Western ways of knowing that then get imposed on everybody else and oppress them. Critical Social Justice advocates do not think we can continue to make progress through liberal methods of reform and may not even believe we have made any. They see a need for a total revolution of thought and an understanding of knowledge as a social construct that is related to identity and position in society. They believe that the only way to liberate the knowledges thus far oppressed is to recognize liberalism as a collection of oppressive power structures that serve the interests of dominant groups. They are particularly opposed to the concepts of color-blindness and meritocracy, believing that these are primarily a way to pretend that racism does not exist and that there is already a level playing field. At root, they believe that liberalism is the belief that society is already liberal and that liberals are essentially conservatives trying to maintain the status quo, which benefits only straight, white men.

How to Respond to This Claim

Highlight that liberalism has produced great progress over the last few centuries, but particularly in the second half of the twentieth century. It was not Marxism or postmodernism or the radical elements of black activism or feminism that gained most public support between the '60s and '80s and initiated important change, but liberalism. The Civil Rights Movement (which Critical Social Justice ideology also critiques), liberal feminism, and Gay Pride were liberal movements, and they won public support by appealing to the liberal values of Western societies. They did not say, "All white people/men/heterosexuals are racist/sexist/homophobic and cannot understand racial minorities/women/LGBT people," and present the campaign for equal rights as oppressed groups engaged in a power struggle. Instead, they appealed to individualism, pluralism, and universalism. They said, "Black people, women, gay men, lesbians, etc., are people just like you with the same desire to live, love, thrive, and succeed. You pride yourselves on founding societies on life, liberty, and the pursuit of happiness, but this has not been extended to everybody. Live up to your ideals, engage your empathy, make the world a fairer and more liberal place."

After legal battles were won, and it became illegal to discriminate against people by race or sex, and when homosexuality was decriminalized, prejudice did not go away. However, neither did liberalism. Since those days, liberalism has continued to erode prejudices and assumptions. Society has continued to become more liberal and less racist, sexist, and homophobic. It is usually easy to observe this by noting differences in attitudes and expectations between generations. These advances weren't made by appeals to a theory that divided people by identity and posited invisible power systems. They were made because of increased adherence to liberal principles and ideas. This created a consistent and growing consensus that it is wrong to evaluate people by their race, sex, or sexuality. Liberalism has not completely eradicated racism, sexism, or homophobia, and it has not magically made all disparities disappear (particularly in the realms of race, whereby, for example, black Americans continue to be hampered by their historical oppression and comparative lack of wealth and opportunity), but it has lessened them decade by decade. With its appeal to our better angels and focus on empirical studies into socioeconomic disparities and what can resolve them, liberalism is far better situated to address remaining bigotry and disparities than theories of invisible systems of whiteness and unconscious bias training.

The biggest misconception that Critical Social Justice advocates have about liberalism is the belief that liberals think society is already liberal, that we are already post-racial, that we already have a meritocracy functioning from a level playing field, and that there is no more work to do. This is incorrect. Liberalism is an ongoing project. Just as "social justice" is not the belief that society is already just and conservatism and Marxism and libertarianism are not the beliefs that society is already conservative, Marxist, or libertarian, liberalism is not the belief that society is already liberal. Liberalism is the aim to make society more liberal. There will always be illiberalism, and liberals will always need to fight it. Unlike many Critical Social Justice advocates, liberals tend to recognize the important progress that has already been made. Liberalism, therefore, is optimistic. That does not mean it is complacent.

Liberals do not want to preserve the status quo as we are so often accused. On the contrary, we are quite concerned that the status quo is getting increasingly less liberal, and a large part of that is caused by Critical Social Justice. While Critical Social Justice sees the status quo as white supremacist, patriarchal, transphobic, etc., and itself as a radical grassroots movement pushing back at the status quo, it is likely to be clear to you by now that Critical Social Justice is today a large part of the status quo. When your ideology is a dominant discourse in universities, schools, government, mainstream media, and social media, and you are able to charge thousands of dollars an hour to teach employees of billion-dollar corporations to dismantle their whiteness, it is time to accept that you are not fighting the establishment. You are the establishment.

Liberals historically have fought oppression and illiberalism by fighting against the establishment, reforming it to make it more liberal. The

Critical Social Justice industry—or what is often known as "woke capitalism"—is currently one of the major forces for illiberalism within the institutions of Western society that we need to fight. It's not the only one we need to fight, however. We must not overlook the illiberal forces from the right currently gaining strength from the public's fear of Critical Social Justice authoritarianism, and so we have a battle on two fronts. We need to try to push back Critical Social Justice from a liberal standpoint while opposing authoritarian forces from the right trying to do the same from an illiberal one. We also need to take care not to become illiberal ourselves in the fight against Critical Social Justice.

The raging political polarization in the United States is frightening in the extreme, with people on both sides becoming increasingly likely to justify violence to defend their cause.[38] Violence is the epitome of authoritarianism and the apex of illiberalism. This can only be prevented if liberals from all over the political spectrum stand against illiberalism consistently. That is what so many of us are doing. If you have picked up this book, this likely includes you. Liberals on the left, right, and center are yet again the reformers and the progressives trying to fix society so that a dominant authoritarian force does not take control and stifle individualism, pluralism, and universalism.

As individuals, there is much we can do in our own personal and professional spheres to push back against Critical Social Justice and fight for liberalism. This begins with uncovering how Critical Social Justice advocates work to indoctrinate people into believing their claims through workplace (re)education—including through unconscious bias testing and training, which, as I will show, are deeply flawed as designed and deployed and thus must be rejected and resisted.

3 Identifying the Problems with Unconscious Bias Testing and Training: Principal Flaws

The concept of "unconscious bias" is something you are likely to have heard of in relation to workplace antiracist training, particularly but also in Critical Social Justice activism more broadly in relation to a wider range of identity-based activism. If you are familiar with the Critical Social Justice concept of unconscious bias, you are likely to associate the term with its core belief that we are all unavoidably socialized into very specific forms of identity-based prejudice but are not aware of it. The ideology relies on understanding society to be thoroughly permeated with various forms of oppressive power systems like white supremacy, patriarchy, homophobia, ableism, fatphobia, and so on. These systems are understood to operate constantly to disadvantage and oppress minority groups but remain hidden beneath a seemingly benign surface. In this reading, racism, sexism, and other bigotries are *the* dominant forces that define our culture and society, but they are seldom overt or obvious. This belief is set out clearly in the book *Is Everyone Really Equal?*, which the Turkish-Canadian author Özlem Sensoy and American author Robin DiAngelo wrote to train teachers in Social Justice Education,

We develop our ideas about people in terms of their race, class, gender, sexuality, ethnicity, religion, ability, and citizenship from the culture that surrounds us, and many of these ideas are "below the surface" or below the conscious level. But we all rely on shared understandings about these social groups because we receive messages collectively about them from our culture. The frameworks we use to make sense of race, class, or gender are taken for granted and often invisible to us.[1]

DiAngelo is arguably the leading figure in "antiracist" unconscious bias training. Her 2018 book *White Fragility: Why It's So Hard for White People to Talk About Racism*, which spent nearly three years on the *New York Times* bestseller list and has sold millions of copies, informs DEI initiatives and practices throughout the United States and increasingly throughout the West, centers on a belief that all white people are necessarily racist and that they are largely unaware of it and resistant to being informed of it. Her assertions include the following:

- Being good or bad is not relevant.
- Racism is a multilayered system embedded in our culture.
- All of us are socialized into the system of racism.
- Racism cannot be avoided.
- Whites have blind spots on racism, and I have blind spots on racism.
- Racism is complex, and I don't have to understand every nuance of the feedback to validate that feedback.
- Whites are / I am unconsciously invested in racism.
- Bias is implicit and unconscious; I don't expect to be aware of mine without a lot of ongoing effort.[2]

Unconscious bias training is considered essential to that effort of becoming aware of one's own racism, and so being able to wrestle with it and dismantle it. This sense of a desperate internal struggle that must take place within all white people to dismantle their own white supremacy is expressed most powerfully by British author Layla Saad in her book

Me and White Supremacy: How to Recognise Your Privilege, Combat Racism and Change the World,

> White supremacy is an evil. It is a system of oppression that has been designed to give you benefits at the expense of the lives of BIPOC, and it is living inside you as unconscious thoughts and beliefs. The process of examining it and dismantling it will necessarily be painful. It will feel like waking up to a virus that has been living inside you all these years that you never knew was there. And when you begin to interrogate it, it will fight back to protect itself and maintain its position.[3]

Within this framework, there is no possibility for any white person to legitimately disagree with the claim that they harbor deeply entrenched negative beliefs about the characters and capabilities of black people within their unconscious minds. Any such disagreement is dismissed, at best, as ignorance due to having failed to engage properly with the training meant to reveal such beliefs or, at worst, as a sign that the individual is invested in maintaining their white privilege and the white supremacist system that harms people of color. People of color who object to these claims fare no better, often being accused of having internalized white supremacy or attempting to ingratiate themselves with the white dominant class.

Unconscious bias training of this kind often gives itself a veneer of scientific validity by relying on the Implicit Association Test (IAT), a tool developed by researchers at Harvard University.[4] This test is designed to capture the automatic associations we have between concepts and attributes. It, for example, measures the reaction times of people associating positive words or negative words to binary categories like "transgender people" or "cisgender people," "fat" or "thin," "young" or "old," "gay" or "straight," "black" and "white," etc. The speed of response in associating positive or negative terms with faces connected to these categories is argued to indicate a positive or negative bias toward people of that gender, size, age, sexuality, race, etc. In terms of the IAT test that looks specifically at race, an initial trial of this test found that 90–95 percent of participants (of all races) had a marked preference for white faces.[5] As this diverged considerably from the participants' self-reported conscious biases toward race, the test was, at first, heralded as a way to detect unconscious bias. However, since then, a mountain of scholarly research has cast so much doubt on the ability of the test to measure unconscious bias in any type of reliable, valid, or consistent manner that it is largely considered unfit for that purpose.[6] As a result, those unconscious bias training courses that continue to use it to assess an individual's unconscious bias do so against a formidable scientific consensus, including the original creators of the test.[7] It is difficult to believe that any responsible trainer would be unaware of twenty years' worth of scholarship on their subject of expertise, so any who are still relying on the IAT and not using more recent and rigorous work on the subject are very likely to be indulging their own (conscious) ideological bias.

It is unfortunate that the Critical Social Justice concept of unconscious bias remains so prevalent in workplaces and is also likely to be what people think of when they hear the term, because unconscious bias does, of course, exist and is relevant in workplaces. It is unfortunate, too, that many employers who are using the Critical Social Justice form of unconscious bias training are unaware of its ideological bias, scientific dubiousness, and the ethical boundaries it crosses in a workplace environment. Indeed, from my work at Counterweight and in my other efforts to help people fight against Critical Social Justice ideology at their place of work or in their school, I know that the managers, administrators, and human resource officers tasked with arranging unconscious bias training often do not understand the problems with the Critical Social Justice varieties of it. Indeed, many of my correspondents reported to me that when they attempted to explain the worldview of Critical Social Justice activists, their approach to unconscious bias training, and the problems with the IAT, they were met mostly with bewilderment. One worker was even accused by a manager of being a paranoid conspiracy theorist for simply quoting Robin DiAngelo accurately on learning that she was to be the primary source for the firm's unconscious bias training. The idea that an antiracist trainer would claim all white people to be racist seemed so outlandish to the manager that he didn't believe the worker—until, of course, the manager actually experienced the training himself.

This chapter, therefore, will focus on three simple objections that can be made to your employer if this kind of unconscious bias training is proposed in your workplace.

1. *Critical Social Justice uses a very limited and flawed approach to unconscious bias.*

2. *The Implicit Association Test is not fit for purpose.*

3. *Critical Social Justice–based unconscious bias training does not work.*

These three points, when presented with the information that follows, will enable you to inform employers about the nature of what they are endorsing without bewildering them or making them believe you to be a reactionary nut.

Objection 1: Critical Social Justice Uses a Very Limited and Flawed Approach to Unconscious Bias.

Unconscious bias is a real and complex phenomenon with multiple causes, including hardwired cognitive flaws, individual experience, and culture. We all have biases, and it really is difficult to be aware of them all and mitigate against them. Some of our cognitive biases are universal evolved traits, such as confirmation bias, in which we pay attention to and find plausible information that confirms our existing beliefs while ignoring or searching for flaws in information that disconfirms them. It is very difficult to avoid these types of unconscious biases and structures in our primitive brain explain why.

As public health specialist Sarah E. Gorman and psychiatrist Jack M. Gorman write in *Denying to the Grave: Why We Ignore the Facts That Will Save Us,*

> If we try to change our minds, a fear center in the brain like the anterior insula warns us that danger is imminent. The powerful dorsolateral prefrontal cortex can override these more primitive brain centers and assert reason and logic, but it is slow to act and requires a great deal of determination and effort to do so. Hence, it is fundamentally unnatural and uncomfortable to change our minds, and this is reflected in the way our brains work.[8]

Why precisely our brains would have evolved to make us experience changing our minds as dangerous can only be hypothesized. One highly plausible explanation comes from social psychologist Jonathan Haidt, who argues that it is more beneficial to a human's survival to believe what her group does than to be a seeker of unvarnished truth.[9]

Other biases we have come from individual experiences and are meaningful only to us. For example, as a young child, I suffered recurrent painful kidney problems. My nephrologist was a very soothing and child-friendly Sikh. To this day, I am inclined to instinctively assess a man wearing a Sikh turban as safe and kind. Meanwhile, the worst "mean girls" in my class at school were a pair of friends named "Kelly," so when meeting someone of that name, I have to fight down an instinctive assumption that she will be horrible. I have these biases even though my rational brain knows that a turban and a name tell me absolutely nothing about a person's manner or character.

Yet more biases come from our natures as pattern-seeing animals. One of my female friends is an electrician, and she tells me that people who have called the large emergency electrical service she works for often look startled or even say, "I wasn't expecting a woman," when she arrives on their doorstep. Such a response could be considered sexist, but I would argue that unless the surprise is accompanied by a belief that a woman cannot be a good electrician, it is simple pattern recognition caused by the fact that all the other electricians they have had have been men.

These kinds of biases are always with us, yet they are not at all what are considered in the Critical Social Justice approach to unconscious bias training. These sessions start from an assumption that everybody will have the same unconscious biases but from a certain position based on their "positionality." Positionality is a term to describe someone's perceived position in relation to power due to their identity. My positionality statement might look something like this:

> As a fat, disabled, bisexual woman, 1 experience various forms of marginalization. I have the lived experience of the microaggressions and discrimination that stems from the unconscious bias of those who benefit from thin privilege, able-bodied privilege, heteronormativity, and male privilege. I can speak to these experiences to people willing to learn to acknowledge and dismantle their fatphobia, ableism, heteronormativity, and misogyny. As a white cisgendered woman, I am aware of my white privilege and cis privilege and acknowledge that I am complicit in upholding white supremacy and cisnormativity. I commit to being accountable to people of color and trans people who are willing to educate me on my racism and transphobia so that I can become more aware of my unconscious biases and learn to do less harm to BIPOC and trans people.

In reality, of course, I do not believe myself to be marginalized or racist or transphobic or to have any special knowledge due to being fat, disabled, bisexual, or female, but in Critical Social Justice–based unconscious bias training, I will be expected to affirm all of these invisible power systems and my position in them. I will be trained to read interactions through these power dynamics and affirm myself to be oppressed in various ways and oppressive in others due to my unavoidable socialization into all those systems. However, in practice, unconscious bias training frequently focuses primarily on race and gender identity or simply on race.

It is typical in an unconscious bias training session for participants to be given an overview history of oppression in their country, followed by evidence that bias still exists. In better courses, empirical evidence of unconscious bias might be presented and discussed, such as studies looking at genuine disparities in the ways employers respond to identical resumes with "black"- or "white"-sounding names or the way we perceive differences in competence or leadership ability based on gender, weight, and height. There is solid evidence for these imbalances and more, and it is important to be aware of them and encouraged to reflect upon your own attitudes. However, very often, examples of biases, stereotypes, and microaggressions that we are all assumed to hold and commonly commit will be asserted as universal in Critical Social Justice–based training. This can be experienced as insulting by the black people being told they are regarded as unintelligent and criminally inclined, the brown people being told they are constantly suspected of being terrorists, and the women being told they are dismissed as incompetent and lacking in knowledge, to say nothing of the white people and men being told they hold these exact views of racial minorities and women and must acknowledge them. Participants are then likely to be divided into groups where they must list their privileged and marginalized identities and describe ways in which their privilege has benefitted them and also led them to mistreat others, as well as the ways in which they have been mistreated by those with privileges they don't have. In such training sessions, there are right and wrong ways to answer these questions and right and wrong beliefs and experiences to claim to have.

People who approached Counterweight for support with unconscious bias training reported the following experiences:

- Being separated into "affinity groups" based on skin color under the assumption that those of the same color will also be have shared values, knowledge, and experiences.

- Being arranged hierarchically in order of each individual's perceived level of oppression, with black people being seen as the most oppressed and Asian people needing to acknowledge their greater privilege and sometimes their own "anti-blackness." Further distinctions were sometimes made between lighter-skinned and darker-skinned black people and between the descendants of enslaved Africans and more recent African immigrants.

- Being assumed to hold progressive views and affirm the ideas of contemporary critical theories of race and intersectionality if you are black or brown, even though black and brown people are ideologically diverse just like white people and often are more likely to be socially conservative due to a statistically greater adherence to religious faith.

- Being expected to affirm your own racism and complicity in a system of white supremacy if you are white with statements like "All white people are racist and I am not an exception" and being asked to list the privileges you have due to being white as well as the assumptions you have about people of other races and the microaggressions you now realize you have committed.

- Being required to pretend to have a gender identity even if you don't believe in the concept of gender and would like to be referred to with the pronouns indicated by your biological sex and to be allowed to use language that reflects your position that "men" and "women" are biological sex categories just as "male" and "female" are.

Unconscious bias training frequently finishes with a number of exercises in which participants are expected to identify unconscious bias and microaggressions in hypothetical scenarios, display an awareness of what are assumed to be their own because of their identity, and also outline ways in which they will try to be more aware of their bias in their working life. Based on these scenarios, we can only assume that it is impossible for white people to go about their lives without constantly being overcome by an urge to touch black women's hair and compliment them on being able to form sentences. They also seem incapable of believing that people of color really do come from the country in which they live, that a black man out for a run is not fleeing a crime, or that their child's Hispanic pediatrician is not the medical clinic's janitor.

Good approaches to understanding unconscious bias must allow for universal cognitive biases and the impact of individual experience and environment rather than laying down one simplistic framework for understanding culture as dominated by oppressive power structures we are all said to be socialized into. Robin DiAngelo (and those who base their training on her work) makes sweeping generalizations about white people with utmost confidence while explicitly rejecting arguments that the individual attitudes of white people may vary significantly. Indeed, she sees any such rejection as nothing more than a defensive move caused by white fragility. Nevertheless, it is very unlikely that all white people in all white-majority countries have the exact same set of racial biases as an Italian American woman born in 1956 to a racist family who admits her own continued struggles with racism.

In her book *Unconscious Bias: Everything You Need to Know About Our Hidden Prejudices*, Annie Burdock writes,

> Amongst the most common sources of deep and unconscious bias are the experiences you have throughout your life. These are incredibly broad; they can include anything from discriminatory things you heard your relatives say while you were growing up to things other kids said

in the classroom or a subject you studied in school.

Every person's life experiences are unique. Your brain develops its new thought processes and reactions based on past experiences. So it's no huge shock that a good or bad experience with someone from a particular demographic group can trigger a natural subconscious association that may persist for years, particularly if that association is enforced by additional experiences or other information your brain receives.

Bias also comes from the people you spend the most time with. Your parents, siblings, close friends and other loved ones have a great influence on the messages you hear and the biases you come into contact with. Everyone knows people in their lives who are openly biased. Think back to the time you spent with them when you were young and learning about the world. How much did their perspectives affect yours?

In a revealing passage, DiAngelo provides a personal answer to that very question,

> From an early age I had the sense of being an outsider; I was acutely aware that I was poor, that I was dirty, that I was not "normal," and that there was something "wrong" with me. But I also knew that I was not Black. We were at the lower rungs of society, but there was always someone on the ladder, just below us. I knew that "colored" meant Black people and that Black people should be avoided. I can remember many occasions when I reached for candy or uneaten food lying out in public and was admonished by my grandmother not to touch it because a "colored person" may have touched it. I was told not to sit in certain places lest a "colored" person had sat there. The message was clear: if a Black person touched something, it became dirty. The irony here is that the marks of poverty were clearly visible on me: poor hygiene, torn clothes, homelessness, rotten teeth, hunger. Yet through comments such as my grandmother's, a racial Other was formed in my consciousness, an Other through whom I became clean.[10]

This is a very powerful passage, and I respect DiAngelo for her insight in recognizing her socialization into believing in white superiority as a way to cleanse herself of the stain of poverty and her honesty in sharing it. But her belief that *her* experience can be extended to *all* white people in white-majority countries is just not credible. My socialization with regard to race was radically different to hers. My parents were wealthy and sent me to a private school in East London. My school was considerably more racially diverse than the majority of state schools at this time, and the black children who attended it were almost entirely the offspring of doctors. My black friends were wealthy, spoke with a middle-class accent, got good grades, and were generally primed for success. I was not socialized to believe in white superiority or to associate blackness with lower intelligence, criminality, and dirtiness. If we were to select another ten white people at random and ask them how they were socialized to understand race, their stories would likely involve neither the coping mechanism of a desperately poor woman born a hundred years ago like DiAngelo's grandmother nor an elite educational environment containing the most economically privileged and intellectually able children of high-achieving professionals like my school.

I would argue that the complete neglect of individuality, universality, pattern recognition, and any kind of bias that does not fit into the theoretical model of oppressive power systems makes the Critical Social Justice approach to unconscious bias training unfit for purpose. This kind of training in which white people are expected to dig deep into their own psyche until they find they do actually hold white supremacist views after all is not only a presumption that denies the variation of individual socialization but is also dangerous. Within this framework, one can either be a racist in denial and complicit in maintaining white supremacy or a racist who admits to believing in white superiority and commits to working on it. It is clearly more virtuous to take the second position. But if the unconscious bias trainers are wrong and white people are not all racist, then they are teaching those who comply with the program to become so by convincing them that they believe themselves to be superior to black people. It is entirely unclear how this will reduce racism.

Unconscious bias training can only be valuable if it enables people to identify and address the unconscious biases they actually have. It would need to accept that some of these will be universal cognitive biases, some will be individual and vary considerably, and some will be cultural. We all have plenty of unconscious biases, and some of them really will be negative views about people with certain identities. Giving people tools to help them recognize this and work on addressing them with honest introspection and practical actions is worthwhile. Critical Social Justice approaches to unconscious bias training do not do this. Instead, they train people to believe they believe specific negative things about specific identity groups that fit within the theories of Critical Social Justice. If these approaches fail, they will achieve nothing. If they succeed, they increase the number of people in a workplace who hold prejudiced views. Surveys into the results of these trainings show that this is precisely what is happening.

Objection 2: The Implicit Association Test Is Not Fit for Purpose.

So many scholarly critiques of the Harvard Implicit Association Test have been made that there is now a repository of publications that demonstrate its problems and shortcomings. This makes these criticisms somewhat difficult to summarize, but I shall form the main points of concern into three clusters.

1. There is a lack of coherence about what precisely the test is measuring.

As one study argues, the IAT has lacked clarity and coherence since its inception for three principal reasons:

a. There is no consensual scientific definition as to what constitutes implicit bias;

b. The definition of implicit bias offered by those who introduced the IAT, including Anthony Greenwald, is logically incoherent and empirically unjustified;

c. Exactly what the IAT measures remains unclear, even after more than two decades of research.[11]

If there is no scientific consensus on the definition of implicit bias to begin with, it is difficult to see how it could be measured scientifically. If the researchers who developed the test are themselves unable to coherently define what they are attempting to measure for the purposes of their study, this casts doubt on whether they will be able to meaningfully measure implicit bias. Indeed, many critics of the IAT have complained of the difficulty in telling what it is measuring. As my colleague at Counterweight, Carrie Clark, pointed out, even if the test does capture a subject's negative biases against a group, it is impossible to tell whether it is conscious or unconscious, or explicit or implicit from a time delay.[12] Indeed, there is also no consensus on where the division between explicit and implicit thoughts lies.

Further, there are no solid grounds to assume that the test is measuring unconscious bias at all because, as Clark also rightly pointed out, the test specifically measures reaction times, and the reasons for those cannot be assumed. People with slower cognitive processing could measure as more racially biased simply because they require more time to follow the rules of the test, while others could appear to be least racially biased simply because they are good at video games and process quickly. It is also entirely possible that people who appear to associate negative terms with racial minorities more quickly may not do so because they hold those negative beliefs but because they are familiar with cultural stereotypes or because they are particularly conscious of negativity toward black people due to strongly antiracist views.

Another study looked into this potential for confusion and found that "[m]any design characteristics of the popular Implicit Association Test appear to make the task highly susceptible to measurement error."[13] This study "provided clear evidence of measurement error confounding IAT scores. Specifically, IAT data was shown to be, on average, comprised of just over 50% random error variance, nearly 30% method variance and under 20% trait variance. These results demonstrate unequivocally that IAT scores are predominantly composed of measurement error not implicit attitudes."[14]

2. There has been a moving of goalposts by the test's creators.

This confusion over what the test is measuring is further confused by its creators appearing to change their minds about what its purposes and capabilities are. The initial trialing of the test was received very positively in some quarters as a potential breakthrough in accessing individuals' unconscious biases and predicting discriminatory behavior, as was the subsequent best-selling book by researchers Anthony Greenwald and Mahzarin Banaji, *BlindSpot,* which described the Implicit Association Test as a revolutionary method for learning about the human mind and exposing our metaphoric blindspots.[15] These very strong claims about the test's capabilities caused much excitement, but following considerable scholarly critique and challenge of it, the creators first defended their claims but later seemed to qualify the claims to a significant degree.

For example, in one of the first interviews after the trialing of the test in 1998, Greenwald said, "The test has the potential to reveal things about people that they may prefer not to know." This appears to be a clear claim that it can be used for diagnostic purposes to reveal an individual's biases. However, in 2015, following scholarly back and forth on this subject, he acknowledged that "attempts to diagnostically use such measures for individuals risk undesirably high rates of erroneous classifications."[16]

Greenwald and Banaji also seemed quite clear on the test's ability to predict discriminatory behavior. But as Olivia Goldhill wrote,

> In *Blindspot*, a 2013 book aimed at general audiences, Banaji and Greenwald wrote: "[T]he automatic White preference expressed on the Race IAT . . . predicts discriminatory behavior even among research participants who earnestly (and, we believe, honestly) espouse egalitarian beliefs. That last statement may sound like a self-contradiction, but it's an empirical truth. Among research participants who describe themselves as racially egalitarian, the Race IAT has been shown, reliably and repeatedly, to predict discriminatory behavior that was observed in the research." So it came as a major blow when four separate meta-analyses undertaken between 2009 and 2015—each examining between 46 and 167 individual studies—all showed the IAT to be a weak predictor of behavior. Two of the meta-analyses focus on the race IAT while two examine the IAT's links with behavior more broadly, but all four show weak predictive abilities.[17]

Greenwald and Banaji have since deemed the test "problematic to use to classify persons as likely to engage in discrimination." When journalist Jesse Singal challenged them on this contradiction, Greenwald replied, "You have to distinguish statements diagnostic of individuals, which we've resisted for multiple reasons, and statements of generalizations about aggregate data based on research of multiple (sometimes many) subjects." But as Singal pointed out, these claims seem quite clearly to refer to individual participants.[18]

These equivocations led Singal to write an article titled "The Creators of the Implicit Association Test Should Get Their Stories Straight."[19] Similarly, Lee Jussim, a social psychologist who heads the Social Perception Laboratory at Rutgers University, has expressed skepticism about the test: "The peer-reviewed scientific literature has witnessed a great walking back of many of the most dramatic claims made on the basis of the IAT and about implicit social cognition more generally." He added, "The point is not that the notion has been completely debunked or the IAT shown to be completely worthless; I even do research using the IAT! Instead, the point is that most of the most dramatic claims about it have been debunked or, at least, shown to be dubious and scientifically controversial. These are not firm grounds on which to sell the public on the power and prevalence of unconscious racism or trainings to mitigate it.[20]

3. There is a pattern of inconsistent results from one test to the next.

The test does not stand up consistently to retesting, which is something we would expect if it were reliably discerning unconscious biases. It seems that people can be racist in the morning and not racist in the evening depending on a number of scenarios that could alter their score, including mood, context, and practice. Having explained that perfect consistency scores as 1 and complete randomness as 0, Jesse Singal writes,

> What constitutes an acceptable level of test-retest reliability? It depends a lot on context, but, generally speaking, researchers are comfortable if a given instrument hits $r = .8$ or so. The IAT's architects have reported that overall, when you lump together the IAT's many different varieties, from race to disability to gender, it has a test-retest reliability of about $r = .55$. By the normal standards of psychology, this puts these IATs well below the threshold of being useful in most practical, real-world settings.
>
> The IAT falls far short of the quality-control standards normally expected of psychological instruments. The IAT, this research suggests, is a noisy, unreliable measure that correlates far too weakly with any real-world outcomes to be used to predict individuals' behavior — even the test's creators have now admitted as such. The history of the test suggests it was released to the public and excitedly publicized long before it had been fully validated in the rigorous, careful way normally demanded by the field of psychology.[21]

German Lopez for *Vox* has also criticized the unreliability of the test, describing his own experience,

> When I first took the implicit association test a few years ago, I was happy with my results: The test found that I had no automatic pref-erence against white or black people. According to this test, I was a person free of racism, even at the subconscious level.
>
> I took the IAT again a few days later. This time, I wasn't so happy with my results: It turns out I had a slight automatic preference for white people. According to this, I was a little racist at the subconscious level—against black people.
>
> Then I took the test again later on. This time, my results genu-inely surprised me: It found once again that I had a slight automatic preference — only now it was in favor of black people. I was racist, but against white people, according to the test.
>
> At this point, I was at a loss as to what this test was telling me. Should I consider the average of my three results, essentially showing I had no bias at all? Or should I have used the latest result? Was this test even worth taking seriously, or was it bullshit? I felt like I had gotten no real answers about my bias from this test. (I recently retook the test a few times—and, again, it was all over the place.)[22]

I myself have taken a version of the test to determine my level of fatphobia and found a different but still inconsistent pattern. I am one of those people with slow cognition when it comes to this kind of test and, thus, liable to come out as highly biased. So terrible am I at video games that my daughter will no longer play *The Witcher* with me as I just con-tinually walk my character into walls. On my first test, I became quite confused by a sudden reversal of sides for good terms associated with fat people and was very slow and received a score of having a significant bias against fat people. However, once I knew that the test was going to make that switch in the last round, I was able to gradually decrease my fatphobia until it disappeared. Yes, I cheated. Perhaps this kind of test cannot prevent itself from being misled by individuals practicing, but this seems like a significant flaw. (Also, I do not have a bias against fat people.)

Is the Implicit Association Test completely useless, then? Jussim argues not. It is no good for measuring unconscious bias but has the potential for measuring something of value to psychology with further experimentation and testing.

> The IAT has many imperfections: dubious construct validity, low test-retest reliability, various other psychometric oddities, its effect size has often been computed in a way that appears to exaggerate its size, it has been almost universally misinterpreted and misrepresented as measuring "implicit bias" when, by Greenwald's own definition, it does not do so, its predictive validity has been found to be modest at best, and even if we ignore all that, its ability to account for inequality in the present is likely to be limited.
>
> This does not mean the IAT is useless. We could generate an equally long list for how cars have been misused. It can be constructively used for both self-insight and research mainly by treating the IAT as what it is—at best, a useful but imperfect measure of implicit *associations*. Each of those imperfections, however, can be a starting point for the next phase of research on and with the IAT. Whether and when such associations reflect norms, cultural stereotypes, social realities, or prejudice remains unclear after over 20 years of research on the IAT. Because so much emphasis was placed on the IAT as a measure of "implicit bias" or "unconscious prejudice," many alternative explanations for its effects received only modest attention. Intensified empirical attention to those alternatives is sorely needed.
>
> Similarly, the IAT is not necessarily even a pure measure of implicit associations, and may reflect response biases, skill sets, and more. It is also possible that they may reflect different sources in different contexts, and some admixture in yet others. These possibilities, too, can serve as inspirations for future research. It is of course possible that in some contexts and under some circumstances, implicit associations *do* mostly reflect bias and such biases contribute to real world inequalities. That, however, requires more evidence than a mere reaction time difference between two IAT's.[23]

In its current state, the Implicit Association Test is entirely unfit for measuring an individual's unconscious bias in a training scenario. The evidence for this claim is overwhelming. It can neither define nor know what it is measuring, as there are too many potential explanations for reaction times. It produces more measurement errors than genuine data, can provide entirely different results on the same day, and is not suitable for use with individuals as it would result in too many erroneous classifications. There is no justification for your employer to inflict it upon you.

Objection 3: Critical Social Justice–Based Unconscious Bias Training Does Not Work.

When I say that unconscious bias training does not work, I mean it does not work to reduce unconscious bias, it does not work to decrease racist behavior, and it does not result in more harmonious workplaces with a greater diversity of staff. Sometimes, it results in a worsening of tensions and a decrease in the diversity of employees. As above, I will present the evidence and arguments for these claims in clusters.

1. Unconscious bias training does not reduce unconscious bias.

Despite the massive scale of the effort to reduce prejudice, whether conscious or unconscious, there have been relatively few attempts to measure success until recently.[24] Findings on unconscious bias training have been disappointing. Two leading researchers into diversity training, sociologists Frank Dobbin of Harvard University and Alexandra Kalev of Tel Aviv University, find that "while people are easily taught to respond correctly to a questionnaire about bias, they soon forget the right answers. The positive effects of diversity training rarely last beyond a day or two." As they caution,

> Current data do not allow the identification of reliably effective interventions to reduce implicit biases. As our systematic review reveals,

many interventions have no effect, or may even increase implicit biases. Caution is thus advised when it comes to programs aiming at reducing biases. Much more investigation into the long-term effects of possible interventions is needed.[25]

The largest and most cited meta-study that synthesized evidence from 492 studies and over 87,000 participants found that "implicit measures can be changed, but effects are often relatively weak" and that there are "limitations in the evidence base for implicit malleability and change."

2. Unconscious bias training does not reduce biased behavior.

The same meta-study cited above found that changes in explicit bias were even weaker and produced trivial effects on behavior.

> Procedures changed explicit measures less consistently and to a smaller degree than implicit measures and generally produced trivial changes in behavior. Finally, changes in implicit measures did not mediate changes in explicit measures or behavior. Our findings suggest that changes in implicit measures are possible, but those changes do not necessarily translate into changes in explicit measures or behavior.[26]

In short, unconscious bias training can make people slightly better at understanding the information provided on implicit bias tests and perform better on tests shortly after the training, but this effect does not last, nor does it seem to have very much effect at all on explicit biases (those openly expressed) or on behavior. As organizational psychologist Tomas Chamorro-Premuzic writes,

> Contrary to what unconscious bias training programs would suggest, people *are* largely aware of their biases, attitudes, and beliefs, particularly when they concern stereotypes and prejudices. Such biases are an integral part of their self and social identity. . . .

This is why you should just ask if you want to find out what people think about something. Sure, there are instances in which they may not want to answer this truthfully, but that is quite different from saying that they are unaware of their thoughts. Generally speaking, people are not just conscious of their biases, but also quite proud of them.

Chamorro-Premuzic also notes the low correlation between attitudes and behavior, further undermining claims made that the implicit association test can predict behavior.

However, there is rarely more than 16% overlap (correlation of r = 0.4) between attitudes and behavior, and even lower for engagement and performance, or prejudice and discrimination. This means that the majority of racist or sexist behaviors that take place at work would not have been predicted from a person's attitudes or beliefs. The majority of employees and managers who hold prejudiced beliefs, including racist and sexist views, will never engage in discriminatory behaviors at work. In fact, the overlap between *unconscious* attitudes and behavior is even smaller (merely 4%). Accordingly, even if we succeeded in changing people's views—conscious or not—there is no reason to expect that to change their behavior.[27]

3. Unconscious bias training does not improve workplace atmosphere or diversity and can make the situation worse.

When there are measurable results of implementing this kind of diversity training, they are usually negative. Dobbin and Kalev attribute much of this to a majority of organizations taking the view that such training should be mandatory. But, as they note,

five years after instituting required training for managers, companies saw no improvement in the proportion of white women, Black men, and Hispanics in management, and the share of Black women actually decreased by 9%, on average, while the ranks of Asian American men and women shrank by 4% to 5%. Trainers tell us that people often respond to compulsory courses with anger and resistance—and many participants actually report more animosity toward other groups afterward.[28]

A UK governmental study into the effects of unconscious bias training similarly concluded that "training interventions do not seem to be effective at improving diversity outcomes within workplaces" and sometimes produce negative outcomes.

> While some types of unconscious bias training may have some limited effects including creating awareness of an individual's own implicit biases and wider diversity and discrimination issues in the very short-term, there is currently no evidence that this training changes behaviour or improves workplace equality in terms of representation of women, ethnic minorities or other minority groups in position of leadership or reducing pay inequalities.
>
> Research which looked at 830 medium to large US companies over 30 years has found that mandatory diversity training either does not change the number of women in management positions, or actually reduces it.
>
> In summary, in spite of a huge number of studies having been conducted on interventions which seek to reduce bias and prejudice, no reliably effective approaches have been established. There is a need for robust, repeated behavioural studies of UBT interventions in UK workplaces before the field can reach consensus on what definitely works and what does not.[29]

Why Does Unconscious Bias Training Not Work?

A number of arguments have been made to explain why unconscious bias training fails to produce any lasting change in unconscious bias, conscious bias, or behavior and sometimes even makes biased attitudes and workplace relations worse.

Firstly, there is the issue of the lack of evidence that biases like racism are unconscious rather than consciously held. As discussed, the IAT cannot show whether people's biases are conscious or unconscious (even if it could detect them accurately), and studies have shown that simply asking people what their biases are is as accurate as trying to divine them via psychological tests.[30] If people already know what their biases are and they consider themselves justified in holding them, as Chamorro-Premuzic says, simply telling them these biases exist and that they hold them is unlikely to do anything to change them.

Some of those who work in the DEI industry as educators and consultants are beginning to accept the flaws in unconscious bias training. In a post titled "The Problem with Unconscious Bias Training" on the website of Tidal Equality, a DEI services firm, DEI strategist Kristen Liesch presents a summary of the arguments against unconscious bias training. She cites studies that show that unconscious bias training can not only increase the salience of stereotypes but also even lead people who hold racist or other prejudiced ideas to justify their beliefs: "It turns out that when individuals are asked to assess their thoughts and behaviours for evidence of bias, this introspection 'reassures people that they have been correct all along and that their conclusions are based on sound reasoning.'"[31] This looks very much like a problem produced by a single focus on culturally formed identity-based bias while neglecting the universal hard-wired human problem of confirmation bias.

There is also the problem with normalizing the idea that people will inevitably hold biases about various identity groups in society. This is a dangerous lesson given the implications. Through unconscious bias training, white people who abhor racism risk internalizing the idea that they unavoidably regard black people as inferior, especially when acknowledgment of their presumed racism is presented as virtuous, and therefore might ultimately learn to become racist. Meanwhile, those who genuinely do hold racist beliefs are likely to find the idea that their racism is inevitable and unconscious validating. As DEI consultant Michelle Penelope King states in an article for *Forbes*, "When participants in training sessions are given evidence that they are biased and told that these biases are unconscious, it encourages them to believe that there is nothing they can do to change their beliefs—they are unconscious after all!"[32]

We can see how Robin DiAngelo enables this thinking:

- Being good or bad is not relevant.
- Racism is a multilayered system embedded in our culture.
- All of us are socialized into the system of racism.
- Racism cannot be avoided.

What a wonderful way for someone who holds racist ideas that they are aware of and feels some shame about to reassure themselves that they are not a bad person but a normal one who cannot help being racist! DiAngelo would like us to rid ourselves of what she calls the good/bad binary, where being racist is bad and not being racist is good. Those of us who believe in individual agency and believe that racism is much more likely to be reduced by maintaining a consensus that it is bad must oppose this idea that it is unavoidable and neither good or bad.

There are two explanations for the negative effects of unconscious bias training that most reflect the experiences of people who came to Counterweight for support with dealing with it at their workplace. These were an increase of awareness of and anxiety around the identities of other members of the workforce, particularly on the grounds of race, and resentment at being told what they believe and feeling they were having their thoughts controlled. These are known as the "rebound effect" and the "backlash effect," and they overlap considerably.

As Liesch writes,

[N]ot only does attempting to suppress bias not work, it can make stereotypes seem more significant and result in an increase in biased decision-making. Scholars call this the *rebound effect* (Think: "Don't think about purple elephants"): the more we try to suppress our thoughts, the more apparent they become. If we're constantly combing through our thoughts to find evidence of a bias, they'll surface faster and faster. Thoughts of bias or stereotypes become more accessible to us than before we tried to suppress them, and begin to influence our other thoughts and behaviour.[33]

Dobbin and Kalev use the same analogy.

[S]ome have argued that antibias training activates stereotypes. Field and laboratory studies find that asking people to suppress stereotypes tends to reinforce them—making them more cognitively accessible to people. Try not thinking about elephants. Diversity training typically encourages people to recognize and fight the stereotypes they hold, and this may simply be counterproductive.[34]

Paula Caligiuri, founder and CEO of Skilify, a digital platform for improving cross-cultural communication, argues that unconscious bias training makes matters worse because

[t]hey cue people in to differences rather than similarities. To rid organizations of discrimination, employees need to see each other as similar, connected, and working collaboratively toward shared goals. A focus on bias—conscious or unconscious—highlights employee differences and, in the end, defeats the program's purpose.[35]

This was a problem reported by many of Counterweight's black members who felt that before unconscious bias training had taken place, they had been seen as part of a team and, in Caligiuri's words, "similar, connected, and working collaboratively toward shared goals." However, after such training, they felt themselves to be racialized in a way that had not happened before and the atmosphere around them to be more self-conscious and uncomfortable. They ceased to feel such a strong sense of belonging and connection with their colleagues,

White people, too, reported a greater consciousness of their race and were inclined to be anxious that they either did hold unconscious biases against people of other races or could say or do something that could be interpreted in that way and thus became much more race-conscious and self-conscious in their interactions. As Caligiuri notes,

> Scoring "poorly" in unconscious bias testing doesn't mean a person is racist, xenophobic, sexist, ageist, or otherwise. Unfortunately, many who have gone through unconscious bias training feel anxious and worry that their so-called "bias" will be apparent to others, causing them to withhold authentic conversations with people who are demographically different.[36]

This observation is supported by a study by psychology professor Jacquie D. Vorauer in which she found that completing the IAT reduced positive intergroup interaction behavior, making white people more cautious and inhibited. She writes,

> It is frequently suggested that increasing awareness of intergroup bias and limited control over biased responses can improve intergroup interaction behavior. Some uses of the Implicit Association Test epitomize this approach to improving intergroup relations. However, if completing the IAT enhances caution and inhibition, reduces self-efficacy, or primes categorical thinking, the test may instead have negative effects. Two experiments demonstrated that when White individuals completed a race-relevant IAT prior to an intergroup interaction (as compared with when they did not), their interaction partner left the exchange feeling less positively regarded. No such effect was evident when White individuals completed a race-irrelevant IAT . . . or an explicit prejudice measure . . . before the exchange, or when their interaction partner was White. . . . Mediation analyses . . . suggested that White participants who completed the IAT communicated less positive regard because they adopted a cautious approach to the interaction, limiting their self-disclosure.[37]

Other studies have pointed to a general increase in anxiety and distrust and damage to previously good working relationships due to the power imbalances and assumptions of bias presented within them. For example, one retrospective study on corporate training found that

> [m]any [white male employees] interpreted the key learning point as having to walk on eggshells around women and minorities—choosing words carefully so as not to offend. Some surmised that it meant white men were villains, still others assumed that they would lose their jobs to minorities and women, while others concluded that women and minorities were simply too sensitive.
>
> Women and people of color did not necessarily leave with positive feelings about the training either. As the minority, some felt pressured to speak for their entire identity group. Feeling misunderstood, they sometimes left thinking that their co-workers were more biased and prejudiced than they had believed them to be prior to the training. When the training event was over, employees went back to their work environments with incomplete knowledge and little understanding about what would be different.[38]

As journalist Joanne Lipman, who refers to this study, writes,

> Training done badly can also damage otherwise cordial relationships. Women and minorities often leave training sessions thinking their co-workers must be even more biased than they had previously imagined. In a more troubling development, it turns out that telling people about others' biases can actually heighten their own. Researchers have found that when people believe everybody else is biased, they feel free to be prejudiced themselves.[39]

Another study compared the performance and cardiovascular responses of white men interviewing at companies that mentioned the importance of diversity against those that didn't, finding that the former caused the men to perform poorly in interviews and have cardiovascular responses that indicated they were stressed. These effects were consistent among men with a variety of political ideologies, including those who felt very favourably toward diversity and inclusion initiatives. Meanwhile, members of minority groups felt no benefits of being informed of a pro-diversity initiative.[40]

Negative results of unconscious bias training are also related to the way they are presented. Citing various studies, Dobbin and Kalev write,

> We know from a large body of organizational research that people react negatively to efforts to control them. Job autonomy research finds that people resist external controls on their thoughts and behavior and perform poorly in their jobs when they lack autonomy. Self-determination research shows that when organizations frame motivation for pursuing a goal as originating internally, commitment rises, but when they frame motivation as originating externally, rebellion increases. . . . [W]hen diversity programs are introduced with an external rationale— avoiding lawsuit— participants were more resistant than when they were introduced with an organizational rationale—management needs. In experiments, whites resented external pressure to control prejudice against blacks, and when experimenters asked people to reduce bias, they responded by increasing bias unless they saw the desire to control prejudice as voluntary.[41]

Unconscious bias training that focuses on differences and assumes specific identity-based biases is highly counterproductive to its aims. People predictably resist any training that appears to try to exert control over their thoughts and beliefs. Such trainings create anxiety, resentment, and alienation among those who attend them regardless of their race, sex, or political ideology. These trainings also create a strong increase in self-consciousness among attendees and a loss of team cohesion. The findings are so consistent that we should expect companies that do not offer unconscious bias training to report better outcomes than those that do. Research bears this out. Strong evidence suggests that companies that have never had unconscious bias training employ and retain more black men and women than companies that have.[42]

Now that you understand the illiberal nature of Critical Social Justice ideology, both its key tenets and claims, and understand the flaws and dangers of one of its primary forms of (re)education, you have the knowledge needed to assess whether there is a Critical Social Justice problem in your organization's diversity, equity, and inclusion initiatives—and, if so, the scale of the problem.

4 Assessing and Addressing Critical Social Justice Problems: Action Steps

Not all equity, diversity, and inclusion programs are equal, and the nature and scope of training can vary widely. But many trainings today are grounded in Critical Social Justice ideology. The implementation of such initiatives inevitably causes anxiety among those who are mandated to participate in them. Although some people are undoubtedly in favor of such training, many are not. For example, white people might fear they will be expected to affirm themselves as unavoidably racist, and "people of color" might worry that they will henceforth be racialized at work and expected to testify to experiences of racism that they might not have had, even if only theoretically. Some people might fear that they will be expected to tell coworkers or even strangers what their sexuality is or whether they have a disability. Others might worry that they will be required to declare their gender identity and pronouns even if they don't believe they have a gender identity or have ethical objections to the concept of gender. Such concerns are often justified, but not always. Ultimately, it depends on whether a training program is based on Critical Social Justice ideology—or whether it is based on a less restrictive ideological framework.

For many people outside of the humanities or activist spaces, the Critical Social Justice ideas that today permeate not only our workplaces and schools but also our broader political, cultural, and social landscape are often baffling. This is because Critical Social Justice ideas ignore accepted standards of evidence and reason and operate on their own logic. If you have worked in an environment not previously bound by any particular ideology of social justice and have simply been expected to treat all your colleagues and clients with courtesy and consideration regardless of their race, sex, sexuality, nationality, religion, or other group identity, you might be unsure how to evaluate a current or new policy or training program in your company or organization. How do you know whether it's based on Critical Social Justice ideology? What indications might there be that you should be worried about it—for example, does it demand you consider all identity categories and consciously privilege members of some groups over members of other groups? And if it does and you have reason to be worried, what can you do to oppose it, opt out of it, or ensure you pass the training without compromising your own principles so that you can be left alone to do your job and continue to have positive relationships with your coworkers?

Because people are increasingly aware of buzzwords that can signal the imposition of Critical Social Justice ideas upon an institution—"diversity," "equity," "inclusion," "unconscious bias," "microaggressions," etc.—it is common for them to fill in the gaps and assume (often correctly) that a policy or training program using them will be ideological and authoritarian. However, it is important not to jump the gun and assume this until there is clear evidence that this is the case. The presence of buzzwords alone does not tell the whole story. Antidiscrimination policies not based on Critical Social Justice ideas often use the same terminology because there is pressure to use them or simply because this is the mainstream language now. This makes it particularly important that people are able to evaluate policies or training programs for ideological bias and respond to them in a thoughtful, knowledgeable, and principled way to promote a more inclusive approach to opposing prejudice and discrimination.

Indeed, there are reasonable, liberal, and ethical policies that institutions can and should adopt to enable them to deal with genuine incidents of prejudice or bullying on the grounds of race, gender, sexuality, etc., and some are already doing so. After all, my argument isn't that racism, sexism, and other forms of bigotry don't exist or have magically vanished; rather, it is that Critical Social Justice approaches to solving such challenges are often themselves prejudiced and discriminatory—and thus counterproductive and illiberal—and that more ethical and reasonable approaches exist. Thus, if an individual goes into strong oppositional mode at a current or perhaps new program that uses some Critical Social Justice concepts but that is not clearly authoritarian or ideological, they risk being seen as a reactionary, someone who opposes reasonable efforts to address racism and other bigotries. This may not only place them in danger of disciplinary action but also reduce their credibility later if there is a clearly identifiable problem that needs addressing. Alternatively, if someone takes a tentative and conciliatory approach to challenging a fully-fledged and committed Critical Social Justice policy or training program, they are just likely to be swallowed by it. At Counterweight, we used a color-coded system to help clients assess potential Critical Social Justice problems in their organizations.

Assessing the Situation

Code Green

If you receive notification of a new policy or program that uses the language of diversity, equity, and inclusion but does not explicitly state that it will be using contemporary critical theories of race, queer theory, or decolonial theory, refer to any of the theorists in these fields, or make any ideological claims about things like "whiteness" or "gender identity" or refer to the Implicit Association Test or unconscious bias training, the best immediate course of action is to seek more detailed information before raising any type of objection. This communication might indicate the beginning of an imposition of Critical Social Justice ideology upon individuals whose own ethical frameworks and worldviews are quite different. However, it might not.

Given the negative attention that Critical Social Justice–based training has increasingly begun to receive, some employers are seeking ways to meet expectations that their company will provide "diversity training" without such illiberal and divisive frameworks. They want to offer training that includes clear and reasonable expectations that employees will not be racist, sexist, or homophobic at work but that also allows them to meet these codes of conduct from their own political, philosophical, or religious worldview. I know this because I have helped some employers to do so and have heard from many others who have already done so or are in the process of doing so. If there is any chance that this type of training is being proposed at your workplace, you will want to enthusiastically support it rather than impede it. Your support of a liberal and inclusive framework will encourage your liberal colleagues to feel more confident to support it, and this will strengthen it against any external or internal pressures to change it into an illiberal and exclusionary one.

More generally, this is the time to exercise a "presumption of innocence" and to seek more specific and detailed information before taking any other action, especially if the proposed policies or training are ambiguous. This is the time to ask questions about the training's definitions of diversity, equity, and inclusion. Specifically, does "diversity" mean accepting and appreciating differences in a pluralistic fashion, as most people understand the word, or does it mean seeking to privilege those seen as marginalized and marginalizing those seen as privileged while enforcing conformity of opinion, as Critical Social Justice understands it? Is "equity" a synonym for "equality" in which nobody will be discriminated against but accommodations will be made for people who need them—e.g., accessibility for the disabled—as most people once understand the word? Or does it mean treating some people more favorably and others less favorably based on their identity as a remedy for disparities, as Critical Social Justice understands it? Finally, does "inclusion" mean welcoming everybody, no matter their political, philosophical, or religious beliefs, as most people understand the word, or does it mean excluding any idea or belief that is theorized to be unwelcoming to those from marginalized groups by Critical Social Justice? You can also ask if the training will be based on any particular programs or texts and what data and measurements will be used to both show problems and evaluate success. By taking a measured approach, you allow yourself the chance to discover whether a Critical Social Justice problem is emerging without coming across as reactionary or resistant to even the most reasonable programs. Should it become clear that a problem exists, that an authoritarian agenda is being proposed that denies your freedom of belief and conscience, you will still have time to elevate your concerns before you are mandated to embrace Critical Social Justice ideology, and your early patience and prudence should, in turn, give you needed credibility when arguing against it later and encouraging your organization to change tack.

Warning signs

- Your organization frames its training in terms of diversity, equity, and inclusion.
- Your organization expresses general support for organizations that promote Critical Social Justice ideology, such as Black Lives Matter, the World Professional Association for Transgender Health, and the Southern Poverty Law Center.[1]

- Your organization requests optional DEI statements in job applications, annual reports, and promotion packages.
- Your organization's training is optional or strongly suggested but not mandated.

Code Yellow

The moment you know for a fact that your organization is subscribing to an unscientific and decidedly ideological approach to advancing diversity, equity, and inclusion in the workplace is the time to take more assertive action. If your organization hasn't already done so, there is a serious risk that it will soon begin imposing policies and training that require you to affirm very specific beliefs—for example, that you have been socially conditioned into white supremacist beliefs or even patriarchal, homophobic, transphobic, ableist, and fatphobic ones.

People with other conceptions of the world or human psychology or different ethical frameworks should not have to pretend to believe in the tenets of Critical Social Justice in a work or educational setting—just as they should not have to profess a belief in Jesus Christ or undergo mandated training in Christianity. They should, instead, have the freedom to believe that individuals have the ability and agency to evaluate and then reject or accept any of the myriad ideas that exist in a pluralistic society. They may believe this for a variety of reasons ranging from the liberal belief in the marketplace of ideas to conservative beliefs in personal responsibility to Marxist beliefs in the dialectic to religious beliefs in having God-given free will. It is essential that employers allow employees freedom of belief and do not coerce them into affirmations of creeds in which they do not believe. Anybody who feels able to push back strongly at this should do so.

However, it is important at this stage not to assume that your employer fully understands the implications of diversity, equity, and inclusion initiatives, the ideological beliefs or the scholars or movements cited, or the unscientific and counterproductive nature of unconscious bias training. Many employers do not have this knowledge and are misguidedly assuming it to be a much more liberal and inclusive thing than it is and are simply box-ticking to meet expectations of good practice. It is best to proceed as though your employer does not know what implementing such policies and trainings would mean in practice and respond in an open and cooperative manner, citing your concerns and suggesting alternative approaches to opposing prejudice and discrimination.

You might frame your concerns by explaining that you are aware that some companies/universities/schools have been using unscientific methods like unconscious bias training and promoting controversial and shoddy racial or gender theories that many principled opponents of racism/sexism/transphobia cannot support. You can give some basic but concerning details about this approach. Do this in a helpful and cooperative manner and help your employer to save face if they are unaware of them by being clear that you do not suspect your own company/university/school would go down this misguided path (even if you do) but simply want to seek reassurance that this is not what is meant by the proposed program or training. By asking questions in this way and emphasizing your own support of ethical policies against racism and other forms of prejudice and discrimination, you can avoid making unwarranted assumptions while at the same time making sure your employer/university/school is aware of how these trainings and programs function in practice. You will also make them aware that you know about Critical Social Justice and can and will oppose it from a knowledgeable and principled standpoint if necessary.

Warning signs

- Your organization not only frames its training in terms of diversity, equity, and inclusion but also references theorists like Robin DiAngelo, Ibram X. Kendi, and Reni Eddo-Lodge and explicitly endorses the work of organizations that promote Critical Social Justice ideology, such as Black Lives Matter, World Professional Association for Transgender Health, and the Southern Poverty Law Center, among many others.

- Your organization recommends that you put your pronouns in your email signature.
- Your organization communicates unmistakable Critical Social Justice tenets and claims in communications (e.g., "All white people are racist) and uncritically accepts the validity of unconscious bias training and testing.
- Your organization mandates DEI statements in job applications, annual reports, and promotion packages.
- Your organization mandates DEI training.

Code Red

If your organization is threatening disciplinary action or other penalties against individuals who articulate principled opposition to Critical Social Justice ideology, this is an urgent situation that requires immediate action. A simple letter explaining the problem with Critical Social Justice methods and appealing for more genuine diversity and inclusion in the form of an acceptance of a variety of worldviews will likely be ineffective at this point. Negotiation on behalf of freedom of belief can and should still be attempted to leave a paper trail of your attempts, but if there is clear evidence that the organization knows exactly what it is advocating and is committed to openly enforcing compliance with it, doing so is likely to be very difficult and needs to be handled with great care. You almost certainly will not be able to make any headway on your own and will need to contact organizations that promote freedom of speech and free expression for legal and logistical support.

Warning signs

- Your organization not only frames its training in terms of diversity, equity, and inclusion, references theorists like Robin DiAngelo, Ibram X. Kendi, and Reni Eddo-Lodge, and explicitly endorses the work of organizations that promote Critical Social Justice ideology, such as Black Lives Matter, World Professional Association for Transgender Health, and the Southern Poverty Law Center, but also demands adherence to the beliefs that they promote as a condition of employment, membership, or matriculation.

- Your organization mandates that you put your pronouns in your email signature as a condition of employment, membership, or matriculation.

- Your organization mandates DEI statements in job applications, annual reports, and promotion packages that are based on a Critical Social Justice rubric, such as the one used by the University of California, Berkeley, that has been adopted by other universities.

- Your organization not only communicates unmistakable Critical Social Justice tenets and claims in its training (e.g., "All white people are racist) and uncritically accepts the validity of unconscious bias training and testing but also demands that you accept these tenets and claims and submit to unconscious bias training and testing as a condition of employment, membership, or matriculation.

Addressing the Problem

Now that you've made your assessment and you've determined that your organization is already pursuing or will soon initiate illiberal DEI trainings or programs, it's time to think about practical steps for voicing your concerns and encouraging your organization to change its approach. Short of quitting, becoming a whistleblower, or being a conscientious objector, there are ways to address planned or ongoing Critical Social

Justice-training and programs in your organization. If you are at code red, you will likely need to jump straight to the last step (7), but if you are at code green or yellow, you should start with steps 1–6. The earlier you take action—and the more strategic and purposeful you are—the better.

Step 1: Understand Critical Social Justice terminology and concepts.

You do not need to have read vast quantities of critical theories of race, gender, sexuality, (dis)ability, or weight in order to have a fundamental understanding of Critical Social Justice. However, you do need to have a basic understanding of the worldview and ethical framework and be familiar with the core terminology and a sound understanding of the ideas that are commonly taught in DEI training programs if you want to address the impositions of those beliefs on you effectively.[2]

People who claim that you do need an in-depth knowledge of the theories, texts, and ethical framework of Critical Social Justice in order to be able to disagree with it, criticize it, or believe something else are often just trying to delegitimize your dissent. This is not how a liberal society that includes people with many worldviews works. One does not have to have read the bible and multiple Christian theological texts to justify disbelief in Christianity or to be a Muslim, Jew, Hindu, or atheist. A non-Christian can have a sound, basic understanding of what Christians believe and what their core moral tenets are and yet have a different set of beliefs and values of their own and expect their right to do so to be respected by a liberal society. Similarly, one does not have to have read everything there is to read about Critical Social Justice to have a sound understanding of its fundamental worldview and ethical framework and yet hold a different set of beliefs and values of one's own. They should also have their right to do so be respected.

Nevertheless, you do need to have that basic understanding in order to critique the belief system accurately and thus make a principled stand against it. This is essential for raising objections that are difficult to dismiss and for being persuasive to others. Just as you could not expect to be taken seriously if you critiqued Christianity by confusing it with Judaism, you cannot criticize Critical Social Justice if you confuse it with Marxism, liberalism, or radical feminism. While it shares some common features with all of them (just as Christianity does with Judaism), it has stark differences with all of them. Those differences are central to understanding Critical Social Justice as a worldview of its own with very specific conceptions advocating for very specific solutions. They must be grasped and understood and responded to as they are.

Step 2: Understand your own principled objections to Critical Social Justice.

This can be harder than you might imagine. For many people, it is just so clearly false to make claims that society is dominated by cultural norms of white supremacy and patriarchy, that penises can be female, or that obesity is healthy, that it seems your objections must be obvious. Similarly, it seems so unambiguously wrong to generalize negatively about whole groups of people based on their skin color (white) or sex (male) that it feels like this shouldn't need explaining. Neither should it be unclear to anyone, many people feel, why it is intrusive and authoritarian to attempt to subject people to "trainings" that aim to access their unconscious minds and reprogram them or that compel them to affirm the beliefs of Critical Social Justice and to follow its tenets. For many, there's a sense that if the problems with these ideas and behaviors aren't already clear to somebody, there is little point in trying to explain them.

This is a misconception. The need to be able to articulate the first principles of empiricism and liberalism and why they are better ways to address issues of inequality than theories about invisible power systems, collective blame, and mind control has never been greater in recent years. Older people may well remember times in which racism and sexism really were social and legal norms, and those who have lived in an authoritarian society will know what it is like to have to pretend to believe in a specific religion or ideology. Their insights into the preferability of liberal societies are particularly valuable. However, most of us who have grown up in a liberal society that increasingly valued science, opposed prejudice and discrimination, and supported freedom of belief have never had to articulate why these are good things. They have never had to argue for liberalism and may well lack the confidence to do so.

Therefore, many people simply remain silent, and this leads to the false impression that there is general agreement with Critical Social Justice methods in a workplace or at a university when this is probably not the case, and a principled and knowledgeable objection could embolden others to speak up. Other people might feel that they need to say something but are unsure where to begin and end up making general objections to "wokeness" or "radical leftism" or "cancel culture" that lack specificity and persuasiveness and are far too easy to dismiss as a general opposition to social justice.

Before addressing the Critical Social Justice problem in your organization, spend some time giving some thought to *why* you feel this worldview is factually wrong, this ethical framework so unethical, and the policies and programs authoritarian and illiberal. Perhaps you doubt that white supremacy is a dominant discourse in society and think that we have actually made much progress as a society toward developing a consensus that racism is stupid and morally wrong? If so, you can find evidence of the changing attitudes that support this hypothesis and argue that we cannot make progress unless we recognize progress to have been made. Maybe you have noticed that identity does not determine one's worldview and that viewpoint diversity exists among all demographics and think that constraining people into certain views based on their skin color is actually pretty racist?

You could be someone who believes that individuals have free will and the agency to reject and oppose racist or sexist ideas. Perhaps you think that collective blame of a whole identity group is both unwarranted and counterproductive to social equality and that history supports this position. You might fear that the identity-based Critical Social Justice approach is likely to lead only to greater racial tensions, worsen the so-called battle of the sexes, and encourage counter identity politics (e.g., Christian nationalism) and counter victim narratives (e.g., white victimhood) and set back progress on racial, sexual, and LGBT equality. You might think that "diversity training" often looks much more like "uniformity training" and want to argue for the value of viewpoint diversity, too, pointing out that marginalized groups are themselves ideologically diverse and are not spoken for by any one ideology. You could think that attempts to get at the "unconscious biases" that people are theorized to have are a serious problem for a number of reasons, including that there is little evidence people have these biases in the first place, that there is some reason to believe that attempting to train them out of people increases actual bias, and that it is a violation of privacy and the employer-employee relationship to seek access to someone else's mind at all.

It is worth spending some time both reading and thinking about what precisely it is about these ideas that are so objectionable to you and how to articulate that. You might find it useful to write your thoughts down and develop a kind of constitution of yourself to enable you to feel much more confident about standing up for what you believe in. Often, people have never thought through their own beliefs and values in a systematic way but simply hold them intuitively and are therefore limited in their ability to articulate them. You can begin by asking yourself questions.

How do I understand the subjects Critical Social Justice tries to explain?

Which of my values and beliefs do I find Critical Social Justice in conflict with and why?

What would I do differently to tackle the issues Critical Social Justice aims to address?

Be able to articulate your own understanding of racism, sexism, homophobia, transphobia, ableism, fatphobia, etc. For example, you might disagree that racism is an invisible power imbalance that all white people are socialized into and instead believe it to be beliefs about the superiority of one race over another that people can and should reject. Alternatively, you might believe that transphobia exists but is defined as hostility to and discrimination against trans people and dispute claims that transphobia is simply believing that there are two biological sexes. Further, perhaps you believe that people aren't unavoidably socialized into racism and do have the agency to reject racist ideas or that the best way to overcome bigotry is to consistently decline to evaluate people by immutable characteristics? Perhaps you believe that class and economic status are the key factors in inequality but that they are neglected by Critical Social Justice and that Critical Social Justice adherents actively divide the working class as they try to address inequality?[3] Maybe you believe that an excessive focus on privilege and marginalization by identity categories is insulting and disempowering to the groups it aims to empower?[4] These objections to the Critical Social Justice approach have been made by liberals, socialists, and conservatives. Such objections do not mean they are not concerned about advancing social justice. In many cases, they object because they care tremendously about ending prejudice and discrimination.

For example, you might object to Critical Social Justice approaches if you believe that less focus on differences and more on commonalities works better for overcoming prejudice and discrimination than dividing people into identity categories and treating them differently depending on those identities. Maybe you think that empirical research into the causes of disparities is a better way to understand and address them than theoretical concepts about unconscious bias and invisible systems of power and privilege. Or perhaps you have other ideas about ways to try to overcome any prejudices members of your organization might have that don't manifest in overt hostility or discrimination or disciplinary action. One of our clients suggested organizing social and sporting events to foster team cohesion. Evidence shows that team activities with shared goals make people very quickly stop noticing what race other people are.[5] Indeed, the best way to reduce prejudice among people from different backgrounds may be to simply have them work together as equals toward some common goal.[6]

Read arguments against Critical Social Justice ideas and evaluate them for yourself, keeping those that you find to be convincing and ethically sound and discarding those that are weak or morally dubious. Try to avoid simply latching onto a simplistic "anti-woke" narrative and repeating its main speaking points. This will result in a stance that is less authentically yours and that will be less genuinely knowledgeable and principled and more vulnerable to inconsistency.

Only once you have made such evaluations and defined your principles and beliefs will you be prepared to argue your case consistently and convincingly.

Step 3: Understand and keep records of the communications and/or policies and programs being proposed.

Once you understand the basic worldview and ethical framework of Critical Social Justice *and* feel confident about your own principles and articulating them, you should be in a good position to look at what is being proposed by your organization and evaluate it. Are your organization's proposed policies or programs based on liberal ideas of social justice or "critical" ones? You can tell by seeing if they focus on the individual and the individual's right to access everything society has to offer based on the premise that all humans have equal worth and if they oppose any barriers that stand in the way of this (liberalism)—or if they focus on invisible systems of power internalized by everyone and make simplistic assumptions about how these relate to immutable characteristics (Critical Social Justice). Do they rely on contested scholarship from authors like Robin DiAngelo? This is a clear sign of a Critical Social Justice approach, and you can suggest broadening their scope to include liberal scholars like John McWhorter and Thomas Chatterton Williams, libertarians like Thomas Sowell, and conservatives like Shelby Steele.[7] Do they appear to believe that the Implicit Association Test and unconscious bias training are scientific and effective? This is also a sign of a Critical Social Justice approach, and you can counter it, if necessary, with much evidence that it is neither.

When gathering this information, read carefully what is being proposed. Look for ideological elements that concern you, but also endeavor to find things you can agree with and support. Determine whether your organization understands the questionable ethics and poor evidence base of Critical Social Justice approaches. Does it fully embrace Critical Social Justice ideas, or has it simply adopted policies that are currently fashionable without doing any in-depth research? Everyone wants to create a welcoming workplace. What values about diversity do you share with your employer that you can begin to build dialogue around?

Here are some questions you can ask yourself:

- Is this a reasonable and liberal approach to antidiscrimination that can be supported by people with a variety of worldviews, or is it pushing one political and ideological framework?
- Does it encourage feedback and counterviews, or is it simply being asserted as the way things are to be done?
- Is the training program voluntary or mandatory?
- Is any reading list balanced or based on one ideological framework?
- Is the organization supporting a certain political or activist organization on behalf of all employees?
- Does the training make truth claims based on empirical evidence or on ideological assumptions?

If you start with the principle of charity and seek to affirm shared values, as you should, this should lead you to end up with notes that might look something like this.

Good

The training welcomes all voices. You are encouraged to give feedback. Antiracism training is voluntary. It cites empirical sources and a broad array of thinkers.

Bad

The language and readings are all that of Critical Social Justice. There are no liberal or conservative black thinkers or ideas included. Training includes the largely discredited unconscious bias training. Several unevidenced ideological claims are made.

If it becomes clear that your employer is pursuing an evidence-based approach to addressing discrimination that is inclusive of a wide variety of political, religious, cultural, and ethical worldviews from which one can oppose racism and other forms of bigotry, you can remain at Code Green. If your employer waffles ambiguously (a very common occurrence), you should probably assume they don't know the ideology very well themselves or are not ideologically committed to it but may still impose it on the organization due to external or internal pressures. In such a case, you should proceed to Code Yellow. But if your employer has already instituted and mandated a Critical Social Justice approach to addressing discrimination that requires individuals to adhere to one political and philosophical framework, you should move directly to Code Red.

Step 4: Network with others in your organization.

One of the most important things you can do is connect with other individuals in your workplace, university, or school who share your concerns.

If you are anxious about doing so publicly, you can approach people privately and sound them out diplomatically.[8] You are likely to find that some, if not most, of them will share your concerns if there is a genuine authoritarian Critical Social Justice issue at play and will be relieved to know they are not alone. This will allow you to coordinate your efforts.

If, at first, it seems as though there aren't any like-minded people in your organization, this is almost certainly a misperception caused by a culture of fear. The percentage of people who genuinely agree with Critical Social Justice ideas is actually very low, even in the United States, where the movement seems to be the strongest and where most of the leading theorists come from.[9] Why, then, do so many people feel as though everybody is on board apart from them? The phenomenon in which people believe that everyone around them agrees with the orthodoxy and so feel pressure to pretend that they do too, thus further perpetuating this impression, is known as "preference falsification."[10] To break this culture of fearful conformity, somebody has to indicate that they are not convinced by the current orthodoxy, thus emboldening others to admit that they also think differently. Although there is a legitimate fear of stigma attached to speaking in contravention of Critical Social Justice ideology, when one person in an organization speaks up in a principled way, more people in the organization will be empowered to do the same. Knowing that you are not alone, and that other people see the same problem as you do, has provided many people with the psychological support, strength, and will needed to resist Critical Social Justice authoritarianism.

Step 5: Determine a strategic response that will be the most effective and least risky.

If you find that you are facing an authoritarian Critical Social Justice issue, you will need to consider many factors when deciding how to respond. You will need to consider how serious the problem seems to be, how well your employer understands what they are advocating and how committed to it they are, how secure your job is, and how likely you will be able to register an objection safely. You will also need to take your own strengths and weaknesses and your own personality and personal situation into account when deciding how or whether to make an objection. There is no shame in considering your need for financial security for yourself and your family and thinking about whether you will have the ability to make persuasive arguments or deal psychologically with any accusations of an insufficient commitment to social justice.

Raising concerns and objections in writing is preferable as a first step because you can take the time to get your tone right and be diplomatic, clear, and firm, and there is less chance of you saying something that could be misinterpreted or misrepresented by the ideologically motivated (see chapter 5).

Often, committed adherents to Critical Social Justice speak in their own technical language and use sleights of hand to frame things in ways that make them appear to be simply opposing racism in a manner no one could object to. This can lead people trying to raise reasonable ethical objections confused and tied up in knots. As noted, you need to have some basic knowledge of this language to untangle it, break it down, and respond to it. However, you do not need to become an expert in the subject to confidently assert your right to your own political or philosophical beliefs, be they well-developed and sophisticated or simple but important to you. Be proactive in engaging with your organization about viewpoint diversity issues and exploring alternatives to Critical Social Justice approaches.

You should make your first approach as friendly and charitable as possible unless you are already clearly in a Code Red situation. Assure your employer that you are for antidiscrimination policies and agree with as much of their DEI program as you can before raising your concerns. Raise issues in a questioning and cooperative way. This will be the most effective and least risky way to start a dialogue. You can get firmer later if this does not lead to a productive conversation. Be prepared to be patient and persistent. While some people are able to persuade their organization to remain open to viewpoint diversity and freedom of belief and speech and to move away from advocating radical political texts and groups and antiscientific forms of training quite quickly, it more often takes several exchanges over several weeks, if not months.

If your employer has already instituted and mandated a Critical Social Justice approach to addressing discrimination that requires individuals to adhere to one political and philosophical framework, you should move directly to Code Red.

Step 6: Be part of ongoing change and build a community.

Consider joining or supporting those organizations that might be in a position to offer legal support should the need arise, and begin making connections with like-minded others outside of your organization, whether on social media or through in-person meetups. Strong networks and coalitions are vital for defending liberal principles and our rights in liberal democratic societies. It is going to take time to make the case for positive alternatives to Critical Social Justice and to change cultural norms to reduce its power and prestige.

Step 7: Seek immediate support from relevant organizations and groups.

Options will vary depending on what country you are in and what security you have as an employee/student/academic/parent. Trade unions may or may not be helpful. The situation can be particularly difficult to navigate safely in the United States with "no-cause" firing policies, and the risk of disciplinary action or job loss is often real. Therefore, we always encourage people to consider their options carefully. It is always valid to consider your own needs and the needs of your family. Organizations and groups to help people in this situation continue to emerge and grow, but you will need to look carefully at their purpose and actions in order to be sure that your values align with them. When looking at organizations and action groups in your country, be careful to check that their goal is to make the field of work, study, or school more open to a diversity of viewpoints and not to replace Critical Social Justice authoritarianism with another form of authoritarianism.

* * *

The sheer volume of suggestions above may make you feel that there are innumerable daunting steps to take before you can start addressing the problem, but this is not the case. If you have read this far, you likely have a better understanding of Critical Social Justice ideology than most employers. And if you use the prompts above to write down a short list of principled objections to the approach that reflect your own moral framework, you will have thought through your own values more systematically than many people ever do. You will likely find that some of your principles may even be protected by legislation or case law in your country (such as the right to believe in free will, which is central to all the Abrahamic faiths but is counter to core Critical Social Justice ideas). My experience with Counterweight is that the risk of legal challenge is more likely to occur to employers if you can articulate a clear, principled objection than if you simply express your intuitive feeling that Critical Social Justice training and policies are authoritarian, nonsensical, unjust, or racist.

The good news is that you are by no means the first person seeking to address the problem of Critical Social Justice in an organization, and there is much to be learned from those who have already taken the steps you are considering today. This includes having a better understanding of how to word a letter of objection or concern to a specific policy or initiative based on Critical Social Justice—which means knowing not only what to say but also what not to say.

5 Stating Concerns about Critical Social Justice and Affirming Principles: Writing Templates

There are two distinct situations in which you might need to put pen to paper to talk about your principles in the context of Critical Social Justice ideology in your organization. The first involves writing a letter of objection or concern regarding training or policies based on Critical Social Justice, and the second involves crafting a DEI statement for the purposes of a job search, job promotion, or grant or school application. This chapter will focus mainly on the first type of writing because there are so many circumstances and variables to consider when voluntarily seeking to address a potential or actual problem with Critical Social Justice in an organization, but I will also address the second type of writing, which is often rightly perceived as a political or ideological litmus test or a form of compelled speech. Options in this second instance are far more limited, especially when the DEI statement will be evaluated according to a Critical Social Justice framework, but even in such cases, there are ways to frame a DEI statement in a way that doesn't necessarily sacrifice your principles.

Letters of Concern

Whether your workplace, university, or school has begun speaking on Critical Social Justice issues in a manner that causes you to feel concerned that it may implement Critical Social Justice policies or it is already clearly engaged in Critical Social Justice–based measures that you think are damaging to the culture of the organization and its employees or students, you may feel you need to express your concerns, seek more information, and, if necessary, push back. The best way of politely doing this (while creating a paper trail that you may need later) is to write a letter—or, in most cases, a formal email. There are better and worse ways to express your concerns, thoughts, and feelings for this purpose, but it certainly is possible to push back at authoritarian overreach in the name of "social justice" and persuade employers, co-workers, or school and university administrators to expand their approach to include more than one ideological perspective in antidiscrimination initiatives.

Since many institutions and organizations begin to implement Critical Social Justice policies in order to be seen to do something rather than due to a genuine understanding of and commitment to what these policies mean and entail, a letter can help alert them to problems. The letter should clarify that the Critical Social Justice framework is built on a very specific ideology that may not benefit the business or organization. It can also help to point out that enforcing that ideology on nonbelievers is a clear breach of freedom of belief and may even be legally actionable. The letter needs to address both principles and practicalities. Whatever your situation, there are two main points that are important to establish.

Point 1: That you are familiar with the main tenets of Critical Social Justice and that you are coming from a place of knowledge, not ignorance.

Among those who believe in Critical Social Justice, there is a strong tendency to dismiss all disagreement as ignorance. This is because the worldview believes people to be unavoidably socialized into invisible, oppressive power systems they are not aware of (as a reminder, the word "woke" is used to describe those who are aware of these invisible systems). Therefore, any disagreement or resistance can be used as evidence of the person's unawakened state. It is therefore important to use language that shows you understand the Critical Social Justice beliefs about invisible power systems, socialization, and unconscious bias and that your disagreement is well-informed. This will also be an effective strategy in the many, many cases in which your employer will be using Critical Social Justice language or programs simply to tick a box without actually understanding Critical Social Justice well themselves. By showing that you do and can speak its language better than they can, you may inspire them to actually look properly into what they are advocating in order to be able to respond to you. This may cause them to realize precisely what they are carelessly endorsing and become concerned themselves.

It is much harder to dismiss you if you say something like this:

> I understand the concepts of power, knowledge, and discourses underlying this approach to <antiracism.> This includes the beliefs that we are all socialized into accepting oppressive power systems as normal and claims that, as a result, we have a difficulty in seeing them that requires special training to overcome. As a <liberal/conservative/libertarian/Christian/Muslim, etc.> myself, I also believe that people can have <racist> biases that are harmful, but I have different beliefs about free will and individual agency, so I cannot subscribe to the simplistic and Western-centric theories of people like <DiAngelo, Kendi, and Eddo-Lodge.> I hope the organization is going to remain open to the variety of worldviews that exist among our culturally, religiously, philosophically, and politically diverse workforce.

Point 2: That you fully support antidiscrimination policies and that you are coming from a place of egalitarian principles, not bigotry.

Another way that disagreement is often dismissed is by attributing it to defensiveness or "fragility." This fragility is understood to be born of the wish to maintain privilege and one's sense of oneself as a good person. True believers in Critical Social Justice often act as though theirs is the only ethical framework from which one can oppose racism, sexism, or homophobia, although, in reality, many frameworks exist for doing so. For example, these prejudices can be opposed from liberal, humanist, conservative, socialist, and libertarian values as well as from many religious belief systems. Many alternative approaches to Critical Social Justice have liberal elements within them—the belief in freedom of belief and speech, equal opportunities and rights under the law, and treating people as individuals—and approaches based on such principles have been the most successful at overcoming racism and other bigotries. Those who acknowledge that liberal egalitarianism exists as an alternative approach to Critical Social Justice will often argue that liberalism is inadequate and not revolutionary enough. However, again, your employer may not know that Critical Social Justice is explicitly opposed to liberalism.[1] They may simply be promoting the currently dominant forms of DEI training. By making its illiberal nature clear, you can alert them to what it is they are actually advocating.

Make it very clear that you are fully committed to nondiscrimination on the grounds of immutable characteristics and in support of all ethical policies to oppose racism and other bigotries. If you then argue that you do not agree with the Critical Social Justice approach, you will be much harder to dismiss as someone who just opposes social justice. The difference between liberalism and current Critical Social Justice antiracism, for example, can be made clear if you say something like this:

The company is absolutely right to assert that black lives matter and anybody who does not believe they do is unfit to work here, but I am concerned about the ideological beliefs held by the Black Lives Matter movement you have shown support for. Obviously, the intention to dismantle capitalism would affect my salary and pension and I'm concerned about what would happen to parental leave if the company fully signed up to the dissolution of the nuclear family. I'm hoping you can reassure me that we can oppose racism without subscribing to any radical movements?[2]

Considered, reasoned queries can be raised effectively and tailored to your scenario. Below, you'll find a simple template that we developed at Counterweight for an introductory letter approaching an emerging issue in an open and questioning way. This is be used for an emerging situation in which you are not sure your employer, university, or school is fully committed to an authoritarian Critical Social Justice approach. You'll also find a second template we developed for a firmer approach addressing a more serious problem or for a follow-up if your initial approach has not been productive.

Template for Raising Initial Concerns

1. *Begin with an acknowledgment of the broad issue and why your organization is making a response at all.* For example: I was pleased to see that <name of organization> takes <racial equality> seriously and is thinking about ways in which to prevent and address <racism.> This is something I very much wish to support.

2. *Move on to specific concerns and potential consequences of narrow or ill-thought-through ideological decisions.* For example: However, I am somewhat concerned by the sources you have referenced and the terminology that has been used. The books and essays recommended seem to point to only one theoretical approach. I'm afraid that this will fail to cover the majority of views held by <racial minorities> and could alienate those whose cultural, religious, political, or philosophical

112 • THE COUNTERWEIGHT HANDBOOK

beliefs differ from those included in your communication. (Note: for those outside of the United States, you might also note that this theoretical approach is an American-centric one.)

3. *Demonstrate that this concern is well founded by explaining your familiarity with the fundamental tenets of Critical Social Justice.* For example: Also, the positions taken by some of the <writers/movements> include some quite controversial ideas on <capitalism/political violence/the nuclear family/Asians/Jews> that I fear will neither be inclusive of the full range of values held by the <employees/students> of <name of organization/school> nor reflect well upon it to the broader public. Also, the reference to "unconscious bias" often refers to the Harvard Implicit Association Test, which is both scientifically discredited and includes ideological assumptions about people's unconscious minds, presupposing the necessity and possibility of intrusion into them.

4. *Request specific assurances.* For example: I am sure that <name of organization> is genuinely dedicated to diversity and inclusion, and so I am hoping that you can reassure me that:

    • A range of intellectual, political, and philosophical thought about <race and racism> held by <black intellectuals and other thinkers of color> will be included, as well as those suggested.
    • The organization will not be aligning itself with any radical political movement but will remain politically neutral and inclusive of a range of worldviews.
    • There will be no unconscious bias training based on the discredited Implicit Association Test.
    • The <antiracist> initiatives will be inclusive of the diversity of thought held by people of all <races.>

5. *Close with a thank you, restate your commitment to ethical approaches to the problem, and indicate openness to discussion.* For example: Thank you for your attention to this matter. Like you, I believe it is very important to

address issues of <racism> and social justice in effective and ethical ways. Please let me know if I can be of any help with any initiatives to achieve this or if you would like further information or evidence of anything I have said above.

Template for Addressing a More Serious Problem
(or If a More Diplomatic Initial Approach Failed)

1. *Again, begin with acknowledgment of the issue and why your organization is making a response at all before expressing concern about the way they are going about it.* For example: It is very important that <name of organization> has strong policies against discrimination and works to include people from a diverse range of range of racial, ethnic, religious, and cultural backgrounds, as well as LGBT people and those who are disabled. I very much want to support all productive and ethical initiatives to achieve this. However, I do not think this is what the current <communications/policies/training> programs are doing, and I wish to express serious concerns about a number of issues.

2. *Indicate specific concerns and give evidence of them as well as a concise explanation of the problem with them.* For example:

   • On <date>, <name of organization> expressed its support for the Black Lives Matter movement on social media. This is not simply a movement of people who believe that black lives matter, which I hope and expect we all do. This is a radical political movement that has justified political violence, expressed a wish to dismantle capitalism and dissolve the nuclear family, and supports figures like the extremist Louis Farrakhan, who has referred to Jews as "termites" and "Satanic." This movement cannot, therefore, be supported in good conscience by those who wish to oppose racism in all its forms, including liberals, libertarians, conservatives, moderate religious believers of all faiths, and, of course, Jews, many of whom are black. (Attached is some information on the Black Lives Matter movement.)

- On <date>, we received emails from <name of the sender> telling us that we <as employees/students> are expected to indicate our gender identity by putting our pronouns in our email signatures in order to support trans people. This, again, is a political statement rather than a simple wish to be inclusive of trans people. In fact, it excludes everybody who does not consider themselves to have a gender identity. It also creates pressure on people to reveal information about their gender identity that they may prefer to keep private and which an employer does not have the right to know. Further, it excludes those who have ethical objections to the concept of gender as distinct from sex, which includes many feminists, Christians, and Muslims, as well as some trans people.

- On <date>, we received notification that there will be mandatory antiracist training. Having looked at the training service you have commissioned for this, I am concerned to see that it takes a purely Critical Social Justice approach as defined by Özlem Sensoy and Robin DiAngelo, excluding all other worldviews held by people of all races. The exclusion of the numerous black intellectuals who address race and oppose racism from a different perspective is particularly concerning as it appears to legitimize some black thinkers and delegitimize others, thus seemingly specifically denying black employees any independence of thought. It also includes mention of unconscious bias training, which has serious flaws and has been discredited. Attached is evidence of the problems with replication, the confusion over what, if anything, it reveals, and the emerging evidence that it increases rather than decreases racial bias.

3. *Demonstrate that your concern is well-founded by explaining your familiarity with the fundamental tenets of Critical Social Justice and illustrate some specific problems.* For example: I was concerned to see that our <social media account/recent communications> have proclaimed support for Stonewall and the World Professional Association for Transgender Health (WPATH) despite their taking a narrowly ideological view of gender that includes truth claims about issues like puberty blockers that are not supported by medical science and trans athletes that have been refuted by sports scientists and which currently face legal challenge from parent groups and detransitioned individuals. I am also confused by the recommendation to base our antiracist views on both Robin DeAngelo and Ibram X. Kendi, even though they are fundamentally opposed on what racism is and whether it is a bad thing that individuals can avoid or an inevitable thing that is neither good nor bad.

4. *Express plainly that you believe that while the current course of action signifies intention to take on problems that you are also concerned about, the approach is a mistake that could exacerbate the issues or create new ones.* For example: While the intentions of this program are clearly good, I am very doubtful that genuine diversity and inclusion can be achieved by using this approach. I, along with the vast majority of the workforce, appreciate and share the aim to ensure that nobody is held back by their race, gender, or sexuality. However, this approach is likely to be counterproductive and raises significant ethical concerns. While those who genuinely believe in the Critical Social Justice approach must have the right to hold those beliefs and have their input included, we must not impose them upon everybody. It is illiberal to expect all <employees/students of color> to hold these particular <antiracist> beliefs just because of <their race.> In reality, <black> intellectuals who address issues of <race and racism> are ideologically diverse and so too are <nonintellectuals of color>. It is il-

liberal to insist that all <white> people affirm the belief that they are inherently <racist.> This will lead people who are not <racist> and who do not believe they are <racist> to pretend to be <racist> to stay <employed/enrolled>. This is likely to only cause greater racial division. Similarly, those who are <LGBT> have a variety of political views and should not be spoken for by one ideology. I fear we are setting ourselves up for all kinds of problems, including that of a hostile <workplace/classroom> and potential lawsuits if we do not allow people to hold their own cultural, ethical, political, and philosophical beliefs.

5. *Provide some examples from liberal, egalitarian principles and make suggestions for genuine leadership training or alternative approaches to engaging diversity successfully.* For example: Please consider some of the options I attach for a more genuinely inclusive approach to leadership training and addressing issues of diversity and inclusion. You will see they allow people to have their own minds and views rather than those the Critical Social Justice approach dictates they must have because of their identity.

6. *Close with a thank you and invitation to more discussion. Express a willingness to take leadership roles with regard to navigating the issue, if needed or appropriate.* For example: I urge you to take these concerns seriously and look at the materials provided. I am more than willing to provide further information, help survey the workforce for the approaches they wish to be taken to oppose <racism>, or help find more genuinely inclusive approaches to diversity issues that recognize the viewpoint diversity that exists within each group.

For full letters objecting to specific topics, see the appendix. No matter the exact problem, keep in mind that you will want to adjust the letter depending on the severity of the problem, your own personal circumstances, and your personality.

DEI Statements

If you are an academic or in higher education, there is a very good chance that you have had to draft a DEI statement of some kind, whether for promotion or tenure, or may soon need to for a job application or grant. While on the surface such a statement may seem innocent enough— perhaps even valuable and necessary—in the same way that a teaching statement might be, in practice, they are far too often used as filters to separate those who subscribe to Critical Social Justice beliefs and those who do not.[3] The (in)famous rubric used by the University of California, Berkeley, for example, which has since been adopted by numerous other universities, gives the *lowest* score possible to those who say they are "willing to supervise students of any gender or ethnic identity" and will "treat everyone the same" regardless of their background.[4] Put another way, such a liberal, individualist, universalist answer is immediately disqualifying. The highest scores are given to those who "convincingly express intent, with examples, to be a strong advocate for diversity, equity, [and] inclusion" and who have "organized or spoken at workshops or other events . . . aimed at increasing others' understanding of diversity, equity, [and] inclusion." In other words, scientists, historians, economists, etc., who are not also Critical Social Justice activists are not welcome.

When used in such a manner, it is not uncharitable or incorrect to refer to DEI statements as ideological or political litmus tests in the same way that Liberty University, a private Christian school founded by televangelist Jerry Falwell, uses a religious litmus test for prospective faculty and students. Specifically, professors "must contribute to the Evangelical Christian mission" of the university,[5] and students must abide by its doctrinal statement, which affirms that "each person can be saved only through the work of Jesus Christ, through repentance of sin and by faith alone in Him as Savior."[6] Whether asked to provide a DEI statement in alignment with UC Berkeley's rubric or to make a profession of faith in alignment with Liberty's doctrinal statement, the individual faced with a litmus test who wants to keep their job, get a job promotion, or get a job is faced with the same type of decision tree. In the case of DEI statements, you can do one of three things:

1. *Tell the truth.* If your views are fully in line with Critical Social Justice ideology, this is the only logical step. But if you are not a believer in Critical Social Justice ideology, telling the truth will almost certainly lead to rejection.

2. *Lie.* If your views do not align with Critical Social Justice ideology, you might profess your belief in Critical Social Justice ideology and deny your conscience in order to make a living, get a grant, get an education, etc.

3. *Mirror.* Tell the truth, but mask it in the language of Critical Social Justice ideology. Even if your views do not align with this ideology, you can craft a response that expresses your true beliefs but does so in a way that mirrors Critical Social Justice ideas, such as by layering in key words (e.g., antiracism, intersectionality, etc.).

Assuming you are someone who is not an advocate of Critical Social Justice, option three is the only chance you have to satisfy reviewers while keeping your conscience clear. I am aware that some people have begun to rely on ChatGPT or other AI platforms when crafting DEI statements. I urge caution with this, having experimented with it myself. It seems even AI gets confused by Critical Social language and becomes inadvertently problematic. It can be helpful if your aim is to lie or to simply generate ideas, but for truth-telling mirroring, you will likely need to do some heavy editing or at least experiment a significant amount with prompts to make the language specific to your past experience, future plans, and research goals. You can use the language in this book's glossary to improve accuracy, but proper execution is tricky and requires basic knowledge of Critical Social Justice ideas and language.

Below is a sample DEI statement couched in the language of Critical Social Justice that is compatible with liberal principles and that illustrates my general point—that it is possible to craft a statement that gives the type of answer a Critical Social Justice–dominated institution will want to see while being fully compatible with freedom of belief and speech and viewpoint diversity. I include commentary throughout to highlight the sleight of hand, which should not need to take place to hold liberal views in a university, but unfortunately does:

> I am strongly opposed to any form of essentialism, whether it be related to race, culture, gender, dis/ability, sexuality, religious or philosophical belief.

The word "essentialism" is generally approved in Critical Social Justice environments but can also refer to opposing the essentialist assumptions of Critical Social Justice ideology—for example, that all black people support Critical Race Theory, for example. You have included philosophical beliefs that includes your right to be conservative or gender-critical.

> In my experience, while most people try to treat everyone as an individual, we are all prone to falling prey to biases that can amount to stereotypes and which can constrain people.

In this way, you are using the word "bias," which is prevalent in Critical Social Justice ideology and relates to specifically theorized biases about identity but can be used to object to unwarranted assumptions being made about people more broadly and include people not considered marginalized by Critical Social Justice and people who hold views that do not align with Critical Social Justice.

> Members of groups that are well represented may still face biases, assumptions, or generalizations about their group, but they are generally more able to challenge this and demonstrate their falsity. This is harder for members of groups that are underrepresented who may feel isolated and unsupported and

then be discouraged from speaking up about their experiences or challenging any prejudice.

This is compatible with the Critical Social Justice thinking around identity groups but also compatible with concerns about the silencing of views held by those who don't conform to Critical Social Justice ideas—for example, conservatives, (real) liberals, dissident black thinkers, gender-critical people, etc. They are typically underrepresented in a university setting.

Therefore, I ensure that I myself work reflectively to minimize my own biases in the classroom.

Again, you are using the word "bias" in its commonly known sense. Reflecting on our biases is something we should all do all the time and doesn't have to relate to Critical Social Justice ideology at all.

I actively take steps to create an environment in which none of my students feel unsafe to speak.

"Unsafe" is often used in Critical Social Justice rhetoric to refer to how certain identity groups are assumed to feel if exposed to views other than Critical Social Justice, but students who are against Critical Social Justice often know their positions at the university could be rendered unsafe if they voice their views and thus remain quiet. The use of "unsafe" in this statement can refer to this context—that you are committed to making those who oppose Critical Social Justice feel safe about speaking up.

I particularly look out for signs of people whom I know or think might belong to an underrepresented group feeling uncomfortable to speak and make efforts to ensure they are given space and encouragement (but not pressure) to share their thoughts, views, or experiences.

"Underrepresented groups" will usually be read in terms of identity by Critical Social Justice believers, but you can also use it to mean people with underrepresented views in a Critical Social Justice environment. At this point, you will probably be asked to draw on your own examples of how you have addressed diversity, equity, and inclusion in the classroom, so the next few passages are examples of possible framing.

> On one occasion, a Black student confided in me that he felt unable to express his views in class because other students (mostly white) expressed biases about how Black people think and experience the world. He feared being ostracized or otherwise punished for speaking his mind. I spent some time with him to understand what kind of comments made him feel this way. It was mostly implication that all Black people held values he did not, while white people were assumed to be individuals. I then challenged students to think about how such statements could be experienced. In this way, the student did not have to challenge them himself, and he did begin to speak up more confidently toward the end of the course.

Such a passage speaks in the language of Critical Social Justice but can easily include the ban on diversity of thought many of our black correspondents felt they had experienced. They were especially frustrated by white Critical Social Justice advocates telling them how they should think and how they should feel. Meanwhile, the capitalization of the word "Black" can be understood as compliance with the Critical Social Justice concept of "grammatical justice" or "orthographic justice." In this context, the word "Brown" is often similarly capitalized in Critical Social Justice literature in reference to race, while "white" is often kept lowercase to avoid white supremacy. Even so, some Critical Social Justice advocates argue that "white" should also be capitalized so that "whiteness" is not seen as the norm or default and so that white people will be more easily held to account for their role in maintaining and perpetuating systemic racism.[7] Note, however, that the capitalization of "Black" need not necessarily be an indicator of Critical Social Justice ideology and that it can be grammatically justified on other grounds. In the field of political science, for example, it is commonly used to refer to a subset of Americans who are the descendants of enslaved people from various regions of West Africa and who today share a distinct sub-culture.[8] Therefore, the capitalization of "Black" can be an ideological choice that aims to racially categorize people for purposes of alleged "antiracism," but in the US context, it can also be used neutrally as a proper noun that identifies a particular cultural group.

> On another occasion, a student who was Deaf told the class she was unable to fully join the conversation because she needed to lipread.

Similarly, the capitalization of the word "Deaf" shows awareness of dis/ability theory.

> Because the way the desks were set out, she could not see everybody's lips. We rearranged the classroom into a circle when possible and when classes were more tightly packed, I asked students to face the Deaf student before raising their point. In this way we improved the equity in the classroom.

Equity is a tricky word to incorporate because in the Critical Social Justice sense it often implies discrimination on the grounds of identity, which is obviously illiberal. However, in some cases, especially in the case of disability where people have extra physical needs, it is entirely liberal to treat people differently in order to enable them equal access to the class.

> In terms of inclusion, I try to pay particular attention to my use of language and endeavor to make as few biased assumptions as possible while being sensitive to difficulties that could arise. For example, I did not assume that an inter-national student from <China> would have any difficulties with English but instead engaged him in friendly conversation, which gave him the opportunity to disclose that he could use support with his written English. Similarly, when a student mentioned their "partner" relevantly in discussion, I did not assume

that their relationship was heterosexual in my response, although, in this case, it was. I have had cause on a few occasions to directly challenge racist and sexist comments on the part of students.

Here, you are using a definition of inclusion that is absolutely compatible with the liberal aim to be welcoming to everyone, and your challenge to racism and sexism can be equally inclusive and object to the denigration of any group.

I have also intervened when students with a dominant worldview are taking up too much time in discussion and always try to ensure that minority voices are also heard in the classroom.

This language is used in relation to identity groups who are assumed to have the same worldviews in Critical Social Justice theory, but dominant worldviews in universities are generally Critical Social Justice ones, and your commitment to encouraging the expression of minority worldviews is a commitment to viewpoint diversity among all demographics.

* * *

While proven letters and tested DEI statements give us something clear to emulate, we can also glean valuable lessons by studying the cases of those who have combated Critical Social Justice in their organizations, especially with regard to strategic questions such as how best to determine the optimal style and manner of approach. This involves an honest assessment of your own strengths and weaknesses, as well as your risk tolerance. After all, the goal isn't just to defeat Critical Social Justice but also to survive it.

6 Choosing the Best Personal Approach for Combating Critical Social Justice: Case Studies

Very often people feel hopeless about addressing an emerging or entrenched authoritarian Critical Social Justice issue in their workplace because they feel they have only two options: oppose it head on in strident and uncompromising terms, or just submit to it. This is not helped by those among the anti-woke who insist that we all need to be brave and forthright. They may even be scornful, treating the reticence of others as cowardice. In reality, it is simply not in everybody's capabilities to be an outspoken anti–Critical Social Justice activist. This could be for a number of reasons.

1. *You could be in danger of losing your job, and you need your job to feed and house yourself and your family.* You are not a coward if you prioritize your responsibility to your family over your responsibility to fight a culture war.

2. *You want to help fix problems in your field, and you know that getting fired would put a damper on that effort.* Sometimes discretion is the better part of valor, and it might be better strategically to bide your time or work more cautiously against the problem. For example, if you are

in teaching, psychology, or healthcare, you might reasonably decide that you can better protect children and those needing mental or physical health treatment from Critical Social Justice–based approaches over the long term if you don't get fired in the early stages of your career.

3. *You might be someone whose skillset does not include verbal argumentation.* You could be more technically minded or oriented toward practical problem solving. If this is the case, you might find yourself tied up in knots by theoretical Critical Social Justice concepts and struggle to clearly make your case against it in the way it needs to be made to be effective. This has been the experience of several engineers and computer technicians we have encountered, as well as people on the autistic spectrum (these two groups have a strong overlap). They have found themselves bewildered when trying to navigate the often illogical and contradictory language of Critical Social Justice. Emergency services personnel have also found themselves in trouble because their skills are more action-orientated than rhetorical, and their tendency toward plain speaking and directness is particularly easy to problematize and misrepresent.

4. *You could be somebody who is conflict averse or anxious and find the idea of causing conflict or opening yourself up to accusations of racism or sexism or transphobia psychologically daunting.* While there are those who would tell you to toughen up, this may not actually be something you can do by sheer power of will if you are, by nature, someone who dislikes conflict, becomes anxious easily, and finds yourself easily upset by false accusations of holding views you do not hold. While many of the toughest clients we had at Counterweight (and, in fact, a majority of the Counterweight team) were women, there is evidence that women are on average more likely to be conflict averse and worry more about social ostracism than men.[1]

For some people, however, it may be possible to take a firm or even a hardline approach to an emerging authoritarian Critical Social Justice issue emerging in their workplace. Speaking out can be feasible for a number of reasons.

1. *You might feel secure in your job or in your financial situation.* For example, perhaps you are a tenured professor, in a senior position, close to retirement, or financially independent, or have highly prized skills that will be welcome elsewhere.

2. *You might feel you must protest because the workplace environment is becoming unbearably toxic and you will be forced to leave if you cannot resolve the problem.* For example, perhaps you have found yourself in a position where the level of stress and anxiety caused by a "walking on eggshells" atmosphere has forced you to the decision that you either must act or become seriously mentally ill.

3. *You might feel that, despite the risk to your security and employability, you have a moral responsibility to oppose the ideology being imposed upon you, your colleagues, and your field, and that you must take an activist approach.* For example, perhaps you believe that the Critical Social Justice antiracist training in your workplace amounts to the demonization of white people and have a deep moral conviction that you cannot stand by in the face of racism against any group. Perhaps you believe that gender ideology in your workplace requires you to fail to protect women's sex-based rights and that you must oppose the endangering of women even at the risk of your job. Or perhaps you work in the medical field or in humanitarian aid and believe that a Critical Social Justice approach to medicine or humanitarianism endangers lives, and you cannot be silent in the face of this.

4. *You might just be somebody who does not have the capacity to hide your true feelings and concerns, keep your mouth shut, or take a slow, gentle, and diplomatic approach to addressing the issue!* Some people simply are naturally blunt

and outspoken and hold strong opinions that they are not willing or able to hide.

We certainly need people like the above who are willing to put themselves forward and raise objections confidently and assertively and take a moral stand against authoritarian and illiberal Critical Social Justice initiatives, especially when they do so to protect more junior colleagues, vulnerable people, and vital professions. In these cases, we just need to help people to frame their objections in the most effective, knowledgeable, and principled way while trying to minimize the damage to their careers.

It is deeply ironic when a "social justice" movement operates in ways that mean only the most powerful and economically privileged feel able to speak up. Yet, even if you feel you can take on an authoritarian Critical Social Justice issue confidently and assertively in your organization, it is not always the best strategic option. In some situations where the problem is not deeply entrenched, an overly assertive approach could lead to defensiveness on the part of your employers, while a gentler and more cooperative approach could yield better results. Similarly, in some situations where Critical Social Justice ideology is deeply entrenched in your organization and you are in a junior or highly supervised position, you may strategically decide not to make waves in order to be able to remain in the field and effect positive change when you are in a more senior, secure, or autonomous position.

Generally speaking, there are three main things to take into consideration when deciding *how* you will go about addressing an emerging problem in your workplace.

1. *The severity of the problem.* If it is only just emerging and your employer is not committed to or knowledgeable about Critical Social Justice ideology, you will want to take a softer approach than if they are

dedicated to enforcing policies and training programs they understand well and are committed to. The consequences of the problem not being addressed—particularly within fields like medicine and humanitarian aid—should also guide your decisions.

2. *The security of your job.* If you are in a junior position or one that is easily replaced, you may need to be more diplomatic than if you are in a secure position or if replacing you would be difficult. You will need to consider how much of a nuisance you are able to make of yourself without being fired, whether you can afford to be fired, and whether your field will suffer if you and other people who oppose Critical Social Justice get fired. If you are more secure or feel your field will suffer more if you don't speak out, you can take a firmer approach.

3. *Your abilities and personality.* You will need to think realistically about what you are able to do both intellectually and psychologically. If you are not rhetorically skilled, are not easily able to grasp Critical Social Justice language and concepts, and are not confident, assertive, or able to withstand a significant amount of conflict and stress, it is okay for you to think about other ways in which you can push back than a direct verbal challenge. If, on the other hand, verbal argumentation is among your skills and you handle stress and conflict well and feel a strong moral obligation to raise objections, you may want or even need to present a strong challenge to Critical Social Justice initiatives.

There are five general styles of approach you can take when pushing back against Critical Social Justice ideas, which I refer to as "gentle," "stealth," "firm," "hard," or "public." Your style of approach should be appropriate to your particular situation and skills, but none are mutually exclusive and you may find you will need to use more than one style over the course of weeks or months.

Gentle

The "gentle" approach is a good one to take if a problem is just emerging and you think your employer or university might be unaware of the full implications of trainings or programs based on Critical Social Justice and would be open to different viewpoints. It is also a good approach if your job is not secure and you need it, or if you are a very conflict-averse person. It is defined by being cautious and asking questions and advocating only when safe and appropriate.

Case study

One of Counterweight's clients, whom I will call "Prisha," was a South Asian woman who was growing increasingly concerned about decolonial and postcolonial narratives and ideas based on Critical Race Theory taking hold in her place of work. She was a liberal humanist who was strongly opposed to racism and imperialism, but she found the theoretical assumptions being made by Critical Social Justice advocates to be quite radical, unevidenced, uncharitable, and counterproductive to a cohesive workplace. However, she was quite a shy person and was reluctant to speak up for a number of reasons, including that she did not want to upset or lose any of her friends who had embraced these ideas, get in the way of well-intentioned aims to oppose racism, be criticized by her employers or colleagues, or be misunderstood not to oppose racism. Her conscience bothered her, though, when she found herself using Critical Social Justice language and pretending to agree with these ideas when she did not actually believe them or find them ethical.

Prisha decided she could not be complicit in theorizing colonial and racist attitudes everywhere even though she did not feel confident enough to challenge them. Her first step was simply to stop using the language herself and to remain silent or noncommittal when other people did, while continuing to speak up against overt racism. She found that she did not get challenged on this. This emboldened her to start making more clearly humanist statements against racism and colonial attitudes in the conversations. This led to another South Asian woman starting a tentative conversation with her in private, in which they both eventually felt comfortable to say they had the same concerns. When they discovered they were not alone, Prisha and her friend then began tentatively sounding out more colleagues and discovering which of them shared their liberal approach to antiracism or were at least accepting of such an approach. They found there were several.

Over time, Prisha grew in confidence and more confidently began to make statements compatible with liberal humanist approaches to antiracism. Although she did not openly criticize Critical Social Justice approaches, the mere airing of her approach led others to feel less pressure to support the Critical Social Justice antiracism and decolonial rhetoric, and so the overall use of Critical Social Justice language in the workplace was reduced. Prisha reported that the gradual change over a period of six months made her workplace a more comfortable and accepting place where people felt more confident to speak freely.

This is an example of a very gentle and minimal approach to opposing Critical Social Justice narratives in your workplace—simply airing alternative approaches or not explicitly supporting them, and so not contributing to entrenching them in your workplace. What Prisha did in her workplace was reduce the pressure on others to engage in preference falsification. This is when people misrepresent their actual views because they feel under social pressure to do so.[2] This then adds to the social pressure for others to do the same. The very simplest way you can push back at Critical Social Justice views is to not espouse the views themselves so that you are not contributing to this pressure to conform. This may not be possible in every workplace where training programs compel people to affirm beliefs they do not have, but it is still possible to signal your lack of enthusiasm for them and encourage others to do the same.

Other ways in which you can gently and cautiously challenge Critical Social Justice ideas include:

- Asking questions about proposed initiatives: "Do you have information on the success of unconscious bias training?"; "Should we make sure we don't assume all people of color think the same way and are inclusive of a variety of views?"; and "Should we be worried that mandatory gender identity declarations might put pressure on people to 'out' themselves?" By asking questions like these, you are issuing only a gentle challenge and not asserting a strong position. Nevertheless, you are signaling that you do not accept everything uncritically, and by doing so, you will embolden others who share similar concerns to raise their own questions and speak up.
- Showing enthusiasm for antidiscrimination policies and recommending some of the ones more focused on empathy and compassion that are compatible with a variety of views. In this way, you do not directly reject Critical Social Justice methods but rather provide better alternatives to them.
- Being friendly to other people in the organization who are making stronger (but still principled) objections to any kind of authoritarian Critical Social Justice initiative. This will offer them some needed support and encouragement without necessarily exposing yourself to any negative response by the organization.

Stealth

The "stealth" approach is a good short-term approach for young professionals, junior faculty, grad students, and those in training whose individual workplaces or fields or university departments are ideologically captured. It enables them to get through the early stages of their career, which will be worthwhile not only to them but also to the field in the long run. For example, if you are a therapist or teacher in training, you might not be in a position to challenge the ideology without risk of risk of being failed or denied certification. By going along with this training in the short term in order to receive a needed diploma or certificate, you give yourself a certain degree of future freedom to speak up as a professional in the field and to steer your own practice or classroom away from Critical Social Justice ideas.

Case studies

"Emma" is a psychology student doing her master's degree and training to become a therapist. She contacted Counterweight when one of her papers was found to be "problematic" because it did not use any critical theories of race and looked at people as individuals. Emma, who is white, did not wish to assume racial power dynamics to always be in play in the problems of her clients of color unless they told her that their experience of racism was a problem they sought help for. She was concerned that she was being explicitly required to always raise the issue of racism and acknowledge her own privileged position when dealing with clients of color. She feared this would damage the therapeutic relationship, make empathy and trust harder, and also assume that the psychological problems of people of color were always explained by racism.

Emma's concern was dismissed as white fragility and her defensive wish to avoid issues of race. This distressed her as her concern was actually that making these ideological assumptions would result in suboptimal therapy for people of color. By seeing the problems of non-white people as homogenous and rooted in racial oppression while recognizing the problems of white clients as potentially stemming from a number of individual causes, she feared that only white clients would receive effective therapy. However, expressing this concern was likely to get her failed from her courses.

Emma, therefore, with some initial help, began to give her professors the kinds of papers they wanted while studying more individual-focused and evidence-based cognitive behavioral therapy approaches on her own. Her grades improved and she will soon complete her program. She intends to go into private practice where she will recognize everyone as an individual and allow them to tell her what their issues are without making any assumptions about them from their race. She believes this temporary subterfuge will allow her to ultimately deliver an individual-centered approach and person-centered therapy for people of all races.

"Jahwar" is a scientist from a Muslim country who moved to a Western one where he applied for a job that allowed him to help save lives. He is a liberal humanist who opposed sexism, homophobia, and antisemitism in his home country. He was asked for a statement of diversity, equity, and inclusion and provided one that was liberal humanist in nature and focused on individualism and universal human rights. At his first interview, it was made clear to him that this was not acceptable. He was spoken to in Critical Social Justice terminology that was unfamiliar to him as he had not encountered the ideology in his own country. He contacted us to ask for help in understanding this and getting through his second interview.

While Jahwar holds his liberal humanist values very strongly, he also really wanted to get the job. By getting the job, he also knew that he would be bringing needed expertise to scientific projects that would benefit people from the poorest countries. With advice, he worked out a strategy in which he would frame his answers in ways compatible with Critical Social Justice without saying anything that went directly against his principles. He practiced this at length and passed his second interview by managing to use approved language without saying anything he believed to be illiberal or antihumanist. Jahwar worried about the ethics of giving a false impression of buying into Critical Social Justice ideology but felt he would be in a stronger position to defend his principles once established in his job. He reasoned that he would not be able to help anyone either with his scientific work or by principled opposition to Critical Social Justice if he did not get the job and had to leave the country.[3]

Other ways in which you can stay under the radar in a Critical Social Justice–dominated environment without compromising your principles include:

- Simply staying silent when you can.
- Referencing the right theorists but using bits of their work that are not incompatible with liberalism. Most theorists will give examples of genuine racism that you can agree are genuine racism. Find some things you can agree with.
- Using ambiguous terminology. For example, you could say that you believe diversity is very important and that people should examine their biases, which is likely to be understood in a Critical Social Justice sense. Meanwhile, you actually mean it in a liberal sense, which is much broader than identity-based diversity or bias but includes viewpoint diversity and the biases inherent in ideological adherence, including to Critical Social Justice.
- Waffle when necessary and answer a slightly different question. For example, a trainee engineer might be convinced by considerable evidence that at least some of the reason there are fewer female engineers than males is explained by differences in interests between men and women on average. However, this would be unacceptable as an answer to a question such as, "Do you believe 50 percent of engineers should be women?" Instead, the trainee could subtly avoid answering the question directly by saying, truthfully, that female engineers are every bit as good as male ones, and that discrimination against them is unacceptable and should not be tolerated. The more wordy you can be at this point—for example, by digressing into excellent female engineering mentors you have had—the better.

Such evasive measures are not ideal but can be navigated in the short term to enable viewpoint diversity to continue to exist in important fields.

Firm

The "firm" approach should be taken if and when you have decided you must register an objection. It is honest, straightforward, and clear while also being charitable and assuming good will in your employer or university. Put another way, it should be undertaken in a cooperative and friendly spirit. This will encourage them to engage you in good faith. If negotiation and reasoned dialogue are at all possible to be achieve, this will be how to do it.

Case study

"Chloe" is an indigenous Canadian woman who works within mental health. When she contacted Counterweight, she was becoming increasingly concerned by the ways in which Critical Social Justice ideology was taking over all approaches to treating patients and staff training at her place of work. She disagreed that seeing everything through Critical Social Justice theories of race and colonialism would be the most helpful thing for purposes of patient care and treatment and completely refused to pretend to believe in them herself.

Unlike many of her colleagues with similar objections, Chloe believed she had some protection from being accused of having white privilege or a colonial mentality and prepared to address the issue in a very practical and organized fashion. She requested a meeting with her manager and went into it with three aims: firstly, to secure her right to decline to take part in any of the Critical Social Justice–based staff training herself; secondly, to raise concerns about the approach itself; and thirdly, to suggest other options. She was very clear in her mind about the concerns she had. A confident speaker, she spent considerable time preparing a structure for the meeting and took control of it, essentially giving a presentation of her concerns in a well-informed but simple and pleasant manner. She was so calm and reasonable and willing to address issues of inequality in other ways and involve herself in projects to do so that she was received well. She was assured that her input was valued and that the alternative reading she suggested would be included in any future training.

However, it frequently happens that initial meetings go well and then days or weeks later, the employee who raised concerns will receive another email requiring them to comply with the same policy or program they had believed they had been assured would not be imposed upon them. Therefore, we advised Chloe to follow up the meeting with an email providing a record of what had been said and promised and push for a response agreeing that her account of the meeting was correct. She managed to do this and is now fully involved in diversity, equity, and inclusion initiatives at her company, where she is able to continue to keep her organization open to diverse viewpoints.

The reason Chloe's situation went so well was because she was calm, cooperative, patient, persistent, consistent, and friendly, and her workplace was not already fully committed to a Critical Social Justice approach. Many workplaces are not yet ideologically captured and, if faced with this kind of confident, resolute, and knowledgeable but non-combative approach, will negotiate, cooperate, and compromise. It is true that Chloe's identity offered her some protection and that she is a particularly articulate speaker, but people with majority identities and less confident speakers have also had success with taking this approach.

No matter your comfort or skill level, there are multiple ways to take a firm but cooperative stance that does not incline your employer to become defensive and that instead encourages them to cooperate with you:

- Show your appreciation that your employer wishes to address issues of inequality and assure them that you wish to support them in this while raising your concerns.

- Show that you are knowledgeable while raising your concerns in a clear and simple way that is easy to absorb. (Avoid overwhelming people with information, but feel free to direct them to additional resources that they might consider.)
- Model the polite attention and careful consideration of your employer's point that you would like them to show you.
- Follow up any meetings with an email summary of what was discussed to ensure that no focus or clarity is lost.
- Be prepared to have to repeat yourself or make the same points repeatedly in relation to different issues and do so patiently and calmly. In a larger organization with different levels of management or administration, you might also need to state your concerns in more than one meeting.
- Offer alternatives that address the same issues in more empirical, liberal, and ethical ways.

Hard

The hard approach is appropriate when your diplomatic approach has not worked or if you are in a Code Red situation (see chapter 4). That is, it is time to be uncompromising when the situation is authoritarian or abusive and you can no longer continue to work at the organization unless the ideological abuse stops.

Cases studies

"Charles" is a dark-skinned first-generation American man. He works in a position of seniority in his company and is recognized as highly skilled. He became alarmed when a white manager sent out a company-wide email acknowledging his white privilege and making a commitment to use it to oppose racism and support employees of color. The manager encouraged white employees to do the same, causing Charles to receive many emails from white colleagues, many of them in a subordinate position acknowledging their undeserved privilege over him. Charles experienced this as deeply insulting, as though they were saying they were better than him despite his achievements because they were white.

Charles first reaction was to compose a very angry company-wide email accusing his manager and colleagues of disrespecting his position and also disrespecting his family, who had come to the country with little money and built a successful business. The disrespect that Charles felt stemmed partly from his cultural background, which led him to interpret any suggestion that he is considered lower status as an insult.[4] But it was also a universal human reaction against infantilization. For example, many women find it insulting and infantilizing to be told they need men to step back and promote them in order to succeed when they are doing just fine and better than many men on their own abilities.

Before hitting send on the email, however, Charles decided to consult with Counterweight. We recommended that he express less anger but remain very clear that he felt insulted by the patronizing messages and that he wanted them to stop. In a revised draft that he ended up sending, he referenced his cultural background and was clear that many others who shared it (and were also not white) would be similarly insulted. He said that the organization was being culturally insensitive in imposing the white privilege concept on him, that it was not acceptable to racialize him at work, and that the emails were getting in the way of him doing his job. His manager issued an apology immediately and stopped the emails and Critical Social Justice–based antiracist initiatives. This was the only occasion on which a Counterweight member succeeded with one email!

"Tom" took a similar hard and uncompromising approach because he—a light-skinned mixed-race man—also found the racial focus in his organization intolerable and because he was confident that his skills would enable him to find another job easily if necessary. Indeed, he had been able to be selective when first choosing his job. In a letter he wrote to his organization, he was outspoken about his ethical objections to the Critical Social Justice approach and defended liberalism, science, and reason (see letter #6 in the appendix). He demonstrated that he was knowledgeable about the core texts of Critical Race Theory and the tenets of various movements his company had been supporting and presented his objections to them clearly.

Tom was polite but uncompromising about his opposition to these ideas being circulated around his work environment and made clear that the environment had become so hostile and tense since their introduction that he was considering resigning. He told his employers that their enthusiastic promotion of Critical Social Justice ideology was inappropriate and provided evidence that it went against existing policies. He objected specifically to training material that negatively generalized about white people and that he regarded as racist. He requested certain assurances that company-wide emails advocating Critical Social Justice ideas would stop, that nobody would be compelled to attend any training sessions, and that no racial segregation of any kind would occur.

Tom's strongly expressed principled objections were compelling but, unlike Charles, he faced opposition from a network of activists within the organization who were putting pressure on the company. Tom's employers, it seemed, were stuck between a rock and a hard place, as some non-white members of staff were putting pressure on the company to implement Critical Social Justice training programs while others, like Tom, were insisting that they must not. Although such an outcome should not be unexpected given that the categories "people of color" (in the United States) and "BAME" (Black, Asian, Minority Ethnic in the United Kingdom) do not represent organic, meaningful communities and only serves to prove how ideologically diverse these "categories" are, this resulted in Tom's employers trying to conciliate him without addressing his points.

If you choose to take this approach, you must be aware that it could work against you, particularly if, like Tom, your employer is facing even more internal (or even external) pressure from Critical Social Justice activists. Nevertheless, it can be successful. These are important points to remember:

- Raise your objections in strong and uncompromising but not rude or angry terms. If you act unprofessionally or lose your temper, you risk being disciplined for aggressive behavior, which is harder to fight than disciplinary action for having a different worldview.
- Don't forget to be clear that you are opposing a certain approach to addressing racism and other forms of bigotry and are fully onboard with addressing prejudice and discrimination in more inclusive and ethical ways. Suggest alternatives.
- Show your knowledge but keep things simple and clear and avoid anything that could be considered hyperbolic. For example, if you overwhelm your employer or manager with information and examples of worst-case scenarios, you risk confusing the message you are trying to get across and appearing paranoid. Catastrophizing is likely to lead to your concerns being dismissed.
- Make your concerns bigger than you. For example, try to include in your arguments concerns that taking the Critical Social Justice route could damage the health of the company, as this possibility is likely to get your employer's attention and also gives you the opportunity to say that you value your company and wish to protect it.

Public

Going public with your concerns is a way to address an issue that simply cannot be addressed internally, but doing so is also likely to end any possibility of continued employment or association with the organization. Going public can take the form of seeking the support of a journalist to bring attention to your case, circulating a petition among those concerned, or exposing the problem to the general public on social media. It can also involve seeking the support of a governing body or external organization to investigate the organization and either require or pressure the organization to cease any authoritarian policies or programs that impose ideological beliefs on its workers, students, or members.

Case studies

Jodi Shaw, then an employee of Smith College, went public with the hostile work conditions she faced due to the introduction and adoption of Critical Social Justice ideology at the school. In a whistleblowing You-Tube video, she said,

> I ask that Smith College stop reducing my personhood to a racial category. Stop telling me what I must think and feel about myself. Stop presuming to know who I am or what my culture is based upon my skin color. Stop asking me to project stereotypes and assumptions onto others based on their skin color.[5]

Jodi decided upon this action following a long series of increasingly concerning events in which she was expected to racialize not only herself but all her colleagues and students. She was told what kind of music she was allowed to perform (not rap) to advertise the library service based on her skin color (white), required to attend essentializing, ideological racial training, and expected to reference her own race and those of other people constantly. Over time, Jodi became increasingly convinced that being coerced into adopting an ideology by her employer infringed on her civil rights and was both legally and ethically wrong. With her internal appeals being ignored or rejected, she determined she was left with no other option but to raise her concerns publicly.

Jodi made sure to exhaust every internal remedy available to her first (and document it all very carefully). She tried as hard as possible to work things out privately before going public. In retrospect, she is glad to know that she did everything in her power to resolve things internally via civil dialogue before resorting to public exposure of the problem. She simultaneously laid the groundwork for coming out publicly if it turned out to be necessary, which, sadly, it did. This included preparing for the worst by talking through possible consequences for her friends and family and how to minimize impacts on them and seeking the support of an appropriate therapist. It also included preparing for achieving maximum impact by setting up YouTube, Twitter, and Facebook accounts and befriending people from Smith and other schools with similar problems.

When she finally posted her video, she was prepared for both a positive and negative response. Going public in this way was very stressful for her. She considers herself a principled person but not a combative one. By nature, she prefers to work cooperatively with people. Despite receiving support from many people who shared her concerns, she also faced a lot of hostility that she had to navigate. This caused significant anxiety and distress and Jodi's psychological well-being suffered. Ultimately, Jodi resigned from Smith College with a principled letter in which she said:

> Every day, I watch my colleagues manage student conflict through the lens of race, projecting rigid assumptions and stereotypes on students, thereby reducing them to the color of their skin. I am asked to do the same, as well as to support a curriculum for students that teaches them to project those same stereotypes and assumptions onto themselves and others. I believe such a curriculum is dehumanizing, prevents authentic connection, and undermines the moral agency of young people who are just beginning to find their way in the world.

Still somewhat shell-shocked from the whole experience, Jodi is nevertheless determined and resilient and now helps and advises other people who feel alone in such situations to connect with others and push back in authentic and ethical ways.

Elizabeth Spievak, a professor of psychology at Bridgewater State University, similarly took a public approach when her school not only failed to support her but also threatened more restrictive research policies after she was accused by racism by students. Rather than go straight to social media to make her case, however, she went to external bodies—in this case, Counterweight and FIRE (Foundation for Individual Rights in Education)—to enlist their assistance in her defense.[6] Elizabeth, who had previously been commended for her work for social justice, came under fire following a research study into how metaphorical rhetoric affects people's perceptions of issues. The study, designed by one of her students as part of a class research project and approved by her university's Institutional Review Board (IRB), presented participants with scenarios in which their local community faced an important issue but framed the issue as either an "open wound that is deteriorating your local community" or a "wild beast preying on your local community." This rhetoric was randomly applied either to Covid-19 or the Black Lives Matter movement. The study then asked participants what should be done to reduce the escalation of the issue. The scenario that described the Black Lives Movement as a "wild beast" was screenshotted by a participant and later shared on social media by another student. Elizabeth and students involved with the research project were named and accused of racism. The university immediately apologized for the "pain and harm" caused by the study, which it also described as "racist," and launched an investigation. Although the student who designed the study is not white, much was made about the fact that Elizabeth is white.

The injustice of these accusations and misrepresentation of the purpose of the study, as well as Bridgewater State's promise to change its research policies so that research would undergo more restrictive (ideological) review before approval, caused Elizabeth to feel the need to object publicly. Previously, Elizabeth had not been fully aware of the threat from the Critical Social Justice movement to scientific research and had been generally in support of initiatives for racial equality, assuming them to be largely liberal. This experience led her to research it more closely, discover decidedly illiberal elements in the movement, and become deeply concerned about the threat to scientific research into important social issues, including racism.

Elizabeth is a particularly strong and resilient individual who was able to argue her case strongly. She presented herself as principled and formidable and showed very little anxiety when defending herself publicly, although she confided to supporters that she had found the whole situation deeply distressing. However, she was determined that scientific research must be defended against ideological censorship. Although justifiably indignant about the defamation of her own character, she was more concerned about the impact on her students and more junior academics without the benefit of tenure. After sending a letter to the university urging them to rethink its policy changes, FIRE published an article detailing some aspects of the case and calling upon Bridgewater State University to recognize that,

> Even setting aside the misrepresentation, that a research project might offend subjects or others does not justify its restriction under the banner of preventing "harm." The proposal that research "do no harm" is admirable as an aspiration, and IRBs undoubtedly serve important roles in evaluating proposed research to ensure that it does not purposefully or inadvertently cause concrete, measurable harm. However, conceptualizing "harm" to encompass offense—however great—to the content of a question posed to a voluntary participant will place considerable constraints on research, including in ways that may not presently be anticipated.[7]

At time of writing, this situation is not fully resolved, although there are grounds for hope. Elizabeth continues to work with senior academics who share her desire to address the threat of Critical Social Justice to academic research and support more junior academics.

Unfortunately, only the most egregious cases of ideological over-reach are usually deemed of sufficient public interest to make much of a splash and inspire opposition among the public. However, this is not the only way to go public. Other correspondents had success circulating petitions or writing open letters that broke down the problem with a particular policy or program. By calling attention to those who would be adversely affected by whatever was being proposed, they managed to gain support and affect some level of change. This included liberal Welsh citizens who opposed a proposed Race Equality Action Plan (REAP) in Wales that took a decidedly Critical Social Justice approach, a consortium of healthcare professionals in Maryland who objected to a new policy that would require them to undergo unscientific unconscious bias training to renew their licenses, and a schoolteacher in Germany who circulated a petition among parents and governors following plans to implement a training program that suggested, among other things, that white people were not fully human.

Things to be aware of when going public:

- If you decide to expose your own organization or publicly cast it in a negative light, know that there is an extreme likelihood that you will lose your job. Most people don't take this route until they have already lost their jobs. It could also cause you problems in finding a future job, and unless you are a particularly sympathetic character whom the public is willing to support financially or a charismatic and confident speaker who is both able and willing to address the problem in a way that people want to support, your financial future could look bleak.

- If you solicit external support, seek out the most serious, principled, and influential organization(s) you can find in order to help you with this. Ideally, the organization(s) should be widely respected and politically nonpartisan. In this way, you will minimize accusations that you are simply a far-right propagandist, which is often the quickest path to having your concerns dismissed.
- If you go with a journalist to make your story public, aim for the most reputable writers and outlets you can find. Avoid any who use hyperbolic language and partisan speaking points so that your concerns are taken seriously.
- If you intend to write or say something yourself on social media, plan your message well and have it looked over by someone who has a strong understanding of the Critical Social Justice worldview and can catch anything that could be misunderstood or twisted and help you present your concerns in the most knowledgeable and principled way possible.

* * *

These five approaches are very broad and general, and you may choose to use elements of one or more of them or even move from one to another. For example, you might choose to remain mostly under the radar while occasionally openly questioning some policies or programs. Alternatively, you could begin gently but find you need to become firmer or must even harden your stance or go public. As a general rule, however, begin with "minimal force." Whatever you decide to do, make sure you do it after considerable thought and plan strategically. Avoid responding when upset or indignant. If you feel yourself becoming angry, it is better to remain silent and then address the matter later in an email or ask for another meeting once you have composed yourself and formulated what you want to say and how best to communicate it.

No matter your approach, however, you will almost certainly encounter resistance, if not from your organization then from co-workers and peers who themselves adhere to Critical Social Justice beliefs. Knowing how to deal with and navigate those inevitable challenges will be important for your success.

7 Dealing with Common Critical Social Justice Challenges: Troubleshooting

Once Critical Social Justice comes to dominate an organization, your work or educational experience will change in unwelcome but predictable ways. No matter your race, nationality, religion, politics, or profession, you will likely face mandatory training from your employer that has little if anything to do with your actual job or research and that may conflict with your own ethical framework, and you will likely have to deal with overzealous coworkers who will be empowered to scrutinize every professional and personal interaction in the workplace or classroom and report any "problematic" behavior. In this new environment, the problems you face will range from minor nuisances that can be easily ignored, such as emails meant to inform you about the importance of "antiracism" or diversity, equity, and inclusion initiatives based on Critical Social Justice, to major threats to your basic rights or job security, such as policies that require you to not only participate in Critical Social Justice–based training but also to profess believe in its tenets and to practice its teachings. I have already laid out some action steps you can take depending on the degree of urgency, but there's a good chance your first attempt to express concern or suggest alternative approaches will be ignored or rejected or be met with equivocation. Even when your employer responds to your concerns exactly the way you'd like, Critical Social Justice can rear its head within your organization in other ways—for example, at the level of co-workers and peers who monitor every word and interaction in the workplace or classroom to ensure ideological conformity. When such challenges present themselves, it is not always immediately clear what, if any, remedy or recourse you might have, but there are ways to troubleshoot such inevitabilities short of giving up or quitting.

Challenge 1: You've made a principled statement of concern about Critical Social Justice ideology in your organization, but you've been met with outright rejection or radio silence by your employer or school and you continue to receive official communications based on Critical Social Justice ideology and to be encouraged if not required to attend mandatory training based on Critical Social Justice ideology.

It is not uncommon for employees whose organization has adopted Critical Social Justice–based ideas and practices to receive countless emails or inhouse communications that are nominally about diversity, equity, and inclusion but that are actually promoting illiberal ideas about race and racism that are foreign to them. For example, they might make assertions about the inherent racism of white people and the need for white people to accept their own privileged whiteness and dismantle it. These messages often announce training sessions that not only express these same ideas but also require compliance for the employee to have satisfactorily completed them. This can feel very unjust and frustrating for white people who despise racism, because even denying one's racism or objecting to being called racist is understood as "white fragility" and evidence of one's racism. This belief is presumptuous, prejudiced, ideologically blinkered, almost certainly erroneous, and certainly unfalsifiable. As a result, such sessions are often seen as a weekly or monthly reminder of their original sin according to a religion they do not share.

It is often more frustrating to be spoken for than to be spoken at. Indeed, perhaps even more concerning is that these emails or training sessions also make assertions about what black people and other people of racial minority think, believe, and experience. These assertions almost always accord with Critical Social Justice beliefs about race and antiracism. Many "people of color" who don't believe or experience any of these assertions do not like being told by their (often white) employer how they should, must, or do think because of their race. Like their white peers, they frequently experience such training as demeaning and invalidating of their own thoughts, beliefs, and experiences. Anyone who objects to the training risks being accused of being an agent of white supremacy.

Other people have found themselves in receipt of many emails informing them that they have a gender identity and should declare it regularly to be supportive of trans people, or that they are expected to attend training where they will affirm their own gender identity and everybody else's. This can be experienced as intrusive and authoritarian by anyone but is a particular problem for those who don't have a gender identity, don't believe in gender identity, or who believe gender to be an oppressive social construct. It requires them to either pretend to have a gender identity and think gender is real or reveal that they don't and be labeled transphobic. It is also a problem for trans people who would really like to just get on with their job and with their colleagues, and who have often had no problem doing so until their employer or school decided to make everybody focus on gender identity and a particular gender ideology. Following this, trans people may well find that the fact that they are trans gains much greater significance in their colleagues' minds. This is particularly unsettling for them if they did not want a lot of attention drawn to the fact that their gender identity differs from their biological sex. In some cases, colleagues may unfairly blame a trans coworker for the initiative even though the trans coworker had nothing to do with it and would much rather it be stopped.

No matter the exact scenario or situation, what can you do short of quitting once you've made your concerns about such training and emails known and they continue to be forced on you, either due to silence or rejection from your employer or school?

How to deal with this challenge

- Firstly, remember that these initiatives and policies are being promoted by people who believe in a certain ideology and not any particular identity group. If you are white or not trans, do not begin to unfairly blame the alleged beneficiaries of this initiative—people of color or trans people—who may well hate it as much as you do even if they are impacted differently by it. Nevertheless, there may well be an activist or group of activists within the workplace that is influencing the employer, and they are likely to be more united by ideology than by race or gender identity. In that regard, recognize that your problem is as much with them as your employer. Although Critical Social Justice advocates are very resistant to considering other points of view, you can try to find some common ground with them, or at least try to reach a détente that allows you to be a conscientious objector to their efforts.

- Because everybody who isn't for Critical Social Justice training and communications is by definition having this ideology imposed on them, try to sound out your colleagues in a friendly and open way. This can be risky, but you are likely to find that more people share your concerns than you realized. It's likely they have been too afraid to say so for fear of being accused of white supremacy or transphobia. If you find that there are a significant number of you and that this number includes a diverse range of people, including those the initiatives are intended to help, you can try to express your concerns again—but this time as a group—in which you collectively share a principled objection to having a political ideology imposed upon you. This type of organizing is especially needed if the employer is overly influenced by an activist group within the organization that is pushing Critical Social Justice ideology. A counterweight such as this will be greatly needed.

- If your initial communication only tentatively expressed concerns and you did not make a specific ask, consider making one that your employer will have to say yes or no to. For example, ask for the option to be excluded from any mandatory Critical Social Justice–based emails or training sessions. If you are able to do this as part of a group, all the better. Collectively write and sign a principled letter explaining your ethical, philosophical, religious, or cultural objections to the training and ask that your request be respected. (See chapter 5 and the appendix.)

- If the training is already voluntary, your ask might be more general. For example, share your concerns about the potential impact of the training on workplace cohesion and ask for confirmation that people will be under no pressure to attend them or to affirm any beliefs they don't hold. If your employer or university has already indicated that nonparticipation will be frowned upon, you might then request that your employer look out for any developing signs of alienation, awkwardness, and fear in the workplace as well as trends of sickness or other absence correlating with the training. Even if they say no to this request, the seed has been planted that the training might lead to negative outcomes, which will make the employer aware of such a possibility and more likely to reconsider training if any of these signs appear.

- If you don't find many people who share your concerns, or even if you do but are not yet ready to make a united objection, keep records of all of these communications with the most concerning bits highlighted. This will be essential for any future objection or action you might wish to make and will make it much easier to counter any claims that you are exaggerating and that you have just been receiving perfectly reasonable emails about treating colleagues with courtesy and consideration.

Challenge 2: You've made a principled statement of concern about Critical Social Justice ideology in your organization, but you've been met with a waffling response by your employer or school and you continue to receive official communications based on Critical Social Justice ideology and to be encouraged if not required to attend mandatory training based on Critical Social Justice ideology.

While good managers or human resource officers who are unwittingly institutionalizing Critical Social Justice ideas without realizing that they exclude all other ethical frameworks from which people oppose prejudice and discrimination will listen to concerns being raised, too many will not. This is true whether or not those to whom you report are themselves ideologically invested in Critical Social Justice. In many cases, those in management or in human resources may not themselves really understand Critical Social Justice even if they use the language of it. They might be a very well-meaning person who misunderstands Critical Social Justice as a much more liberal and inclusive thing than it is and genuinely think it will be good for the company even if they don't really understand it. Equally, they might be someone simply box-ticking and making the right noises because there is pressure on them to do so. That is, they want to be seen as doing something, even if they don't fully understand what they're doing. Such individuals, whom I refer to as "buzzword wafflers," contribute to the problem in workplaces not because they are ideological zealots, but because they want a quiet life. However, they can be very difficult to deal with because they generally want to avoid any conflict, evade the concerns genuinely being raised, and refuse to speak straightforwardly and therefore make any attempts at reasoned conversation and resolution infuriatingly circular and unproductive.

The buzzword waffler is particularly frustrating to employees who do understand Critical Social Justice ideology and would like to speak plainly to their employer about why the things they are saying, texts they are recommending, policies they are implementing, or training programs they are initiating present a problem for freedom of belief and viewpoint diversity. Typically, what happens is that having taken great efforts to spell out the problems with the approaches in a principled and knowledgeable way in writing, the employee will be invited to a meeting where they will be "buzzword waffled" at. One employee who came to Counterweight told his employer, "I am concerned that diversity, equity, and inclusion seem to all be about diversity of identity and not very inclusive of a diversity of worldviews." This was responded to by a meeting in which the employee was reassured that this was precisely what the organization intended to resolve and then waffled on about the need to be inclusive of marginalized voices and worldviews. They then returned to promoting just one worldview —that of Critical Social Justice.

Another of our correspondents said, "I am concerned that you keep sending emails out recommending unconscious bias training because (a) UBT is unscientific and (b) it is not appropriate for an employer-employee relationship for you to demand access to our unconscious minds." The individual was reassured repeatedly that the employer did not advocate unconscious bias training and did not believe in it as a method. He then received several more emails talking about the importance of unconscious bias and expectations of employees to address theirs via Critical Social Justice methods. Each time, the employee responded by reminding the management that they agreed they did not believe in the efficacy of unconscious bias training only to receive a managerial response stating that management have already confirmed that they don't believe in it. Yet, management would continue to send emails recommending it.

One of our correspondents told his HR manager, "I am concerned that you are pressuring employees to read Ibram X Kendi's *How to be an Antiracist* when it claims that people can only be racist or antiracist and that being 'not racist' is not possible. I am also concerned that you promote Robin DiAngelo's work when it claims that all white people are racist. I believe people have free will to reject racist ideas and be not racist. Is that an acceptable stance?" This individual then showed us a waffly response by the HR manager claiming that neither of those theorists said either of those things and that, of course, the company accepted that people could be "not racist" and did not believe that all white people were racist. When we recommended sending in cited passages from the books in question where these claims were made,[1] the employee was ignored. He followed up again and was told the claim that the books said the things they actually said was right-wing propaganda, that the matter was closed, and that disciplinary action could be taken if he made such (accurate) claims about the contents of the books the organization was recommending again. This response contained a higher ratio of evasion and denial to waffling but such tactics are all linked and usually indicate an employer whose commitment is more to a quiet life than Critical Social Justice.

This is all infuriating, and we heard frequently from people dealing with this kind of evasive, waffly nonresponse. If employers deny that they are promoting the things that they are promoting or that the things they are promoting contain the content they demonstrably contain, it is impossible to reach any kind of resolution. Sometimes, this is done as an intentional motte-and-bailey move but more often than not it is simply a matter of the managers needing to tick the right antiracist boxes and make the right noises. In such cases, staying the course for them is simply a matter of expediency or even laziness. They might have little incentive to revise or change what they've already planned, even if they accept that your principled criticisms are valid.

But no matter the exact reason for the waffling, what can you do short of quitting when you have trouble getting a direct, unequivocal answer from your employer regarding your concerns?

How to deal with this challenge

- Direct your queries and concerns to others in the organization who might be in a position to offer greater clarity. Start by assuming that anyone else you might approach has not fully realized the problems with the Critical Social Justice–based training and messaging that the organization have been pushing and try to inform them in a helpful, friendly, and cooperative way.
- Avoid meetings if at all possible and try to raise your concerns by email, with the support of colleagues, where waffling is harder and there is a written record of the points being made.
- If you cannot avoid a meeting, prepare for it by having two or three simple questions that you would like answered or points that you would like addressed in mind. Solicit direct answers to keep the officer or manager on the subject. If they try to waffle or use vague buzzwords and nice-sounding platitudes, avoid going down any rabbit hole yourself and respond by assuring your employer that you share their concerns about racism and that you'd like to focus on your core questions and points.
- Follow up the meeting with an email that contains the two or three simple questions or points you wanted addressed. If you feel they were addressed even in a waffly fashion, write what those responses were. That could look something like this:

Thank you for our meeting today. I thought it would be useful to follow up by email. I met with you to discuss three concerns and you were able to reassure me on the matter. These were:

1. I was concerned that there had been talk of mandatory unconscious bias training and provided evidence that this is both ineffective and intrusive. You assured me that no such mandatory training will take place.
2. I was concerned that the organization had signaled its support for a radical political movement on social media when, given our mission, we have a responsibility to remain politically neutral. I showed you evidence of the political nature of the movement and received your assurance that the organization is committed to keeping its commitment to be politically neutral so I am glad that this will not be happening again.
3. I was concerned that you were recommending all employees to read a book that claimed all white people to be racist while our code of conduct states that all prejudice on the grounds of race is unacceptable. You assured me that you intend to adhere to the code of conduct so I am glad that no such generalizations about any racial group will be made in future.

Your employer will then have to correct you in writing if they don't intend to keep to those assurances or call you in for another waffly meeting, which you can follow up with another email summary.

If you feel your points were not addressed, your email can simply restate the points and request clarity again. This is the best way to cut through a buzzword waffler's equivocation and get them to address the issue you want them to address. The same email can be sent as many times as necessary. In this way, if the employer is unwittingly leading your organization into an authoritarian Critical Social Justice situation by trying to tick antiracist boxes with the least effort possible and not looking properly at what they are promoting, you will make this much harder for them to do. On the other hand, if minimal effort is their motivation, your polite persistence in search of unambiguous answers could make them expend more effort in continuing to evade your concerns. This can make them realise that to look at the material and address your concerns sincerely is the quickest way of getting rid of you and restoring a quiet life.

However, making a (polite and reasonable) nuisance of yourself as a strategy for getting your employer to pay proper attention to what they are advocating is a risky maneuver, particularly in those locations where there are "no cause" firing policies. Therefore, while this kind of patient persistence is the best way to get your box-ticking buzzword waffling manager or HR person to reconsider authoritarian or illiberal policies and plans, it is only to be undertaken when you are confident that your job is secure, or if it has come to a point where you no longer care if you lose it.

Challenge 3: You've made a principled statement of concern about Critical Social Justice ideology in your organization, but you continue to experience problems with Critical Social Justice in the organization because one or more co-workers or peers "problematize" all professional and personal interactions in the workplace or classroom.

Problematization is the process of revealing something to be an ethical problem when this is not immediately apparent. Within Critical Social Justice ideology, something that is not clearly racist or sexist can still be considered "problematic" in relation to race, gender, sexuality or some other identity issue because of assumptions or connotations claimed to exist within it. For example, use of the term "pregnant women" can be considered problematic because it relates pregnancy to women when trans men can also get pregnant. Although an individual who says "pregnant women" has not said "I believe trans men to be women," the statement is problematic because it can be argued to imply this. This also happens in even more tenuous ways. For example, it has been claimed to be problematic for a white person to compliment a black speaker on her speaking because this allegedly reveals surprise that a black person can be eloquent.[2] It doesn't matter if the white individual would have complimented a white speaker who had given the same talk in exactly the same words. This is because impact matters more than intention,[3] and it is theorized that black people would be impacted negatively by assuming the compliment to indicate surprise.

Problematizing is a particularly difficult issue to deal with. It occurs in a situation where there is a committed and knowledgeable Critical Social Justice activist in the workplace or classroom. They are usually highly skilled in the methods of unfalsifiable accusation making and Kafka trapping.[4] In a work setting, sometimes it is the manager of the company, in which case it is a particularly difficult situation to deal with. More often it is an employee or group of employees putting pressure on the employer, which can be countered by gaining the support of the employer, but this is still not easy. Employers can be afraid of challenging a problematizer. We heard both from individuals who had been targeted for problematization by a co-worker and from employers who have a problematizing employee. It is always a very challenging situation.

More often than not, problematization occurs when somebody with knowledge of the Critical Social Justice conceptual framework and some rhetorical skill targets an individual with the intention of showing him or her to have ideas that are problematic—that is, they do not adhere to the ideas or language of Critical Social Justice. Often it is someone who has directly challenged Critical Social Justice beliefs in some way, but it can be anyone. Sometimes the problematizer will go for someone who is not highly verbally skilled or has a particularly literal and systemizing mind and is easy to tie up in theoretical knots.

One of the people who came to us was problematized because he criticized the Black Lives Matter movement. He is black and absolutely believes that black lives matter, but he couldn't agree with the organization's aim to dismantle the nuclear family (a goal that was included on its website at that time).[5] His cultural background was religious and socially conservative, and the concept of family was very important to him. Nevertheless, he was accused of not believing black lives matter and everything he did subsequent to announcing his disagreement was problematized by a small group of activists within the organization. All his words and interactions at work were interpreted as bigoted in some way.

Another person we assisted never challenged any Critical Social Justice ideas at all. He made the "mistake" of asking a black colleague out on a date while being white. She didn't see him in a romantic way and declined, and he never mentioned it again. After some initial awkwardness, their friendship resumed. All was well until a Critical Social Justice activist joined the company and accused him of being a sexual predator for having asked out a non-white colleague. The activist then proceeded to problematize everything he did. He was accused of not responding as well to black service users as white ones in various subjective ways until his employer was pressured to send him for antiracist training. This client had had an exemplary record of helping people in need, most of whom were not white, and he resigned in protest at the injustice of this.

True problematization is more than just mere language policing. It is better understood as a form of bullying. Someone who is very well versed in Critical Social Justice ideology and highly rhetorically skilled can take perfectly ethical and normal language in relation to something like gender, race, or disability and twist its use into a grave and unforgiveable offense in ways that are simply incomprehensible to anyone not already familiar with the highly obscure and contentious theories based on Critical Social Justice. No one is immune from problematization, but some will be more vulnerable to it than others given Critical Social Justice ideas about intersectionality and positionality. But as with all types of bullying, the shy and socially awkward are particularly vulnerable to being problematized. One caring and conscientious woman whom we helped was close to a nervous breakdown when she approached us. She had had the misfortune of attracting the attention of a problematizer at her place of work even though she herself had never challenged Critical

Social Justice ideas and had, in fact, supported many of them, believing them to be more liberal than they were.

It is extremely difficult to resolve a situation successfully when somebody clever, dishonest, rhetorically skilled, and knowledgeable of Critical Social Justice has decided to problematize you unless you yourself are equally knowledgeable and skilled at sophistry. Few people are, and this is a good thing. There are some ways to minimize the damage done by a problematizer, however.

How to deal with this challenge

- Engage as little as possible. Think of some of the situations you have seen on social media. Someone is problematized and then there is almost nothing they can do to save themselves. Blood is in the water and the activists will circle, picking on everything that is said afterward. Even the most groveling apology will be found to be problematic. There simply is no saving oneself. Defend yourself once with a single dignified statement of your principles and then, if you can, simply ignore any further accusations. The best thing to do in this kind of situation is to disengage, even though our instincts may push us to do the opposite. The intention is to provide as little blood in the water as possible and hope the problematizer gets bored.
- If you have to engage because this is your work colleague and you have a manager who is receiving complaints about you, retain the same principle. Remain calm. Do not allow yourself to be stung by the injustice and respond angrily or emotionally. Instead, state your genuine position simply and with confidence. Affirm that the accusations are not true, that they are a misrepresentation of your words and beliefs, and, if possible, say that you will not defend yourself against any accusations of beliefs you do not hold.
- Do not lose your temper. This is very important, even if you are accused of really morally abhorrent beliefs. This is much easier said

than done but it helps to remember that the problematizer will be quite happy if you lose your temper and yell at them or thump your fist down on a table. They can then pursue you for intimidating behavior. Instead, maintain the moral high ground and say something like, "That is a very serious accusation and I am appalled by the beliefs and motivations you attribute to me. They are not something that exist in my mind and I'm sorry they exist in yours."

- Try to avoid being drawn down any rabbit holes of subjective interpretation or engaging with activists in their own theoretical economy. Instead, remain outside it. If you are someone who instinctively feels cowardly remaining silent in the face of injustice and as though you *should* defend yourself against every false accusation, try reframing your thinking. Try imagining yourself as a firm rock standing strong amid a raging sea of ideological zealotry. This image was helpful to a firefighter who came to Counterweight for help. His strong sense of justice and action-orientated nature made him particularly vulnerable to speaking hotly and playing right into a problematizer's hands. Try to be firm and confident but polite and co-operative. Make brief principled statements. For example:

  - If someone says, *"All white people are racist. You need to accept that and work to dismantle it."* You can say, "I don't share that belief. I believe that people have the agency to accept or reject racist ideas. I respect your right to your belief system and ask that you respect my right to mine. We can both oppose racism without believing exactly the same thing."

  - If someone says. *"You disagreed with that colleague because she was a woman. As a man you need to accept that women have knowledge and expertise you might not."* You can say, "I am well aware that many women have knowledge and expertise that I do not. In this case, we both had expertise and we both put forward suggestions. That's a productive work environment."

- If someone says, *"Calling something stupid or crazy is ableist against those with learning disability or mental illness."* You can say, "I would not call someone with a learning disability stupid or someone with a mental illness crazy and I suggest you don't either. That would be ableist."

In all these cases, the problematizer is likely to end up at a place where they claim something like: *"Your beliefs and language contribute to an oppressive culture that is hurting <black or trans or other identity groups> and you need to be accountable for it."* In which case you can respond with, "I understand that theoretical framework and respect your right to believe in it. I do not share your beliefs but will join you in opposing all prejudice and discrimination. I don't think it's appropriate for us to try to convince others of our own political or religious beliefs at work, so we should leave it here."

This is not remotely likely to satisfy the Critical Social Justice activist, but if, like most, your employer is not a Critical Social Justice activist but is simply trying to do the right things for ethics and optics, your calm, principled reasonableness will make the ideologue's hyperbolic, inconsistent zealotry stand out more clearly to them. It will be clearer to them that the person making their lives difficult is not you. The Critical Social Justice problematizers are a menace to any organization, and employers are increasingly seeking ways to prevent them from destroying their companies from the inside. As long as they have a presence in your organization, though, this type of calm and principled response remains the best course available to you as an employee or student, I'm afraid.

* * *

Although these are the most likely challenges you will encounter in the workplace, there are others. No matter the challenge, however, best practices remain fairly consistent.

These are summarized best as:

- Always raise objections in writing where possible.
- Attempt to do so in concert with colleagues who share your concerns.
- Follow up any meetings where you raised concerns with emails restating them and how they were responded to.
- Be patiently and politely persistent with employers or HR managers who do not appear committed to a Critical Social Justice worldview and whom you wish to make aware of the potential problems they are setting up for the organization (if you can do so without losing your job or don't care if you lose your job).
- Avoid engagement with a problematizer who uses dishonest tactics to twist your words and respond only with minimal, dignified, and principled statements, if at all.
- Do not allow yourself to be needled into losing your temper. Remain calm outwardly and seek moral support as needed.

Many of the challenges you will encounter when combating Critical Social Justice are due to the very nature of Critical Social Justice. Put simply, they are extensions of its built-in defense mechanisms, which, as you now well know, includes rejecting any criticism of its tenets as "white supremacy" or "whiteness," rejecting evidence and reason in favor of "other ways of knowing" and "lived experience," and rejecting liberalism itself. The good news is that due to its destructive nature, lack of limiting principle, and internal contradictions, it will ultimately collapse in on itself even if we ourselves are unable to directly defeat it. The bad news is that until that day arrives, it can do untold damage, and we thus must do all we can to curb its reach and keep it from dominating our lives and institutions any more than it already does.

Conclusion: The Fall of Critical Social Justice and How to See It Out

The Waning of Woke?

Many social scientists, as well as political and cultural commentators of various kinds, have begun to argue that Critical Social Justice (usually referred to as "wokeness") "peaked" in 2020 and has since been on the decline. There is evidence to support the position that there is a growing resistance to Critical Social Justice and a general sense of culture war fatigue. The overall attrition rate for DEI roles was 50 percent higher than non-DEI jobs in 2022,[1] as many companies began phasing out certain DEI positions. Further, while job postings for DEI positions expanded by nearly 30 percent between 2020 and 2021, they dropped by almost an equal percentage between 2022 and 2023.[2] Support for the Black Lives Matter movement declined from 67 percent at its peak in 2020 to 51 percent in 2023, and a majority of Americans say the increased focus on race since the 2020 George Floyd protests has not improved the lives of black people.[3] There are also signs that other areas of Critical Social Justice focus have decreased in popularity. Analysis by sociologist Musa al-Gharbi, arguably the most meticulous documenter of this trajectory across many spheres of society, reveals, among much more, a decline in relevant journalistic word usage as well as a drop in cancellation events, a decrease in academic output using Critical Social Justice theories, a greater confidence of students to express their views, and a greater push-back against DEI from both employers and mainstream outlets.[4] This is supported by research examining the language of 725 corporate social responsibility communications undertaken by Adam William Chalmers and Robyn Klingler-Vidra. Whereas companies once primarily used the term "civil rights movement" when discussing issues of social justice, their language shifted in 2015 and became dominated by "wokeisms" such as "allyship" "diversity equity," "equity and inclusion," and "racial justice." Since 2021, this language has been in decline.[5]

There is certainly room for optimism that Critical Social Justice is losing its social prestige. Some portion of this shift was inevitable be-cause Critical Social Justice has always been destined to implode for three primary reasons: Firstly, Critical Social Justice has a concept of society that is not rooted in reality and relies on methods that do not work. The need to take the claims of the theorists and activists on faith is one of the reasons it is often likened to religion. Unlike religion, however, we do not have to wait until after our deaths to find out if its texts and prophets have steered us right. The failure of Critical Social Justice to accurately describe social reality and effect positive change is becoming increasingly hard to deny. Its DEI programs have spectacularly failed to decrease racism or reduce disparities in workplaces and instead either had no effect at all or worsened them (see chapter 3). Its intense and divisive focus on racial and LGBT identity politics has not improved race relations or the acceptance of sexual minorities but contributed to a resurgence of race-consciousness, white identity politics and a reduction of support for same-sex relationships.[6]

Secondly, Critical Social Justice is too unstable and cannibalistic to become a long-term ethical framework for most people. Because it works on "problematizing" everything, including itself and its allies, its ideas become complicated, contradictory, and confusing and change at a rapid pace all the time. Terms and concepts that were acceptable a few months ago may not be so today. "Allyship" and "checking one's privilege" were once required signs of commitment but have since been problematized in some quarters (but not others) as performative and self-centering and better replaced with "solidarity" and "complicity."[7] "Diversity" has been a core feature of Critical Social Justice activism, but, in some circles now, it can be seen as an attempt to make members of marginalized groups conform to white, Western ways of knowing and avoid the hard work of "decolonization."[8] This is not user-friendly for real people, most of whom have jobs and cannot keep up with all this. It also creates a culture of fear where committed and well-intentioned people can be problematized and even canceled for making a verbal slip or missing a metaphorical memo.

Thirdly and relatedly, Critical Social Justice has alienated too many people. It gained some general popularity in the first place because it contained a kernel of truth. It is genuinely naïve to think we can just change laws and prejudice and discrimination will just go away. If biased attitudes remain, and they do, discrimination will still happen on a more covert level, and there is a need to be alert to that. Following the rush of equality laws in the 60s and 70s, which included the decriminalization of homosexuality and made discrimination on the grounds of race and sex illegal, many liberals on both left and right were concerned about the way in which such discrimination had just been accepted for so long. What were we still not questioning? People looking into this is surely a good thing.

Nevertheless, the methods of Critical Social Justice in practice have been steadily alienating more and more people. White women have been consistently problematized not only by Critical Social Justice scholars and activists for their voting patterns but also in the popular press, as evidenced in the birth of the "Karen" meme.[9] Gay men have been scorned for failing to be consistently intersectional (or queer[10]), while the visibility of lesbians among gender-critical feminists (colloquially known as trans-exclusionary radical feminists or, disparagingly, TERFs) made them increasingly suspect as a group.[11] Parents of all political persuasions and races have become alienated from the movement after raising concerns about their children being taught that their race determines their values, beliefs, and experiences and their interests decide their gender identity and after being informed that it is they who hold regressive views and are racist or transphobic.[12] Artists like Adele and Rebel Wilson have been criticized by Critical Social Justice advocates for simply losing weight,[13] thereby alienating those who think managing one's weight and being attentive to one's health is important.

Critical Social Justice took a particularly steep nosedive in credibility as an ethical movement for social justice following the response on elite university campuses to the October 2023 attack by Hamas on Israel that often extended beyond anti-Israel protests to antisemitic slurs and abuse. The congressional testimony by presidents of three such American universities made international headlines when they all equivocated when asked if calls for the genocide of Jews would be considered harassment according to their campus policies. The uproar in the wake of this testimony led to the forced resignation of two of the presidents, Liz Magill of the University of Pennsylvania and Claudine Gay of Harvard University. The presidents' responses made perfect sense in the logic of Critical Social Justice, and the entire episode called considerable attention to the ways in which DEI policies and activist Critical Social Justice scholarship, particularly in the form of the "decolonize" movement, have contributed to this hostile atmosphere by framing everything in a simplistic oppressor/oppressed binary. Renowned cognitive psychologist Steven Pinker, a long-time member of the Harvard faculty, beautifully summed up the reaction to Gay's testimony given Harvard's well-earned reputation for promoting, if not enforcing, Critical Social Justice ideology on campus: "The fury was white-hot. Harvard is now the place where using the wrong pronoun is a hanging offense but calling for another Holocaust depends on context."[14]

As Pinker noted, the negative response to the testimony wasn't coming simply from a narrow range of liberal writers or from conservative reactionaries. It was also alumni, donors, faculty, and citizens from all over the political spectrum voicing considerable concern, including a White House spokesperson and the second gentleman of the United States. A significant number of individuals across the mainstream have begun to openly and urgently ask: how have we reached a point in which a university's administration does not support a biology instructor who is forced from her job for saying sex is a binary while at the same time, it says students can call for the genocide of Jews without censure or penalty?[15] As Pinker rightly pointed out, it was not that Gay was wrong to defend the rights of academics and students to argue even abhorrent ideas like this in the appropriate setting, but rather that they or their universities had demonstrably not defended this freedom for those who contravened the rules of Critical Social Justice—and, in the case of Gay, had reportedly even played a role in punishing insufficiently "woke" faculty herself.[16]

The growth of negative perceptions of the Critical Social Justice movement is demonstrated by the negative connotations of the term "woke," which has increasingly been used and understood as a term of disparagement to the point where some people believe it to have been invented by its critics. This shift began because people who understood, if not directly felt, the negative effects of the Critical Social Justice movement needed a word to identify the ideology they sought to criticize but often didn't have the precise academic language or knowledge to do so. This was especially important because, unlike longstanding political and philosophical movements like conservatism, liberalism, or socialism that describe specific aims to conserve cultural traditions, oppose constraints on freedom, and seek social ownership of the means of production, respectively, the Critical Social Justice movement has tended to give itself titles that encompass the values of anybody who isn't a hateful extremist —Social Justice, Black Lives Matter, Antifa (i.e., anti-fascism), etc. When it first emerged, this made it difficult for those concerned about growing illiberalism to criticize it without seeming to be against social justice or to disagree that black lives matter or that it is good to oppose fascism. The term "woke," which captured its identifying feature of theorizing largely invisible power dynamics to exist everywhere and always but that are undetectable to the untrained and uneducated, was thus seized upon as a means of naming the ideology so that it could be better identified and resisted. Today, 40 percent of people in the United States would regard being thought "woke" as an insult, while 32 percent would see it as a compliment.[17] Americans are similarly divided over whether it simply means being informed on social injustice or whether it means policing others' words. Comparable percentages are found in the United Kingdom, with 42 percent of Britons saying they would regard being called "woke" as an insult (up from 24 percent in 2020) and 27 percent saying it would be a compliment (up from 26 percent). One in seven now identify as "anti-woke."[18]

As a reflection of this growing expression of public opinion, we are seeing small, if symbolic, moves away from Critical Social Justice in areas where it was once uniformly accepted, including in the entertainment and media industries, where consumers make their opinions known with their wallets. Netflix shelved a plan to adapt Ibram X. Kendi's *Antiracist Baby* and streamed a stand-up special by unapologetically "problematic" comedian Dave Chapelle in the face of an employee protest, telling employees to find another job if its decision was intolerable to them. Its subscriptions increased by 7.6 million, which may not have been a coincidence.[19] Similarly, Disney responded to accusations of political bias with the reinstatement of Bob Iger as CEO and a promise to "quiet things down" on the culture war front and to respect its audience.[20] These moves correspond with changes in the broader cultural mood. For example, the percentage of the American population that believes transgender athletes should participate only on teams that align with their biological sex has risen from 62 percent in 2021 to 69 percent in 2023.[21] Meanwhile, the predominantly left-leaning *New York Times* has responded to open letters from both GLAAD and its own employees demanding greater conformity with Critical Social Justice ideas, particularly around transgender issues, with statements asserting its commitment to free speech and viewpoint diversity, informing employees that it would not tolerate attacks on colleagues.[22] The *New York Times* has also increasingly started to feature pieces that openly question issues that Critical Social Justice has tried—and largely succeeded in—making unquestionable. For example, in February 2024, it published a lengthy article titled "As Kids, They Thought They Were Trans: Now, They No Longer Do" that raised concerns about the popular narrative that children with gender dysphoria should undergo transition and called attention to the ideological bias of gender clinics.[23] Although the story ran as an opinion piece, this sort of coverage, which included interviews with detransitioners, has been notably absent in mainstream US media in recent years.

How Do We See Critical Social Justice Out?

There is reason to be optimistic that Critical Social Justice is losing its social prestige, but there is no cause to be complacent. The ideology remains well-entrenched across institutions, and troubling trends continue. The Foundation for Individual Rights and Expression (FIRE), for example, continues to record a growing trend of deplatforming in universities,[24] the usage of terms related to queer theory and related trans activism appears to be continuing to rise,[25] and some have argued that, far from declining, "woke" is becoming the new normal.[26] Also, while

Critical Social Justice terms have begun to recede in usage among companies in the United States and the United Kingdom since 2021, their use has accelerated among companies in Canada and parts of Europe over the same time period.[27]

Even though the movement is too divorced from reality, chaotic, contradictory, ethically inconsistent, and alienating to survive, it has done a great deal of damage socially and will likely do a lot more before it falls. Precisely how it will fall and what will move into its place are now matters of grave concern. We are already in a very politically fraught situation due, in part, to the social expectations around issues of social justice that the movement has re-engineered. Its focus on its own unique form of identity politics that not only divides people into groups but also claims them to have opposing knowledges, values, and goals requiring different moral rights, responsibilities, and rules to be applied to them has been very harmful. As I and others have long argued, the identity politics of Critical Social Justice does not continue the work of the Civil Rights Movement. Rather, it betrays its universalist values. Consider the following passage from an article I wrote with fellow author James Lindsay in 2018,

> It is generally a terrible idea to have different rules of behavior dependent on identity because it goes against the most common sense of fairness and reciprocity which seems to be pretty hardwired. It is also antithetical to universal liberalism and precisely the opposite of what civil rights movements fought to obtain. . . . If most people are now working on an understanding of fairness, equality, and reciprocity as individual, this mentality can be incomprehensible and alienating.
>
> It is in this way that identity politics is the most counterproductive and even dangerous. We humans are tribal and territorial creatures, and identity politics comes far more naturally to us than universality and individuality. Our history bears the evidence of humans unapologetically favoring their own tribe, own town, own religion, own nation, and own race over others and creating narratives after the impulse to attempt to justify doing it.

The universal human rights and principles of not judging people by their race, gender, or sexuality—which have developed over the modern period and resulted in the civil rights movements, legal equality, and much social progress—are much more uncommon to us and must be consistently reinforced and maintained. If we allow identity politics in the form of [Critical] Social Justice to undermine this fragile and precarious detente, we could undo decades of social progress and provide a rationale for a resurgence of racism, sexism, and homophobia. Given the novelty of egalitarian society, it is not at all clear that women and racial and sexual minorities could easily win these losses back.[28]

In the six years since those words were written, these important and foundational principles have been considerably undermined, and society has become increasingly polarized into "in-groups" and "out-groups." Not all of this is down to Critical Social Justice, of course, but we have seen a rise of a new form of counter-identity politics using its language that, if not created by Critical Social Justice, has been enabled by it. Because the Critical Social Justice movement has taken great efforts to conflate its own theories of race with black people and its own theories of "queerness" with LGBT people, it has enabled those who quite possibly were already inclined to be racist or homophobic to do the same and attack black people and LGBT people and their full rights under the law under the guise of critiquing Critical Social Justice theories or being "anti-woke."[29] Overt expressions of racism are becoming more common on social media. As the black conservative Adam Coleman has argued,

> In their desperation to fight the left, [some of the anti-woke] became just like them. They're now race-conscious and they still think they're winning the culture war. But when you discard your principles, you lose every time. Quit staring into the abyss because it always stares back.[30]

At the same time, anti-LBGT sentiment has increased, as evidenced by a dramatic seven-point drop in the percentage of Americans who believe same-sex relationships are morally acceptable.[31] This is almost certainly, at least in part, a backlash against the excesses of Critical Social Justice in the form of queer theory–based trans activism. As the political writer and podcaster Alexander von Sternberg put it,

> It's clear that the worldview emerging from this reactionary backlash is one that does not merely resist Critical Social Justice but also devalues sexual freedom, LGBT rights, and women's rights. We need better than one sick, illiberal cult mentality supplanting another.[32]

These reactionary attitudes have the potential to have consequences that impact the liberal commitment to treating all people as equal under the law. Consider how the founder of Turning Point USA, a group originally formed to protect conservative students' interests on university campuses, has gone from supporting the "color-blind" approach of Martin Luther King Jr. to launching a campaign to overturn the Civil Rights Act of 1964, claiming that it ushered in the DEI bureaucracy of Critical Social Justice.[33] While his is surely a minority view rejected by the vast majority of conservatives, it is deeply alarming that it is now a view being advanced by the head of an organization that has a place in mainstream conservative discourse. Meanwhile, perhaps more urgently worrying, Republicans who openly oppose liberal reforms that have given the same rights to same-sex attracted people as heterosexuals are gaining strength from legitimate objections to Critical Social Justice trans activism that impinges on women's rights and children's bodies.[34] If *Obergefell v. Hodges*, the 2015 US Supreme Court case that determined same-sex couples have the right to marry in the United States, were to be overturned, the thirty-five US states that still have same-sex marriage bans on the books would be reactivated.[35]

These attitudes have the potential to grow and spread via a process that I have called "reactive overcompensation,"[36] when people take an extreme view in direct opposition to an equally extreme view on the other side as though this can somehow balance things out and restore order. Of course, it really does the opposite. The metaphor of the pendulum that swings back and forth is particularly useful. Imagine trying to stop a pendulum swinging by pushing it back harder in the opposite direction. This can only make it swing ever more wildly, and it careens madly back and forth between the extreme ideological poles, taking out innocent bystanders in its path.

A milder form of reactive behavior coming from a more thoughtful and ethical right is also, I would argue, short-sighted and counterproductive and perhaps even more worrying because it has more mainstream support. There are those who believe that it is necessary and compatible with freedom of belief and speech to use state power to ban Critical Social Justice books and ideas specifically from public institutions.[37] Unlike the reactionaries who want to overturn the Civil Rights Act, they well understand the difference between ideas and people and point out, rightly, that banning books that reference something like Critical Race Theory represents an opposition to ideas, not to people of a certain race who may or may not endorse Critical Race Theory. They further argue that it cannot be illiberal to ban ideas that are themselves illiberal. Some become impatient with liberals who argue that giving governments the power to decide what may or may not be taught in universities or workplace training sessions or what may be stocked in libraries is not the way to overcome bad ideas. Some even perceive us as suggesting we all sit around and have civilized discussions about why Critical Social Justice ideas are factually and ethically wrong for another decade while academics continue to get canceled, employees continue to be compelled to affirm their racism or belief in gender identity, and children are indoctrinated into highly dubious or age-inappropriate theories of race and gender. This is not the liberal position.

The primary liberal opposition to banning any ideas is that it makes them very difficult to criticize or defeat. There is almost never a justification for banning ideas in institutions for adults (exceptions include things like bomb- or drug-making instructions), and no good justification for removing ideas from children can ever be based on partisan politics. There are good justifications for protecting children from sexually explicit content or graphic violence, but this is something else entirely. There are also good arguments for not teaching younger children political ideologies of race or gender at all at an age where they do not have the skills to evaluate them. Older children who will soon be entering university or work and can be expected to encounter Critical Social Justice ideas there are not at all benefited from an education that has not prepared them for this. The liberal stance, therefore, would be to present older children with a variety of political and philosophical views and an educational environment that encourages them to compare and critique them. Adults may choose which ideas to critique for themselves, and I am particularly glad to have had access to all the core texts of Critical Social Justice scholarship in order to write *Cynical Theories*. Yet, some older children in Texas may today not have in-school access to my critiques who otherwise might have had it if not for reactive government interference. The book, presumably because it discusses Critical Race Theory, was among the list of 850 titles that Texas state representative Matt Krause sent to school superintendents in October 2021 asking if they were on library shelves. Although the book has never been formally banned to the best of my knowledge, the message and consequence of such an investigation are abundantly clear.[38] How many public school libraries in Texas would risk putting the book on its shelves after receiving such a pointed query?

A primary liberal objection to ever giving governments or the public (backed by government) the power to decide which ideas may or may not be taught in universities or workplace training is that we simply do not know what kind of government or public we are going to get in the future. When thinking about how to address illiberal ideas, it is essential that we do not focus narrowly and act reactively to ban those ideas but instead think broadly of what will serve us well in all contexts and in the long term. Interestingly, this attitude that seeks to avoid radical action that damages social norms and institutional structures of society that we wish to conserve is typically associated with conservatism, and yet it is conservatives at the forefront of giving governments the power to ban ideas and books, typically in "red states." This is unlikely to serve their interests in the long term. One particularly useful book that addresses this problem is *The Cancelling of the American Mind* by Greg Lukianoff and Rikki Schlott of FIRE. They write,

> Even those strictly dedicated to advancing a conservative agenda are being shortsighted when they advance bills like the Stop WOKE Act. They're ignoring the dangerous precedent being set. Handing administrators the right to fire professors who think the wrong way is something that with near certainty will backfire on conservatives by legitimizing speech codes that will be used against them.

They quote Will Creeley, FIRE's legal director, who notes,

> No matter what your beliefs, no matter what your party affiliation, you should be very nervous because that axe swings both ways. Today, folks are coming for books dealing with the LGBTQ community, tomorrow they'll be coming for books dealing with faith. . . . Once you start banning books, it is a very slippery slope.[39]

This does not mean that liberalism has no way to protect academic freedom (or employees' freedom of belief and speech). On the contrary, the key purpose of liberalism is to protect the individual from coercive control, and the purpose of government in a liberal society is to devise ways to safeguard those liberal freedoms. One way to do this is being trialed in the United Kingdom with the appointment of a Director for Freedom of Speech and Academic Freedom within the Office for Students, whose sole responsibility is to ensure that academics and students are not having their academic freedom curtailed in any way. Appointee Arif Ahmed describes his mission this way,

> [T]he role exists to protect and to promote freedom of speech within the law. And freedom of speech is not just one political position or value among many. Supporting freedom of speech is not like supporting Scottish independence or opposing an increase in VAT. Nor is it like socialism or one-nation conservatism. The reason is that freedom of speech, like democracy, is—although it may not only be—what you might call a process value rather than an outcome value. It does not tell you what the outcome of any political or scientific debate should be. What it tells you is how that dispute should be conducted: namely, through open and tolerant discussion in which all sides both feel and really are free to express their views.
>
> So, what matters to us, within the confines of the law, is not what side you take—what matters is that you get to choose what side you take.[40]

This is the fundamental essence of liberalism. When Ahmed speaks of freedom of speech as being, like democracy, a "process value" rather than an "outcome value," he is speaking of protecting academic freedom in the long term rather than playing Whac-A-Mole with illiberalisms that crop up and, in the process, further undermining academic freedom in a way that is certain to backfire and further damage our liberal democracies.

Another benefit of the consistent application of the liberal principle of freedom of belief and speech is that it is much simpler than trying to enact laws to ban specific ideas that might be illiberal, including those that aim to suppress other ideas. A principle that political and ideological views should not be censored but also must not be imposed upon anyone or taught as true to children is so much more easily upheld as a default response than the drafting of particular laws that try to set out the ideas that must not be spoken. Such laws necessarily end up being vague and subjective and cause great anxiety on the part of school-teachers, librarians, administrators, and HR departments, who are typically not lawyers. Lukianoff and Schlott address this problem, too, and point out that the fear of being sued is likely to lead to the over-policing of ideas, the eroding of education, and the silencing of students and parents.[41] So confusing has legislation on the acceptable content of books been that, in one county in Florida, schools afraid of falling foul of it removed from shelves Anne Frank's *The Diary of a Young Girl*, Agatha Christie's *Death on the Nile*, *The Guinness Book of Records*, *Ripley's Believe it or Not!* and Douglas Adams's *The Hitchhiker's Guide to the Galaxy* as well as five dictionaries and eight encyclopedias.[42] When elements on both the left and right take steps to bias children's libraries or remove perfectly age-appropriate books from them on political grounds,[43] it is children's education that suffers most.

While it clearly seems to some that addressing the problem of authoritarian impositions of Critical Social Justice might be more easily achieved by forbidding the Critical Social Justice ideas rather than the authoritarianism, this position is not supported by evidence. Banning ideas simply doesn't work; it also undermines the foundations of liberal democracies. Banning the authoritarian imposition of ideas, on the other hand, has a much better track record of success and upholds those all-important foundations. The concept of "secularism," in which religious believers have the right to their beliefs but no right to institutionalize them or impose them on other people, is something the United States does particularly well, and there is no reason to think it and other countries could not expand this concept to political ideologies too. Seeing the bigger picture and standing by the principles that underlie one's society is not a weak position but a strong and lasting one. Bad ideas come and go, but liberal democratic ideals can outlast them all. They contain within themselves the tools to defeat bad ideas as long as we stand by the principles that have protected the freedom of belief and speech that enables this. As Lukianoff and Schlott argue,

> [T]he unfortunate truth is that while these bills are predicated on legitimate concerns, they are ultimately mere Band-Aids being placed over a deeper societal issue. Legislators are playing Whac-A-Mole with divisive concepts on behalf of parents while losing sight of positive, restorative visions. Laws won't make these ideas go away.[44]

OK, But What Do We Actually Do?

To see Critical Social Justice out without replacing it with anything else authoritarian or undermining academic freedom, artistic freedom, and freedom of belief and speech generally, we will need both principled big-picture thinking and specific policies. We must take direct action now to reform ideologically captured institutions using the precedent of secularism. I have worked with numerous employers to reform their policies and advise on their training programs, so I am most qualified to speak specifically to that issue, but I shall also offer some thoughts on the issue of schools and universities based on general principles and the insights of parents, teachers, students, and academics who came to Counterweight.

Schools

Schools should not teach any political philosophy as true, just as they should not teach any religion as true (note: the US school system offers perhaps the strongest model for this, as state schools in many countries, including the United Kingdom, do teach one religion as true). With younger children, there is frequently no need to teach any political or philosophical framework at all. A focus on primary subjects like math and language alongside a general rule against bullying is generally sufficient. Of course, teachers will need to respond to any racist, sexist, or homophobic bullying specifically, and policies will be needed on how to do this. No teacher should be encouraging a child to share any thoughts they might be having on their sexuality or gender expression, and any concerns a teacher might have about comments made by a child related to either should be reported to the same professionals who already support children showing signs of anxiety, distress, or difficulties at home. Teachers are not psychologists trained to deal with difficulties experienced by children in relation to their sexuality or sense of gender, and the poor current standards of such services are a separate issue to be dealt with and not a reason for any teacher to feel she must attempt amateur therapizing or an excuse for her to do so based on her own beliefs. It is essential that removing any expectation of sexuality or gender therapy from schools does not tip too far in the other direction and cause any child to feel that they must hide the fact that their parents are the same sex or perform any conventional gender roles.

As children get older, they will need to encounter political views, probably first in history and then in more advanced studies like sociology and media, and they will need to feel confident to think critically about them and begin to form opinions. Schools should make the same effort they do with religions to teach *about* political views without teaching them as true. While finding the right balance in any curriculum will always be difficult, certain stances are recognizably political and should always be framed as opinion if discussed at all depending on the age of the students, such as "All white people are racist," "Anti-discrimination law is forced association," "Property is theft," "Taxation is theft," "Everybody has a gender identity," "Gender roles are good and must correspond with biological sex," "We live in a patriarchy," and "We don't live in a patriarchy but we should." Teaching children these as true should be as clearly understood to be as wrong as teaching them that "Jesus is the son of God," "Jews are God's chosen people," or "There is no God but God, and Muhammad is his prophet." Parents must be able to report any concerns they have about ideologically biased teaching and expect to be taken seriously, but they must also not have the power to pressure schools into adopting their own political bias.

Universities

Publicly funded universities must be reformed to make them fit for their purpose of knowledge production, which requires the active mitigation of ideological bias. Methods for doing this will vary across disciplines. While academics in the hard sciences and many of the social sciences must try to eliminate as much bias as possible by adhering to scientific methods specifically set up to minimize human bias or error, this is not the case in all subjects. Many disciplines within the humanities and social sciences, particularly, benefit from scholars arguing from a variety of political, philosophical, or ideological standpoints. This benefit is, of course, lost if they all adhere to the same set of biases or feel under pressure to pretend they do. Universities should be able to show that they have taken steps to foster viewpoint diversity and balance their academic faculty for the benefit of rigorous collaborative research and their students. While certain subjects tend to attract more scholars on the political left, if a political science department has no political scientists who are conservative, liberal, or libertarian, it should be expected to show the efforts it has made to recruit some and also what those professors and instructors in the department are doing to ensure they provide their students with counterviews to their own perspectives.

There should be an expectation of academics that they will engage with critique from colleagues working in the same area but from a different ideological standpoint. There should be no subjects that are "not up for debate" in a university. In the area of social justice, differences in, for example, analyses of disparities in society can be regarded in the same light as competing hypotheses. This is particularly important within scholarship that seeks to better understand our social reality for the purpose of addressing disadvantage faced by various groups. As biometrician Darryl I. MacKenzie and his coauthors explain, speaking from species and community ecology, "Science can be viewed as a process used to discriminate among competing hypotheses about system behavior, that is, discriminating among different ideas about how the world, or a part of it, works." They go on,

> The key step in science then involves the confrontation of these model-based predictions with the relevant components of the real-world system. . . . Confidence increases for those models (and hence those underlying hypotheses) whose predictions match observed system behavior well and decreases for models that do a poor job of predicting.[45]

This basic scientific principle holds true for any rigorous scholarship that seeks to obtain factual knowledge about the workings of the world. While humans are a particularly messy and complicated part of the world and our behaviors can be hard to measure and interpret directly, predictions can still be made and compared to measurements from the real world. This has been done with the predictions of Critical Social Justice (see, for example, the discussion of Dobbin and Kalev in chapter 3), and it is not shaping up very well. It is essential that other hypotheses are also able to be raised and tested. It is quite possible that Critical Social Justice does have valuable insights to offer because even when general theories do not stand up to scrutiny, specific hypotheses within them may still do so,[46] but we cannot know this unless the scholars accept that critique and comparison with both competing hypotheses and empirical measurements of social reality can be legitimate and respond to any critique or criticism of their work with counterevidence and counterarguments.

Workplaces

It is utterly reasonable and, indeed, necessary for there to be workplace rules against displaying prejudice or hostility to people or discriminating against them because of their race, sex, sexuality, nationality, religion (or lack of religion), gender identity, disability, weight, etc. What is illiberal is imposing one ideological framework for doing so upon everybody and requiring them to affirm it to keep their job. A truly inclusive workplace would accept that there are many moral frameworks from which it is possible to oppose bigotry and that diversity includes diversity of viewpoints.

Taking racism as an example, liberals might say that evaluating people by their racial category rather than as individuals is likely to result in both factual error and illiberal stereotyping. They may also say that the best way to combat racism is by opposing evaluating others by their race consistently. Socialists might say that social class is the major cause of inequality and factor race into that framework while arguing that a primary focus on race divides the working class and makes remedying class-caused disparities harder. Critical Social Justice advocates might say that opposing racism requires all of society to become aware of the unconscious racial biases that they believe we are all socialized into and that we should work to dismantle them. Meanwhile, conservatives or libertarians might argue that people need to take personal responsibility not only to treat all races equally but also for much of their own success and that placing too much responsibility on society is disempowering to individuals. Somebody whose primary ethical framework is religious might argue that racism is wrong because we are all God's creations or draw on theological texts from their specific faith tradition as grounds for opposing racism. It is likely that most people would simply say that racism is stupid and hurtful and that we should be thoughtful and kind to our fellow humans generally, not only our work colleagues. Some people may prefer not to share their views at all, and this position must be respected as well because it is illiberal for an employer to demand to know the inner values, thoughts, and beliefs of employees.

Recommendations for Workplace Policies

There are genuinely inclusive and productive ways to address bias in the workplace. Based on my work with employers and my years-long research on the impact of DEI programs, I have found that policies generally work best when they are (1) kept simple, (2) in accordance with any local antidiscrimination law, (3) clear that people are entitled to oppose discrimination and prejudice in a way that aligns with their own personal political, philosophical, and religious beliefs, and (4) based on traditional liberal principles. Specifically, employers might do the following:

1. *Make a general statement of adherence to relevant antidiscrimination law.* Such laws typically involve straightforward opposition to discrimination on the grounds of characteristics like race, sex, age, sexual orientation, gender identity, national origin, disability or genetic information, pregnancy, and marital status. Antidiscrimination law in some countries explicitly includes political beliefs or philosophical beliefs, but some do not and some vary from region to region.

2. *Make a commitment to treat all employees with equal courtesy and consideration and to refrain from any prejudice or hostility on the grounds of the above and ask all employees to do the same.*

3. *Take care to specifically state that employees are free to oppose discrimination on the grounds of their own political, philosophical, or religious beliefs, which they need not share publicly.*

4. *Make a commitment to not impose any religious, philosophical, or political beliefs on others at work and require employees to do the same.*

5. *Make a commitment to not tell employees that their particular religious, philosophical, or political beliefs are false or immoral and ask employees to do the same when at work.*

6. *Make clear that any demands that the company adopt any particular religious, philosophical, or political belief that goes beyond existing antidiscrimination law*

or company policy and that is contradictory to other lawful religious, philosophical, or political beliefs will be rejected.

7. *Make clear that these statements and commitments are taken very seriously and that any contravention of them will lead to appropriate disciplinary action.*

Recommendations for Training

When it comes to training, I am often asked if I know of any liberal DEI training programs. I do not know of any and there's a good reason for that: liberals don't tend to train people in what they should think. They require people not to engage in prejudiced or discriminatory behavior that harms, disadvantages, or denies the rights of others while leaving them to comply with this from whatever ethical framework they hold. However, when we look at elements of programs that have worked to increase workplace harmony and decrease discrimination, there is a pattern that diverges considerably from the Critical Social Justice approach and is entirely consistent with liberalism. They have these key shared features:

- A commitment to voluntary attendance so that people do not feel coerced.
- A discussion of the various kinds of biases that might affect a workforce, including ones based on our hardwiring, our cultural expectations, and our individual experiences.
- A process that focuses on shared workplace goals.
- An avoidance of essentializing or stereotyping any group.
- A focus on fostering a sense of belonging and team cohesion rather than difference.
- A focus on overall improvement of processes rather than on the presumed biases of problematic individuals due to their identity.
- A universal commitment to inclusion—including of white people and men—as part of building a truly diverse workforce.

It might seem odd that these need to be stated as productive ways to go about having a discussion of antidiscrimination policy and reduction of bias in the workplace. Indeed, as Dobbin and Kalev report, "people react negatively to efforts to control them."[47] But we needn't review a wide body of organizational research to discover this. Anyone who has ever encountered humans before already knows this to be the case. Similarly, the finding that human bias exists on a universal, cultural, and individual level should come as a surprise to no one. Those are the levels on which humans exist. Do humans respond better when work meetings are relevant to their work? Yes, I expect they do. I am also unsurprised that not essentializing and stereotyping demographics results in fewer essentialist and stereotypical assumptions. And *of course* an approach that focuses on shared goals and purpose and similarities rather than differences and does not single any demographic out as a problem is going to bring people together better than one which does the opposite. The reason that this all needs to be stated today, however, is because Critical Social Justice has done the opposite of all of this and significantly damaged human relations in the workplace and throughout society.

What to Do with the Woke?

It is possible that by this point some of you might be thinking, "But what about the woke? They're hardly going to just sit back and allow a return to liberalism in schools, universities, the workplace, and beyond, are they? And assuming we can push them back and undertake liberal institutional reform, what do we then do with them? They're single-minded zealots." Well, no, Critical Social Justice scholars and activists are not likely to be at all receptive toward attempts to re-liberalize the institutions on which society most depends. They will be very unlikely to accept their ideological position as just one among many that has no special authority over everybody else. That is the very nature of authoritarianism, and unfortunately, we cannot make them feel differently. We can only defend and uphold liberal principles on a legal level, on an institutional level, and on an individual level and require Critical Social Justice advocates to accept that views other than their own may exist and that attempts to prevent them from doing so will not be tolerated. Every time Critical Social Justice retreats or pauses to regroup in our institutions, we must be prepared to put liberal policies into every little space it concedes.

The Critical Social Justice movement has now alienated and infringed on the fundamental rights of so many people that it is not uncommon to hear calls that the woke must be punished in some fashion. Given the way that Critical Social Justice has adversely affected lives and livelihoods, some people become angry at the very idea of a liberal plan that would simply require the woke to stand down and take their place with the rest of us. At the very least, they demand mass firings of Critical Social Justice ideologues, and that is likely to be the fate of those who refuse to accept that they can no longer impose their ideology on everybody else.

However, this is not a realistic or even an ethical approach for everyone who has taken on the ideology. The employers I speak to overwhelmingly do not wish to fire all their "woke" or "woke adjacent" employees. They typically give two reasons: firstly, quite a lot of the "woke" are otherwise good at their job, and secondly, very many of them are not single-minded zealots by nature. Many of them are young and have been failed by the educational institutions that should have been expected to teach them that a variety of worldviews from which to seek a more just society exist. The most common "SOS" email I receive from an employer can be paraphrased as "How do I get these people to tell the difference between their ideology and just being a good person? I don't want to decimate my workforce, but I can't go on like this."

In one case, an employer contacted me for help with a very clear policy because he was having a particular problem with a young woman who worked on the company's social media. She was very good at her job and was generally a sweet and earnest person, but she had difficulty with the company's "no political messaging" rule. Specifically, she did not understand the difference between "Black Lives Matter" messaging and the company's anti-discrimination policy, which said the company recognized the value of everybody regardless of their race, gender, sexuality, religion, etc. She wasn't being manipulative or disingenuous. She had been in a bubble where she did not recognize the difference between supporting a very specific political movement with some fairly radical aims and being a decent person who opposed racism, including, of course, against black people. She apologized when informed she'd broken the "no political messaging" rule but remained quite confused.

A very similar problem occurs with employees who agitate for the inclusion of pronouns in emails and at meetings. They insist they just want to be inclusive of everybody and fail to realize that they are demanding conformity with a particular position on sex and gender. Such a policy is not inclusive of people who do not consider themselves to have a gender identity, who disbelieve in the concept of gender identity, or who have a conscientious objection to the concept of gender identity. Some people have been so deeply embedded in their own ideological bubble that they are genuinely unaware of a very strongly held principled opposition to pronoun mandates on the part of a subset of feminists, some social conservatives, some religious believers, and miscellaneous other people, some of whom simply don't think that their beliefs about sex and gender are any of their employer's business. "But it is so easy to just put pronouns in your email signature and it makes doing that so much easier for trans people" is a common refrain. Yes, it would be very easy for a Jew or Muslim to just say, "Jesus is the son of God," or to add Luke 1:35 to their email signature, but that doesn't mean they should be compelled to do so. Here, the issue is not finding it difficult to produce words or wanting to make it harder for anyone to express their personal beliefs. The issue is that not everyone has the same philosophical or religious beliefs, and no one should be forced to state a philosophical or religious belief that is contradictory to their own beliefs, especially those that are important to them.

When thinking about the "way out of woke," we have to remember that there are very many relatively young people who graduated from a university captured by Critical Social Justice over the past decade and have remained in its bubble fortified by the social prestige afforded to the political ideology ever since. This is, after all, what so many of us have been concerned about and what we have argued to people wondering why we are so worried about the culture within elite universities. If we accept this concern about university capture to be valid, we must also accept that there are now many people in their twenties who are genuinely unable to distinguish between Critical Social Justice ideas and just being a good person and who may be entirely unfamiliar with the rest of the world of political and philosophical thought. This is a problem we are going to have to grapple with as a society when the Critical Social Justice movement finally falls. Any practical, ethical, and compassionate way forward will have to catch these young people and show them that other views exist (they might even consider them in the process) and that they have a responsibility to consider them when operating in an ideologically diverse workplace.

This problem is something I am working on at the moment, and my first thoughts involve developing the older concept of "cultural competency," which was also largely swallowed up by the advent of diversity, equity, and inclusion. Cultural competency involved training people who worked with people from a variety of cultural backgrounds to have a base knowledge of different cultural beliefs and customs. I undertook some of this training myself when working in nursing and social care. It was a very practical course that included things like how to observe kosher or halal dietary requirements when working with an elderly observant Jew or Muslim with dementia and how to recognize and respect differences in formal manners and physical contact. The good thing with cultural competency training is that it does not require anybody to affirm any of the belief systems they learn. People only have to know they exist and incorporate this into their work in a way that understands and respects the freedom of belief of others. The benefit of expanding this concept into the realm of politics and culture would be twofold: (1) such training would be precisely what is needed to fill the gaps in the education and real-life experience of those who have been trapped in a Critical Social Justice bubble and (2) it would also remove all plausible deniability from those who know full well that other worldviews exist but believe they have the right to overrule them.

This point is illustrated by a case in Georgia in 2023, in which an elementary school teacher was fired for reading an illustrated book about gender fluidity to her students titled *My Shadow Is Purple*.[48] "A heartwarming and inspiring book about being true to yourself and moving beyond the gender binary," per the book's descriptive text, it presents the idea that children need not be a boy or girl. ("My Dad has a shadow that's blue as a berry, and my Mom's is as pink as a blossoming cherry. There's only those choices, a 2 or a 1. But mine is quite different, it's both and it's none.") In the book, gender identity is imagined as a shadow, and our protagonist's is purple because the child likes some pink things and some blue (like most children). In this regard, the book encourages children to think in terms of gender stereotypes that are coded pink for girls or blue for boys and then determine their own gender identity based on how closely their own interests align with these stereotypes. Citing district policy that banned the teaching of "divisive concepts" and the promotion of a teacher's "personal political beliefs" and that affirms the right of parents "to direct the upbringing and the moral or religious training of his or her minor child," the school board voted to fire her along strict party lines.[49] But in defending her decision to read the book, the teacher argued that she couldn't possibly know what was allowed or not under such a vague policy. Put simply, she did not realize the book could be considered divisive or that any parents could object. This is a legitimate defense given the way many of these laws are written and framed, as I noted earlier, but in this particular case, is her claim credible? This seems unlikely as very many parents object to gender roles and stereotypes and more would object to their child being encouraged to consider whether they were a boy or a girl or nonbinary depending on those stereotypes, but for the purposes of this discussion, let's take her at her word.

Why did she not know? How could a teacher working in a suburb of Atlanta not know that feminists, social conservatives, and various religious people, as well as people who simply dislike facile gender stereotypes, exist? This is the type of situation that could have been avoided with a bit of cultural competency training of the sort I describe above. Without such training, the ambiguity of the wording of the "divisive concepts" policy gave her plausible deniability to claim she did not know what books contain concepts that people are divided over. Teachers should be expected to know that the families of the children they teach hold various religious, philosophical, and ethical beliefs and that they have a responsibility to respect that their beliefs have the same right to exist as their own do. Basic cultural competency training in the place of DEI training would not only help pop the Critical Social Justice bubble of many young teachers but also allow for the sending of a clear message, "If you do not recognize and respect the existence of worldviews that are entirely compatible with antidiscrimination policy and law but not compatible with your views and insist on imposing your own ideology on others, you will need to leave."

Let's be clear: requiring Critical Social Justice advocates to accept that other worldviews have as much right to exist as theirs do and requiring those who work with people to have some idea of what they are to enable them not to trample all over the freedom of belief and speech of others is not authoritarian, although it may well feel like it to believers. The expression, "When you are accustomed to privilege, equality feels like oppression" (author unknown), which is so often used by the Critical Social Justice movement, also applies to it. Those who have been accustomed to their own political ideology being allowed to dominate over all others are likely to experience having that special privilege revoked as a form of oppression even when their own right to continue to hold and express their views is not denied to them in the way they have denied such freedoms to others. I, for one, am not very inclined to be sympathetic to their plight. I may even allow myself the tiniest amount of schadenfreude when an employer tells me of the incredulous, entitled moral outrage of an employee, when the employer has been able to respond to an attempt to impose Critical Social Justice beliefs on the workforce with a firm "No."

Nor is "merely" reforming systems on a legal, institutional, and individual level so that there is no tolerance of authoritarian institutionalization of political ideologies or imposition of them on others a weak position. There are people who would like to fire all those who have ever espoused Critical Social Justice views and demand "consequences" for those who have contributed to a culture of fear and cancellation. This is neither workable nor ethical, except in cases where someone has broken the law or the policies of their organization to abuse a position of power and been shielded from consequences by the dominance of the ideology. We cannot apply reforms retrospectively, and accusing others of having once contributed to a cancel culture would likely escalate into something that looked very much like a cancel culture, given the subjective nature of such accusations. Yes, it might take out some bullies who will always be bullies, but it would also adversely affect young people who had been sucked into an ideology and shielded from any other ideas, misguided people who initially believed the ideology to be much more benign than it was, and those who had themselves been bullied by activists and went along with the ideology simply to keep a roof over their family's heads, which is precisely what critics of the movement have long warned is happening. Further, any suggestion of a "witch hunt" would be likely to reignite sympathies for Critical Social Justice advocates among those who have finally been convinced that it is not simply an attempt to make society more just and that its authoritarianism does need to be checked and its social prestige reevaluated. The identitarian left, like the identitarian right, is unlikely to simply go away even when we marginalize it to the fringes. To avoid a resurgence, possibly under a different name with different terminology but with the same illiberal concepts and drives, we must not enable it to take on an oppressed status and reactivate the liberal center and center left's sympathies and set the pendulum swinging again.[50] To ensure that the movement's defeat, when it comes, is lasting and not replaced by another form of authoritarianism, those of us who are liberal in that broadest sense of being anti-authoritarian will need to put our strength behind ethical policies against authoritarianism that will work in all contexts and stand the test of time.

In the meantime, we can all continue to do our part to hasten the demise of the Critical Social Justice movement by pushing back against it in principled and knowledgeable ways in our own institutions and lives. Understand what Critical Social Justice is and be able to articulate your own principled objections to it clearly. Assess the problem arising in your organization accurately and formulate a plan to address it that is appropriate to its severity and your own position, personality, and skillset. Sound out your colleagues and peers and address it as a group where you can. Be polite and persistent in your objections, be clear in your support for ethical and effective anti-discrimination policies, provide your employer or educator with information on what they are promoting, keep records of all communications, and leave a paper trail of your own. Genuine, knowledgeable commitment to the political ideology of Critical Social Justice is relatively small. By taking a principled, informed stance against it yourself, you will embolden others to do so. As others work to address the problem from the top down, whether on legal or institutional levels, join the groundswell of people pushing it out from the bottom up.

Be part of the counterweight. Thank you.

Glossary of Common Critical Social Justice Terms

Many of the terms below have everyday meanings and Critical Social Justice meanings. The definitions given are the ones used by adherents of Critical Social Justice.

Accountability. This refers to an assumption that everybody, regardless of their own principles or beliefs, should be held accountable for upholding the views of Critical Social Justice ideology. If your employer announces an intention for the organization, the managers, or the employees to be "accountable" or "exercise accountability" in relation to Critical Social Justice issues, this usually indicates that they intend to accept ideological complaints as valid and endeavor to "do better" rather than evaluating the reasonableness of any interpretation of any behavior or utterance.

Allyship. An ally is someone who endeavors to offer support via Critical Social Justice–approved methods to any group (outside the one they themselves belong to) that is perceived as marginalized. For example, a "'trans ally" will be a person who is not trans but takes it upon herself to call out any language or belief seen as transphobic in Critical Social Justice terms. The rationale for this is that it is done in order to spare trans people from having to do all the work of "educating" and "calling out" themselves. The trans ally is someone who will object to any views that differ from Critical Social Justice views about gender identity regardless of whether any of their trans colleagues themselves subscribe to Critical Social Justice views or wish to compel everybody else to do so. Many trans people do not and this can lead to trans allies calling out trans people for holding the wrong views on trans identity.[1] This also happens when "white allies" practice Critical Social Justice versions of antiracism by only supporting the black people who share those views and condemning those who do not.[2] Allyship, therefore, is best understood as allying oneself with an ideology rather than with a marginalized group of people.

Antiracism *(see also Racism)*. "Antiracism," in Critical Social Justice terminology, relies upon the definition of racism as an oppressive system that permeates everything and results in unequal freedoms, rights, and opportunities for people according to their race. Antiracism is thus a commitment to regarding all disparities as a manifestation of racism and, crucially, actively attempting to correct for them on a systemic level from a top-down approach. Within this approach, only this kind of antiracism is valid and there is no way to be simply "not racist" and commit to rejecting racial prejudice and discrimination consistently.[3]

Bias. The belief that everybody is biased in very specific Critical Social Justice identity-based ways. They may be unconscious of this and need to be made conscious of it, affirm their bias, and work to dismantle it. Everybody is believed to have some unconscious biases and be racist, sexist, transphobic, ableist, etc. The only difference is whether one admits it and works against it, which is good, or denies it and thus perpetuates it, which is bad. Any claim that one does not have any particular bias is regarded as defensive denial and probably a product of fragility *(see Fragility)*.

BIPOC. This acronym stands for Black, Indigenous, and People of Color. The term "people of color" has until recently been used to refer to all non-white minority groups, but more recently, a need to distinguish between the three groups has been seen as necessary. This is because black and indigenous people are seen as specially oppressed but in different ways, while other people of color face racism that is seen as less severe or less entrenched in American society.

Blackness. Blackness is seen as the opposite to whiteness *(see Whiteness)* and the foil by which the oppressive system of whiteness is enabled to operate. Blackness is therefore believed to be perceived negatively as an essence of dark-skinned people that makes them bad and inferior to white people. We most often hear the term prefaced by the prefix "anti-." However, black activists have celebrated blackness (or, in earlier times, "negritude"[4]) as a positive and empowering identity, and we may also hear it spoken of in this sense.

Cisgender. To identify as a man or a woman while having the reproductive systems generally understood as those belonging to a man or woman. That is, to be cisgender—or just "cis"—is to be "not trans."

Cissexism. To assume that being cisgender is normal and natural and, therefore, better than being trans. Just as sexism is understood to be the belief that men are innately superior to women, cissexism is understood as the belief that cis people are innately superior to trans people.

Critical. "Critical" is a term that gets placed before many other terms related to issues of social justice, and this is how you can tell it is a form of Critical Social Justice—for example, Critical Race Theory, critical pedagogy, critical studies of ableism. In this sense, "critical" refers to beginning with the assumption that society is dominated by very theoretically specific power dynamics.

Critical Race Theory. This was originally a form of critical *(see Critical)* legal studies related to race that emerged in the 1970s. It holds that racism is ordinary and/or permanent and all-pervasive; that white people don't oppose racism unless it suits them; that there is a unique voice of color that is represented by Critical Race Theory; that lived experience and story-telling are primary ways of revealing racism; and that liberalism and the Civil Rights approach are, at best, inadequate and, at worst, reinforce racism.[5] Critical theories of race have since evolved, simplified, become more dogmatic, and are found more in cultural studies and pedagogy than in legal studies.[6]

Decolonize. The aims of the "Decolonize" movement are to reinterpret and "deconstruct" everything from the curriculum to hair. It goes beyond the aim to include more non-Western intellectuals and artists, as well as non-Western customs and traditions in the Western world. In fact, it is contradictory on these grounds, claiming both that there needs to be more inclusion of these in the West and that the use of them by white Westerners is cultural appropriation. The "Decolonize" goals extend into the realm of knowledge and include the claim that science, reason, and liberalism are white and Western and that the whole of Western modernity, including nearly all its key figures, should be understood as racist and oppressive.[7]

Dis/ableism. Ableism refers to the assumption that everybody is able-bodied or that it is better to be able-bodied. Disableism is prejudice against disabled people and believing them to be inferior to the able-bodied. The aims of disability activists go beyond opposing prejudice and discrimination against the disabled or increasing their access to all that society has to offer. Rather, they claim that we generally only regard it as better if all of one's body parts work because we have been socialized into prejudice against disabled people. This leads to activism that opposes aims to treat or cure disability and even conflates this goal with wishing disabled people (rather than their disability) did not exist. It centers around the belief that "disabled" is not something an individual is but rather something that has been done to a person by a society optimally designed for able-bodied people.[8]

Discourse. Ways of talking about things. Within Critical Social Justice, references to discourses focus on ways of talking about things that are understood to either uphold oppressive power structures like white supremacy, patriarchy, and transphobia or disrupt or resist them. Discourse analysis is the scrutinization of language for power dynamics. This understanding of language as the primary source of maintaining oppressive power structures underlies much of today's language-policing, no-platforming, censorship, and coerced affirmations of certain beliefs and concepts like microaggressions, whitesplaining, and mansplaining.

Dismantle. The term "dismantle" is often used in relation to whiteness, masculinity, imperialism, heteronormativity, cisnormativity, ableism, etc. It is related to the invisible systems of oppressive power we are all believed to have been socialized into internalizing and now need to become able to see—become critically conscious of or "woke" to—and then work to deconstruct internally. This is an evolution of the "deconstruction" approach of the postmodernists known as "poststructuralists." When you see some kind of policy or training program that claims to help you dismantle your whiteness or other unconscious biases, it generally means it will assume you to hold the prejudiced beliefs that have been instilled in you by dominant discourses and expect you to affirm that you have them and commit to trying to unlearn them.

Diversity. This refers, in principle, to diversity of identity and the unobjectionable claim that the inclusion of people of diverse races, both sexes, all sexualities, gender identities, and abilities in any organization or initiative is a good thing. In practice, diversity often focuses mostly on race and increasing representation of non-white people. This is why we can sometimes hear an individual referred to as diverse when, in fact, they are still an individual who has just one race that isn't white. The aim for diversity does not include diversity of viewpoint.

Equity. Equity is understood to be different from equality—while equality aims to treat everybody the same, equity aims at fairness by evening up the playing field by giving people seen as marginalized pref-erential treatment. This can be reasonable when it comes to things like allowing wheelchair users to access elevators or diverting more resourc-es to poorly funded schools, but in practice, it often refers to trying to even up outcomes by identity group rather than ensure equal access to opportunities. This can take the form of affirmative action or positive discrimination in which people are hired or promoted on the grounds of their marginalized identity. Critics of this have pointed out that this identity-based approach mostly results in benefitting middle-class white women and racial minorities who were already likely to succeed in the first place and does little for upward mobility for economically disadvan-taged groups.[9]

Erasure. This is when a certain identity group is considered to have been neglected and left out of any account or endeavor., i.e., some-body who identifies as "nonbinary" could be claimed to be erased by the address "ladies and gentlemen." Similarly, women of color could be claimed to be erased if any feminist initiative does not make specific mention of issues of racism faced by women of color.

Fragility. People are understood to be fragile if they defend themselves against accusations of racism or other bigotries, or even if they just don't affirm themselves to be racist or have other prejudices. "White fragility" is heard most commonly and refers to the belief that white people can-not bear to be confronted with their own racism, which is assumed to be inevitable, and respond by becoming defensive.[10] Since racism and other bigotries are presumed present, any defense is invalid and can, therefore, only be explained by fragility. "Fragility" has also been applied to masculinity when men have objected to wholly negative portrayals of masculinity or men.

Inclusion. Inclusion, in Critical Social Justice terms, often means the exclusion of any ideas considered problematic or people who hold them.

To be inclusive is not simply to be welcoming of everybody in any environment (which is liberalism) but to monitor and ban the use of language or expression of beliefs that could make anybody feel excluded according to Critical Social Justice ideology. For example, the no-platforming of a gender-critical feminist could be done in the name of being inclusive of trans people.

Indigeneity/settler colonialism. Indigenous people are understood to be the first people to inhabit a certain land. However, the term is only applied and considered meaningful when other people have come later and taken governing power of that land. For example, the Māori people of New Zealand, originally from Polynesia, are considered to be indigenous because they arrived in the fourteenth century but were then superseded by European settlers who took control of the region in the eighteenth century. The European settlers are considered to be settler colonialists because they imposed their own governing structures on the people already living there. White people of Europe are not considered indigenous because later immigrants have not taken control and imposed their own governing structures on them. Within Critical Social Justice, claims about the knowledges (various systems of knowledge and "ways of knowing") and power structures of indigenous peoples and settler colonialists are often reductionist and mirror the decolonial theories.

Intersectionality. A framework that looks at ways in which people can be members of more than one marginalized group and which argues for the need to consider this compounding effect. For example, black women are said to suffer both from being black and from being women, and that these intersect to produce a unique form of oppression. There is validity to this claim as negative stereotypes about African American women are distinct from negative stereotypes about African American men and white women. However, in practice, intersectionality often devolves into an ever more complicated mess of competing claims to marginalized status, a process that has been disparagingly referred to as the "Oppression Olympics,"[11] as well as criticized for locking people into stereotypes.

Microaggressions. These are understood to be small and often unintentional insults that have plausible deniability on their own but amount to a constant onslaught of assumptions that negatively affect people's lives. For example, asking a non-white British person, "Where are you from?" could be seen as implying that they are not really British, and if they get asked this a lot, it could result in the black Briton feeling as though they are not accepted as belonging. However, microaggressions are deeply subjective things. Increasing numbers are discovered all the time and include statements that people should be allowed to believe, like "The best person for the job should get it," and statements that would have to be read extremely uncharitably to be seen as an insult of any kind, like "I love your hair."[12]

Minoritized. The word minoritized is used in place of "minority" to refer to identity groups. It is intended to convey that the minority status accompanied by oppression has been imposed upon such groups by society rather than being simply an objective measurement of their percentage of the population. This can then be used to refer to groups who are not literally a minority, like women. It can also be used to indicate that the "minoritized" group has been rendered as something "other" and lesser (than the group seen as dominant) by the group perceived to have more power.[13]

Misogyny. This literally means "hatred of women." However, like "white supremacy," it has been loosened considerably to become a largely subjective and ideological definition claiming that countries like the United States and the United Kingdom have deeply entrenched social systems in which women face hostility, hatred, and subordination because the society is set up for men.[14]

Normativity. This refers to something having been rendered normal, natural, and therefore good by powerful forces in society. Heteronormativity refers to the assumption that most people are heterosexual and that this is how people should be. Similarly, cisnormativity refers to the assumption that most people are cisgender (not trans) and that this is natural and good. Thin-normativity is the assumption that not being obese is the optimal condition for humans and, therefore, good. When Critical Social Justice activists add "-normativity" to terms like "hetero," "cis," and "thin," this usually means not that they wish to challenge prejudice against LGBT or obese people but that they have read oppressive homophobic, transphobic, and fatphobic power systems into a statement or occurrence and wish to problematize it.

Positionality. This is related to standpoint epistemology, where people are understood to have certain social statuses related to their identity. These are arranged hierarchically in society, and this affects the knowledge individuals have of the world and the things they have authority to speak about. That is, they have a position of privilege or marginalization because of an aspect of their identity and should bring this to bear on what they speak about and how. For example, I am oppressed because I am disabled, fat, and a woman but privileged because I am white and cisgender. Therefore, I can speak to ableism, fatphobia, and misogyny from my lived experience but must defer to people of color and trans people about racism and transphobia while also addressing my own racism *(see Racism and Fragility)* and transphobia.

Privilege. This is understood to be an unearned advantage associated with identity and relates closely to positionality *(see Positionality)*. Somebody who is white is understood to have white privilege and/or male privilege and certain nebulous benefits accruing to those from a society that is believed to favor white men even if they are poor, disabled, and homeless. While prejudice certainly does exist and affects some groups more than others, Critical Social Justice activists tend to have a simplistic and naïve stance on the matter that generalizes to an inordinate extent. It frequently neglects socioeconomic status or pays passing lip service to it and utterly neglects other unearned advantages such as intelligence, attractiveness, or a loving family.

Problematic/problematize. The term "problematic" is used to describe anything that can be argued to contain implications or connotations of racism, sexism, homophobia, transphobia, ableism, or other bigoted ideas. This is obviously highly subjective and interpretive. This term is used when there is no clear evidence of racism or other prejudiced assumption, but an argument can be made that it speaks into an oppressive discourse using the methods of Critical Social Justice theories. The process of making something appear to be a problem ethically via the application of theory is known as "problematization." Because of the belief that invisible systems of oppressive power underlie everything, spotting a "problem" in this way is seen as virtuous. For example, it's problematic to speak of "standing up" for a cause because it assumes all allies are able-bodied and erases those who cannot stand.[15]

Queer. This refers to any sexuality or gender identity that stands outside the most common combination of "feminine woman attracted to men" and "masculine man attracted to women" and has a political connotation. While "queer" used to be a reclaimed word for homosexuality, it is now used to represent a much broader range of sexual and gender identities, including some that are not anything to do with homosexuality or gender identity, such as asexual—not being interested in sex—or demisexual—only being interested in sex when an emotional bond has been established. To describe oneself as "queer" rather than "gay" or "lesbian" or "trans" generally denotes a political commitment to challenging perceived norms around gender and sexuality rather than a neutral statement of one's sexuality or gender identity.

Racism *(also see Antiracism)*. A system of power and privilege that affords certain races advantages over others in either overt or hidden ways. This stands in stark contrast to the common understanding of racism as prejudice and discrimination on the grounds of race. It enables Critical Social Justice activists to claim that racism can only be perpetrated against racial minorities and that it is impossible to be racist to or about white people because of the way power dynamics work. This makes it difficult to argue for not evaluating people by their race consistently as a way of opposing racism and instead facilitates generalizing negatively about white people as a way of opposing racism. This tends to further entrench racial categories as real and socially significant things and thus works against the goal of overcoming a racialized society.

Saviorism. This is usually related to race and so we most often hear the term "white saviorism." This is understood to be a form of racism in which white people take part in initiatives to help non-white people in order to validate their own sense of being a good and nonracist person and to feel superior. For example, somebody who dedicates their time to humanitarian aid projects like helping to build wells or supply medical aid to poor communities in Africa can be accused of indulging in white saviorism rather than dismantling their own assumed white supremacy. It is a particularly uncharitable and nasty ideological interpretation of an individual's motivation to help others.[16]

Social justice. When used by Critical Social Justice adherents alone and without the word "critical" or any other qualifier to denote it as their own theoretical approach, this is a presumptuous term that assumes that only adherents to Critical Social Justice seek a just society and everybody else has some other agenda. By appropriating the concept of social justice to one theoretical approach, liberals, Marxists, libertarians, and conservatives who all also seek a just society are then put in the position of appearing to oppose social justice itself when arguing against Critical

Social Justice when, in fact, they are opposing a particular approach that they don't believe results in a more just society.

Socialization. The belief that we are all conditioned into certain beliefs and values by society. Although it is true that culture does have great influence on beliefs and values, Critical Social Justice adherents tend to take an extreme and dogmatic approach to this and make strong claims about all white people having been socialized into white supremacist beliefs, or all men having been socialized into misogynistic and abusive ones. A white person or a man may claim that they do not, in fact, instinctively devalue black people or women but naturally assume them to be equally valuable and competent human beings and individuals whom they may or may not respect depending on their personal qualities. Any claims of this sort are interpreted as defensiveness and fragility. So, too, is any attempt to suggest that white supremacist and patriarchal views are not actually social norms at all and that they are widely regarded as negative by society.

Systemic. When something like racism or sexism is claimed to be systemic in Critical Social Justice terms, this does not necessarily indicate a belief that systems within institutions are overtly set up to discriminate against certain groups in society. The "systems" being referred to are the invisible systems of power like whiteness, patriarchy, and transphobia claimed to exist in everybody's unconscious minds and to be perpetuated by ways of talking about things and interactions. This is why asking for evidence of racist or sexist policies will be seen as missing the point. Therefore, claims of systemic racism or sexism of this type are unfalsifiable, and when asked for evidence of them, advocates will gesture at disparities and assert that only systemic prejudice on the part of dominant groups could cause them.

Violence. The understanding of violence in Critical Social Justice ideology has been expanded to include anything that could be considered to do harm. For example, the statement "White silence is violence" means "Unless all white people agree with Critical Social Justice ideology and adopt its antiracist approaches, they are complicit in a system of oppression against black people that results in their deaths." Similarly, an argument made by a gender-critical feminist that women's spaces and sports need to be reserved for biological females for reasons of safety and fairness is argued to contribute to a culture of hostility against trans women. A Critical Social Justice interpretation argues that this results in trans women's murder even though no trans women have been murdered by gender-critical feminists or, as far as we can tell, by people influenced by feminism.

White adjacent. This term is used to explain why some groups who are not white are successful financially and professionally and may also not support Critical Social Justice approaches to opposing racism. Most commonly, these groups are East Asians or, occasionally, South Asians. Jews are sometimes considered white adjacent, but more often now, they are not considered to be a marginalized group at all, despite the rise of antisemitic hate crime and sentiment. Instead, they are considered a particularly privileged subset of white people (if they are white). The accusation of being "white adjacent" is made to enable the accusation of "perpetuating whiteness" to be applied to people who are not actually white.[17]

Whiteness. This is another nebulous concept, and it refers to a more subtle form of white supremacy or an underlying system of discourses and attitudes perpetuated by white people in support of white supremacy. Whiteness was originally understood as the process of deeming certain groups to be white and others not in order to overtly determine social status and rights in the United States. This understanding is historically accurate. However, in current Critical Social Justice ideology, this process is considered to continue covertly through secretive and hard-to-detect means by which white people conspire in unspoken ways and maintain solidarity with each other to deny people of color equal access to the best opportunities in life. Because whiteness operates as a subtle and unspoken ideology, it needs to be uncovered through "critical" theoretical perspectives *(see Critical)* and the digging out of unconscious bias. The concept of whiteness allows theorists and activists to claim that they are not attacking people with white skin but rather an ideology of whiteness when they generalize negatively about white people.[18]

Woke. Woke is the African American Vernacular English term that correlates with the theoretical concept of critical consciousness. If one is "woke" (or critically conscious), one has become aware of the invisible systems of power that permeate everything. As a result, one is more able to see them and more committed to making others see them, affirm them, and share a commitment to dismantle them. Because the term has been so useful for defining the core concepts of the world and the ethical framework of Critical Social Justice, it has been picked up and used by most critics of Critical Social Justice as the target of their criticism. This enables them to demonstrate more clearly that they are not opposing social justice but a specific worldview that sees oppressive power systems everywhere, justifies using negative identity-based stereotypes, and advocates for authoritarian means to impose this worldview on others. Consequently, there is now a misconception that the word "woke" was created by its critics as a pejorative and an attack on any form of opposition to racism or other prejudices.[19]

X. Some of you will have noticed the letter "x" replacing vowels in certain words like "Latinx" and "womxn" and "folx." The "x" represents a political commitment to gender-neutral language and is now more commonly associated with queer politics, although it began in radical feminism to prevent the word "women" from including the word "man" and being a derivation of it (and thus theorized to be dependent on it).

Radical feminists who used "womxn" or "womyn" often do not support the queer and trans movements who now use the letter X to represent a neutral gender or an unknowable and ambiguous one. Within queer spaces, the "x" (or sometimes an asterisk) is often used to refer to the indefinable and fluid as well as changing words from being straightforwardly masculine or feminine. It indicates inclusiveness of queer and transgender identities, but this attempt at inclusiveness has itself since been problematized for implying trans women are not women.[20] The way the "x" is pronounced in speech when it cannot be phonetically is by using the name of the letter and saying "ex," so, for example, Latinx is pronounced "Latin-ex." Similarly, "womxn" can be pronounced as "wom-ex-n" (or as "woman-ex" or "women-ex") but is today often just pronounced as "women" or "woman." "Folx," meanwhile, is pronounced phonetically as "folks" because it can be. "Latinx" is the word you are most likely to hear in Critical Social Justice discourse, although very few Hispanic or Latin American people use the word "Latinx," and a majority of them have never heard of it.[21]

Appendix: Sample Letters

The letters shared here include those written by me or another Counterweight team member and those that have been written and successfully used by people who came to Counterweight with specific issues. Most of our correspondents prefer to remain confidential but have given me permission to share their letters. No matter your situation, you will find helpful framing, lines of argument, and passages in these letters that you can use in whole or part and otherwise adapt for your own purposes.

Letter Objecting to Mandatory Gender Pronoun Declaration
Letter Objecting to Ideologically Biased Readings on Race
Letter Objecting to Support for Radical Political Movements in Public Organizations
Letter Objecting to Affinity Groups or Other Racial Segregation
Letter Objecting to Claims That All White People Are Racist and/or Socialized into White Supremacy
Letter by Non-White Writer Objecting to Critical Social Justice Approaches to Antiracism
Letter Urging Caution over Voluntary Meetings Discussing Race and Racism
Letter to a School on Antiracist Teaching
Letter to a School Teaching about Gender Identity
Letter by a Non-White Writer Objecting to Antiracism Training

Letter Objecting to Mandatory Gender Pronoun Declaration*

Dear <name of employer>,

I write to express my concerns about requirements for people to state their gender pronouns in their email signatures or in meetings. While I understand and share the desire to be inclusive of people with diverse identities and worldviews, I think this could serve the opposite purpose as well as be an invasion of privacy for people for whom this is a private matter. Also, many people do not feel they have a gender identity separate from their biological sex. This requirement to provide gender pronouns amounts to requiring them to pretend to hold beliefs they do not hold about gender. They may even have ethical objections to this policy for philosophical or religious reasons.

Declaring one's pronouns is not, in itself, a political act, but it does convey a certain position on gender that is widely read as having political and philosophical connotations. In the same way, someone could declare her own identity as "adult human female," and this also conveys a political and philosophical position on gender even though it appears to be a simple statement of fact. Due to the sensitive nature of this and the political connotations, I believe it is better to remain, in all official communications, politically neutral. I don't think it serves the purpose of inclusion if we were to mandate such identifications in email signatures or include them in meetings. It could, in fact, cause people to feel excluded or under pressure to reveal their political views or their views on gender, which they should

---

* This letter, or a variation of it, can be used by people who have gender-critical views, religious views about gender, or simply don't wish to imply any particular view on gender. It can also be used by trans people where it is often most effective. In a Twitter (now X) thread starting "Why do I hate being asked my pronouns?," Dr. Jen Manion, who identifies as trans, gives a number of reasons, including, "The expectation that I answer on demand (to strangers) about something that is personal, complex, and traumatic." This perspective is often neglected by employers or trainers who can simply assume that all trans people appreciate the sharing of pronouns. Jen Manion (@activisthistory) started the thread on September 9, 2021, at 6:12 p.m., twitter.com/activisthistory/status/1436090050144526338.

not have to do at work as both are private matters.

In the same way, I think we should be welcoming of people with a variety of religious, political, cultural, racial, or philosophical identities but not require them to declare these in their email signatures. It is more in keeping with the spirit of inclusiveness for people to simply share their names and positions in signatures, and not to be under any pressure to reveal more about themselves than that. Everyone should, of course, remain free to disclose any aspect of their identity or any worldview they might hold to colleagues with whom they have developed relationships where this personal information is shared by mutual consent.

Yours sincerely,

Letter Objecting to Ideologically Biased Readings on Race

Dear <name of employer, school, or library>,

I note with interest that you have recently begun promoting/recommending books on race and racism. I support this decision as this is an important subject about which people should read. However, I am a little concerned that the books you promote seem rather limited ideologically and thus might fail to be inclusive of the ideological, political, religious, and cultural diversity of black intellectuals who address race and racism and the people who might like to read them.

For example, I notice that *White Fragility,* a book by a white professor of multicultural education, Robin DiAngelo, is recommended/available but not *Woke Racism*, a book written by a black professor of linguistics, John McWhorter, who most strongly disagrees with her approach. Equally, Ibram X. Kendi's *How to be an Antiracist* is included but not the work of the liberal intellectual who most disagrees with him, Thomas Chatterton Williams (see, for example, his book *Self-Portrait in Black and White*).It would be wonderful to get a full range of black intellectual thought in there ranging from Erec Smith's advocacy of a three-pronged understanding of empowerment in *A Critique of Anti-racism in Rhetoric and Composition: The Semblance of Empowerment* to Thomas Sowell's empiricist argument for a multivariate analysis of demographic data in *Disparities and Discrimination* to Shelby Steele's appeal to the individual, merit-based ethos of the American Dream in *Shame: How America's Past Sins Have Polarized Our Country*.[1] All of these books oppose racism and argue for a variety of ways to do this. By including a wide range of texts like this in its recommendations, <name of employer, school, or library> could avoid inadvertently giving the impression that there are only a few core texts on race and racism and missing out on a wide range of black intellectual thought.

Yours sincerely,

Letter Objecting to Support for Radical Political Movements in Public Organizations[†]

Dear <name of employer>,

I was concerned to see that our <social media accounts/recent communications> have proclaimed support for the Black Lives Matter movement. As a publicly funded organization, we have a responsibility to be politically neutral. While the belief that black lives matter is certainly politically neutral and any employee who did not believe this would be unfit to serve the public, the movement called "Black Lives Matter" is a political movement and makes public political stances that employees must be free not to take. These could include the aims to dismantle the nuclear family,[2] overthrow capitalism,[3] or defund the police.[4] Black Lives Matter owes much to the Marxist thought of the Frankfurt School, entering the American Black Radical Tradition via such figures as the Communist intellectual Angela Davis, which was then combined with postmodern theory around 1990 by intellectuals like Kimberlé Crenshaw, who developed Critical Race Theory and the concept of intersectionality. Please note that Critical Race Theory explicitly opposes the liberalism, equality under the law, and civil rights values that so many citizens and members of our organization, including black ones, have fought for and remain committed to.

My concern is that taking such an overtly radical political stance is not only likely to be incompatible with the ethical values of many of our members but is also likely to undermine public confidence. Public support for the BLM movement is mixed, including among racial minorities.[5] I urge you to recognize that we have a responsibility to ensure that black employees and members of the public are equally well served by us and that we can recognize that black lives do indeed matter without supporting a movement that espouses specific and radical political values.

Yours sincerely,

[†] This can also be adapted for private organizations.

Letter Objecting to Affinity Groups or Other Racial Segregation

Dear <name of employer, university, or school>,

I am writing to express my concern about the plans to segregate <employees/students> into racial groups for the purposes of discussing racial issues. While I understand that some people of color have expressed a preference for discussing issues of racism in the absence of white people, this is by no means a universal feeling. For those who do not hold this view, segregation by race can feel like a deeply regressive step that recalls a deeply racist history. Equally, the idea that "affinity" can be decided by a person's race is a form of racial essentialism that I cannot ethically support. It implies that people's primary identities and experiences must be racial when there is, in reality, so much more to people than that, and many people prefer not to be racialized <at work/in university/in school>. I believe that it is better to allow affinity groups—better known as friendship groups—to form naturally over shared values, interests, culture, religion, politics, or philosophical beliefs or simply the enjoyment of each other's company.

[If white] For myself, I cannot agree to be part of a white affinity group. I do not believe there is any merit in forming groups around a white identity, and there is much evidence that white identity politics have been the cause of much racial oppression throughout history. I ask that you allow me (and others) to decline to partake in this on precisely those ethical grounds. I understand that the purpose is meant to be to enable white people to examine their role in historical and current racism and it is believed that by racializing themselves, white people will be better able to understand the racial experiences of others. However, I do not share this belief, and I do not believe there is any evidence that forming white identity groups has ever reduced racism.[6] I would be interested to see any evidence you have to the contrary. In the meantime, please allow me to continue not to racialize either myself or any of my non-white colleagues or friends in this way.

[If not white] While others may wish to form groups based on their racial identity and believe this can help to address racism, I myself do not

wish to be racialized in this way and request that you allow me to abstain from joining any group based on my skin color. I am concerned about the potential consequences of dividing people in this way at all, but I recognize that if some people wish to do so, they must be allowed to. I wish <the organization/university/school> would not encourage this, however. I do not believe there is any evidence that forming racial identity groups has ever reduced racism. I would be interested to see any evidence you have to the contrary. In the meantime, please allow me to continue not to racialize either myself or any of my white colleagues or friends in this way.

Yours sincerely,

Letter Objecting to Claims That All White People Are Racist and/or Socialized into White Supremacy

Dear <name of employer>,

I am pleased to see that we are addressing issues of racial equality. However, I have some significant concerns about some very strong claims being made which seem to deny individual agency. The claim that all white people are socialized into holding racist assumptions about non-white people is an ideological one strongly influenced by the best-selling book *White Fragility,* by Robin DiAngelo. It cannot be accepted by anybody who believes that individuals have different backgrounds and experiences and also possess the ability to evaluate and then accept or reject certain ideas. It is a problem, in essence, for those who believe in free will, which includes liberals, conservatives, and believers in the Abrahamic faiths, as well as for anyone who believes that individual thought and viewpoint diversity exists within racial groups.

It is undeniable that our country has a deeply racist history in which non-white people have been horrendously oppressed and that individuals with racist ideas still exist. White supremacist discourses have been dominant in society, and they have not entirely disappeared. Nevertheless, we live in a society that has made significant racial progress both legally and in attitude and that contains more than one discourse. Anybody born since the beginning of the Civil Rights Movement has had the opportunity to evaluate antiracist discourses as well as racist ones. Very many white people have been raised to believe that racism is wrong, and even those who have not cannot have escaped exposure to arguments to this effect. To claim that <we/they> have all nevertheless internalized white supremacist ideas and are unavoidably racist is not supported by evidence. It is also deeply offensive to those who believe racism to be both stupid and unethical.

It is unclear what white people who do not hold white supremacist views and do not automatically associate non-white people with negative characteristics are expected to do in this kind of training. Will <we/they> be allowed to openly disclose <our/their> genuine views and <our/their> principled opposition to racism? There is some implication that <we/they> will need to try to pretend to hold racist views or genuinely work to convince <ourselves/themselves> to hold racist views to comply with the assumptions set out in this training.

[If white] I would appreciate your clarification on this issue as I have ethical objections to trying to become racist or pretending to be racist. Nor do I think that doing so will in any way reduce racism in the workplace.

[If not white] I would appreciate your clarification on this issue as I have ethical objections to encouraging my friends and colleagues to become racist or to pretend to be racist. Nor do I think that doing so will in any way reduce racism in the workplace.

Yours sincerely,

Letter by Non-White Writer Objecting to Critical Social Justice Approaches to Antiracism[‡]

Dear <name of employer>,

I am very glad that you are addressing issues of race and racism seriously and developing policies and training programs to address them. I realize that your intention is to benefit people like me who have historically been disadvantaged and are still more likely to face racist discrimination. However, I have some concerns about the way you are going about this.

The recent communications, policy changes, and training initiatives intended to benefit people of color and ensure diversity and inclusion have focused on one specific ideological approach to antiracism. This is an American-centric approach that centers on the work of theorists like Ibram X. Kendi and Robin DiAngelo. I am afraid that such a narrow focus neglects the intellectual and ideological diversity of people of color and the work of many other black intellectuals and intellectuals of color. The idea that all people of color can be spoken for by one Western ideology is constraining and limiting and also a little presumptuous. While white people are understood to be ideologically diverse and can range from Marxist to conservative, black people and other people of color are understood to be represented by one school of thought. I urge you to reconsider this racially essentialist approach, recognize the intellectual and political diversity of people of color, and include a greater range of ideas and thinkers in your communications and initiatives if you truly want to honor diversity and be inclusive.

The adoption of one specific approach to addressing issues of race and racism that focuses on progressive left-wing politics and intersectionality has been particularly difficult for people of color who are believers in the Muslim, Christian, Sikh, or Hindu faiths. Indeed, such individuals

---

‡ This letter has been assembled from the objections raised by black, South Asian, and other people of color who have come to Counterweight for help with addressing their concerns. Their experiences and objections vary, and so I present the most common, repeated concerns and the most effective way they have been presented.

are more likely than white people (who have lower degrees of religiosity) to hold beliefs that are socially conservative and to believe in traditional family structures. This has led many non-white religious believers to feel unable to support the Critical Social Justice approach to antiracism not only because they oppose racism from a different ethical framework but also because they do not share the largely atheistic views of white, Western progressives about gender and sexuality.

Some employees of color would prefer their workplace not to put them in the position of having to declare or deny their political or religious views, which are private matters. They may feel under pressure to attend antiracist meetings and pretend to agree with ideas they do not agree with because these are the ideas claimed to be held by people of color. Others have found themselves in the position of having to be the ones to raise objections to this ideological approach to race and racism because white people are too afraid of being accused of racism to do so. This gets in the way of advancing in our careers.

Furthermore, many people of color have found that the new intensive focus on race in the workplace has led the workforce to see them as racial categories rather than as individuals as they had done previously. This is deeply uncomfortable for those who do not wish to be racialized at work. It has caused barriers to form between them and white colleagues with whom they previously had good relationships.

I urge you to rethink this approach to addressing the important issue of racism in the workplace and how to counter it. I recognize that you are trying to make things better for people of racial minority by listening to us more, but this racially essentialist approach is counterproductive to that aim. Please consider a more inclusive approach to addressing the issue that does not assume that all non-white people hold a particular concept of social justice and approach to antiracism. Instead, please implement policies that recognize the intellectual and political diversity of people of color and allow us to retain our own ethical frameworks. Any policies should encourage us to oppose racism and support social justice from our own diverse perspectives that may differ from the Critical Social Justice one.

Yours sincerely,

Letter Urging Caution over Voluntary Diversity, Equity, and Inclusion Meetings[§]

Dear <employer>,

I note with interest that you are setting up some voluntary meetings to discuss diversity, equity, and inclusion in the workplace, particularly in relation to issues of racial equality. I am fully in support of all initiatives to eradicate racism and to be inclusive of more people with a diverse range of racial, religious, cultural, and sexual identities as well as viewpoints. I would like to take part in any initiatives to achieve this. I also appreciate that these meetings are voluntary, thus removing any pressure or expectation from any individual to discuss matters upon which they would prefer to keep their views private.

However, I am a little concerned due to my familiarity with problems that have arisen with these kinds of meetings in other organizations when one particular approach to antiracism came to dominate the meetings and push out all other approaches. Specifically, the approach best known simply as "Critical Social Justice" (see Sensoy and DiAngelo, *Is Everybody Really Equal,* 2017) is often taken as the best or even the only approach to antiracism, despite it being a political and theoretical approach that is not accepted or even known by the majority of people of all races.

Therefore, I provide a list of indicators that the meetings might be becoming counterproductive to the goal of diversity and inclusion and succumbing to pressure to conform to a single ideologically narrow orthodoxy. This has, in some workplaces, resulted in the uncritical acceptance of racial essentialism, the pressure to accept a belief system involving invisible power structures, an increase of racial prejudice, a growing alien-

---

[§] This is a letter I wrote for an employee drawn from the various problems people who came to us described most consistently. You can adapt the letter to refer more obliquely to "self-reported indicators collated by people who study diversity initiatives." It is generally safer not to cite me as a source directly given my profile and my involvement in, among other things, the so-called Grievance Studies Affair, which has plenty of supporters but also many detractors.

ation between colleagues, resignations, and an uncomfortable working environment.

Please look out for things like:

- People promoting only one kind of antiracist thought within meetings—for example, authors like Ibram X. Kendi, Robin DiAngelo, Layla Saad, Reni Eddo-Lodge, and Akala, but no Thomas Chatterton Williams, Glenn Loury, Shelby Steele, or Chloé Valdary.
- People uncritically accepting claims that people of a certain race hold certain beliefs—aka racial essentialism. For example,
  - People saying only black people who have American-centric DiAngelo–style views of antiracism are authentic.
  - People seeing all white people as having been socialized into white supremacist beliefs and harboring inherently racist ideas.
- People becoming angry and abusive to those expressing ideas they disagree with or saying that people of a certain race have no right to express any ideas. For example,
- People saying, "Your view is damaging" or "You are a racist for having that view" or "You should just sit down and shut up because you are a certain race," rather than saying, "I disagree very strongly with that view because . . . ," or presenting actual arguments that can be discussed and debated.
- People using racial slurs to describe other people with certain views— for example, Uncle Tom, coconut, c**n, Karen, etc.
- People advocating for training everybody in their own preferred "antiracist" way to think about race
- People implementing antiscientific unconscious bias tests to examine their colleagues' minds and beliefs rather than just allowing them to express their own views and accepting that other people have different ones.
- People pressuring the organization to make commitments to certain political groups.
- Some people being very vocal and confident while others seeming fearful or reluctant to speak.

- People affirming certain beliefs while appearing very tense and anxious.
- People beginning to self-segregate into racial groups during breaks or in situations where seating is self-selected or ceasing to socialize with colleagues of a different race after work.
- People becoming angry or withdrawn at work and having more sick days, particularly on the grounds of mental health and particularly on days when meetings are happening.

I hope you take this communication in the spirit of cooperation and helpfulness in which it is intended. Although I have looked quite deeply into these issues and read about these problems arising, I do not doubt that you have too. As anyone with years of experience managing a racially and ideologically diverse workforce and fostering workplace cohesion knows, these indicators presage an incoming ideological conformity drive. You will likely know that such a drive creates a hostile environment and intimidates less confident members of the workforce, particularly women and minorities, into self-censorship. I very much value the workplace atmosphere we currently have and the good relationships and social cohesion among the workforce. I would like to be part of any effort to increase this and oppose any prejudice or discrimination.

Yours sincerely,

Letter to a School on Antiracist Teaching

Dear <school official/head teacher/school board>,

Thank you for your communications that you have been teaching about racism and the importance of opposing it. I heartily support this endeavor. It is very important that children have an understanding of history and the ways in which black people and other people of color have been oppressed. They need to know not only the importance of ensuring that this never happens again but also the importance of continuing to oppose evaluating people's moral worth and social status by their race. We will support any ethical approach to conveying this important message in age-appropriate ways to our child.

However, I am somewhat concerned about the ways in which this is being done. I am sure you are aware that the school is made up of children from diverse cultural, religious, and ethical backgrounds and that there are a variety of ethical frameworks from which to oppose racism. Nevertheless, it seems that the children are being taught only one way of understanding race and racism and that this draws heavily on currently popular critical theories of race, whiteness, and antiracism, most commonly known as "Social Justice" (as opposed to "social justice") or "Critical Social Justice." This could inadvertently cause problems in which white children are led to believe that black people and other people of color are ideologically monolithic and that there is only one authentic black voice. This form of racial essentialism excludes the thought of all black intellectuals who address race and racism in other ways and will necessarily exclude many children of color who have been raised with different beliefs.

[If white] I am particularly concerned about concepts of whiteness and white supremacy and the claim that all white people are socialized into holding racist beliefs. We have not raised our child to hold such beliefs, but now <she/he> believes that <she/he> should because <she/he> is white. Children are very impressionable at this age, and I must object to you trying to convince my child that <she/he> holds racist beliefs. We must

request that you stop undermining the antiracist values we have raised our child to hold and replacing them with racist ones.

[If black] I am particularly concerned that my child is being taught that society is stacked against <her/him> and that <she/he> is unlikely to be able to succeed no matter how hard <she/he> works. While racist attitudes do still exist, and we do have to prepare our child to face them, this fatalistic and defeatist attitude undermines the values and confidence we have worked to instill in our child. Children are very impressionable at this age, and I must object to your encouraging them to believe they will fail in life simply because of their skin color. We must request that you stop undermining the strength, ambition, and hope we have instilled in our child and attempting to replace it with resentment and despair.

[If mixed race] We are particularly concerned that our child is being taught to associate whiteness with being an oppressor and blackness with being oppressed. It is entirely possible to teach the deeply racist reality of history accurately without including this kind of racial essentialism that can only cause deep confusion and distress for a mixed-race child. Children are very impressionable at this age, and I must object to you undermining the antiracist values <she/he> has been taught at home. We must request that you stop counteracting the values of racial equality and unity we have taught <her/him> at home and replacing them with simplistic racial power dynamics that negatively impact the way <she/he> sees <her/his> parents and <herself/himself>.

Yours sincerely,

Letter to a School Teaching about Gender Identity

Dear <school official/head teacher/school board>,

Thank you for your communications about the teaching of sexuality and gender identity you have been doing and the importance of accepting LGBT people. We support this endeavor. It is very important that children know that it is wrong to bully people who are gay, lesbian, bisexual, or gender nonconforming. It is particularly important for children who will be LGBT themselves to receive the message that there is nothing wrong with them. We will support any ethical approach to conveying this important message in age-appropriate ways to our child.

However, I am somewhat concerned about the way in which this is being done. There are a number of ways to be supportive of LGBT people, and there is no need to take any specific ideological approach to this. Nevertheless, the information we are receiving indicates that a particular theoretical ideology of gender and sexuality is being foregrounded. It seems to be that which is promoted by the "Critical Social Justice" approach to LGBT activism and particularly to trans activism. You should certainly be aware that this approach is far from universally supported by people who are lesbian, gay, bisexual, or transgender/transsexual. We would prefer you to take a more neutral approach that does not politicize LGBT identity, especially given that LGBT people are politically diverse, and very many of them prefer not to politicize their sexuality or gender identity at all.

We are concerned that gender-identity affirmation seems to be being promoted to children who are of an age where they are still discovering and exploring all aspects of their identities and discovering who they are. They may well not yet know what their sexuality is or have formed a well-thought-through understanding of the nebulous concept of "gender." Furthermore, child psychologists and sexologists who deal with issues of gender dysphoria are still working to understand how best to address and, if necessary, treat it, and there is not a consensus on the issue.[7] It is concerning, therefore, that children and adolescents who are known to quite naturally "try on" a number of identities in the process of discovering their adult selves are being pushed toward understanding gender nonconformity only in terms of trans identity. We understand that this is done with the intention of being supportive of children with gender dysphoria who may experience considerable distress. However, it would be much more ethical and in the best interests of any gender dysphoric child to simply show them kindness and acceptance and leave any "diagnosis" of their struggles to qualified psychologists.

Yours sincerely,

Letter by a Non-White Writer Objecting to Antiracism Training[¶]

Dear <name of employer>,

I hope you are well.

In our last meeting, you said to me, "I think we have been clear about what is important to us and what we believe is right for the company," and, of course, I respect the right of the managers of a company to decide its values and direction. However, you have also, at times, given assurances that you are also willing to listen to employees. Most recently, you have expressed a commitment to listen to <BIPOC/BAME> employees. I am one such employee and I have done a lot of listening to you telling me how I should feel about race. I am hoping that you might make some time to read this letter by me telling you how I actually *do* feel about it. Not just because you're white, not just because I'm not, but because if you are serious about your commitment to antiracism, it does require listening to people of different races having different views about how to address racism.

I am afraid I do not feel the same as certain others on this matter and wish to have a more open discussion about the ongoing politicization in our company and the implications of defining our strategy on diversity and inclusion by applying one particular antiracist methodology. Our understanding and usage of terms such as "whiteness," "white privilege," antiracism, etc., are important to understand, especially in their relationship to data and policy. I have read quite widely into the scholarship that underlies these terms and their meanings, and I think I have a stronger understanding of them than most of the people in management who have been using them. This is not a racial issue. I do not believe my skin color gives me greater authority to interpret these texts than you. I just think I've read more of them.

¶ The bulk of this letter was written by an employee who would probably be recognized as a light-skinned black man in the United States and as mixed race in the United Kingdom, although his actual heritage is more complex than that. Even so, much of this letter can also be used by white people.

At our company, the methodology being used is known as Critical Social Justice (see Sensoy and DiAngelo 2017)—a broad umbrella that includes a wide range of "critical" movements, including Critical Race Theory, Critical Gender Studies, Critical Pedagogy, and more. This is being led by a vocal group within the company, with the unfortunate support of the leadership team, and it is creating quite a hostile environment for those who disagree with this theoretical approach to handling matters of discrimination, racism, sexism, and other hateful bigotries. I cannot support this approach with its use of divisive and explicitly discriminatory and reductionist generalizations because it goes against my own antiracist principles. I cannot support its logical fallacies, its unfalsifiability, or its use of circular reasoning.

I don't want to work in an environment where my race is noticed but my individuality is not. Like many <insert nationality> of all races, I support the universal civil rights approach to equality, respect merit and hard work, and consider liberalism and reason to be the very best approach to handling interethnic interactions and differences. I *do not* believe that I or my colleagues have "internalized" or been "socialized" into racism as claimed by those who hold the beliefs and values of Critical Social Justice. I don't believe this as a liberal <nationality> man, and I don't believe this as an inheritor of my family's faith tradition, which holds, like all the Abrahamic religions, that I have free will to reject immoral ideas like racism. It is, then, of great concern to me that our company is proselytizing these American-centric Critical Social Justice views onto others who, like me, may have different beliefs and ethical frameworks related to their own individual or cultural backgrounds.

It is through my study of Critical Race Theory and critical discourse theorists such as Robin DiAngelo, Ibram X. Kendi, Richard Delgado, Jean Stefancic, and numerous others in this field—as well as my study into activist outfits such as Black Lives Matter and their close ideological and tutorship relations to groups such as the Marxist-Leninist revolutionary Weather Underground—that I have become quite familiar with this belief system. The approach of Critical Race Theory "question(s) the very foundations of the liberal order, including equality theory, legal reasoning, Enlightenment Rationalism and neutral principles of constitutional law" (Delgado and Stefancic, *Critical Race Theory: An Introduction*, p. 3). I do not. Nor do most people. I don't believe in "discourse theory," a key component on which modern Critical Race Theory or, indeed, the wider Critical Social Justice movement relies today. This is the belief that language itself is a tool of oppression that taints the very knowledge and things we perceive as truth as inherently racist/sexist/homophobic/ableist/fatphobic, etc., and therefore inaccessible. This worldview arose in an atheistic context in France during the postmodern movement and draws on earlier theories of conflict that originated in an atheistic context in nineteenth-century Germany during the height of Marxist thought. Not only does this make it unsuitable for many people whose values arose in other parts of the world or within religious traditions, but it also makes it unsuitable for many Western liberals, rationalists, and empiricists. This is because it closes down the possibility of genuine empathy between groups and calls into question the very validity and nature of objectivity. It places pressure on individuals to identify themselves and evaluate each other by race and other identity categories and to do so in binary oppositions and hierarchies.

In the case of race, through the application of Critical Race Theory and "whiteness studies," this places those who are white or have what is known as "proximity to whiteness" in opposition to those who are not white or are considered to have what is known as a "minoritized positionality." Those who are said to be aware of their positionality in an ostensibly oppressive society are said to have critical consciousness (or, in African American Vernacular English, to be "woke"). Robin DiAngelo, a *New York Times* best-selling author, declares that a "positive white identity is an impossible goal" and that ". . . White identity is inherently racist; white people do not exist outside of a system of white supremacy" (*White Fragility*, p. 149). Is this really what is important to you or right for your company? I am a part of this company, and I reject it just as I expect my white colleagues to reject negative stereotypes about me.

Whilst I have confidence that the leadership team is attempting to do the right thing, I am concerned that it is unwittingly opening the door for these important and highly charged issues to be monopolized by those whose viewpoints, language, approach, and prescriptions are highly divisive, politically radical, and are often without any rigorous foundation or respect for logical consistency. All of these ideas cause overwhelmingly more harm than good, are disempowering for those of us who fall into "marginalized" groups, and are alarmingly anti-intellectual and shoddy methodologically.

I consider the application and promotion of such an ideology in the workplace to not only be inappropriate and wholly dismissive of my agency and achievements but also a source of a great deal of personal trepidation. In addition to my concerns for myself and other non-white employees, it is distressing to know that my white colleagues, for many of whom I have a deep respect and admiration, are being smeared as irredeemable racists by virtue of their skin color alone. If you believe, as do Delgado and Stefancic, that minority status brings a presumed competence to speak about race and racism, please listen to me when I use mine to tell you that this never ends well. I'd rather, however, that you considered my argument and not my skin color when evaluating my competence.

I very gladly joined this company, turning down other competing offers, because of the excellent interactions I had—and continue to have—with the people I work directly alongside (be they of any race, ethnicity, sex, religious belief, orientation etc.), and I genuinely enjoy my work and the constant challenges it brings. However, the environment I value so much is in danger of becoming hostile.

In order to address my concerns, I would appreciate your responses to the below:

- I would like your assurance that I will not keep receiving emails telling me what my race makes me believe and feel and that all employees have the right to opt out of this.
- I would like your assurance that neither I nor any of my colleagues will be under any pressure to attend any meetings proselytizing any belief system we do not share.
- I would like your assurance that at no point will the company consider segregating me or any of my colleagues by our race, requiring us

to affirm any beliefs we do not hold or to evaluate ourselves or each other by any of our identity categories.

Kind regards,

Notes

Introduction

1. Some organizations employ longer acronyms like DEIA or DEIB that include additional descriptors like "accessibility" and "belonging," but for the purposes of this discussion, we will use the umbrella term DEI to refer to all such offices, programs, and trainings. In the United States, 95 percent of highly research-intensive institutions had a senior DEI executive in 2022. One such school, the University of Michigan, had 142 DEI administrators with combined salary and benefits of $18.1 million that same year. Diana Ellsworth et al., "Racial and Ethnic Equity in US Higher Education," Executive Briefing, McKinsey and Company, July 18, 2022, www.mckinsey.com/industries/education/our-insights/racial-and-ethnic-equity-in-us-higher-education; Adam Andrzejewski, "University of Michigan Spends $18M on Equity Administrators," *Real Clear Politics*, February 13, 2023, www.realclearinvestigations.com/articles/2023/02/13/university_of_michigan_spends_18m_on_equity_admins_881064.html.

2. Rachel Minkin, "Diversity, Equity and Inclusion in the Workplace," Pew Research Center, May 17, 2023, www.pewresearch.org/social-trends/2023/05/17/diversity-equity-and-inclusion-in-the-workplace.

3. I have written extensively about this ideology elsewhere, notably in Helen Pluckrose and James Lindsay, *Cynical Theories: How Activist Scholarship Made Everything about Race, Gender, and Identity—and Why This Harms Everybody* (Durham, NC: Pitchstone Publishing, 2020). Many other books have since been written about the illiberal and authoritarian nature of this ideology, including, among others, John McWhorter, *Woke Racism: How a New Religion Has Betrayed Black America* (New York: Portfolio, 2021); Andrew Doyle, *The New Puritans: How the Religion of Social Justice Captured the Western World* (London: Constable, 2023); Yascha Mounk, *The Identity Trap: A Story of Ideas and Power in Our Time* (New York:

Penguin, 2023); Tomiwa Owolade, *This Is Not America: Why Black Lives in Britain Matter* (London: Atlantic Books, 2023); and Coleman Hughes, *The End of Race Politics: Arguments for a Colorblind America* (New York: Thesis, 2024).

4. See the chapter titled "The Misguided, Dystopian Goal of Equity" in Ronald A. Lindsay, *Against the New Politics of Identity* (Durham, NC: Pitchstone Publishing, 2023) and the concerns raised by a group of physicians and health-care professionals who raise awareness about the ways in which Critical Social Justice ideology negatively affects medical education, training, practice, research, and policy. Do No Harm, donoharmmedicine.org.

5. See, for example, Jonathan Ames, "I Help Thousands of Britons Fight for Social Justice, Says Anti-Woke Campaigner Helen Pluckrose," *Times,* October 15, 2021, www.thetimes.co.uk/article/i-help-thousands-of-britons-fight-for-social-justice-says-anti-woke-campaigner-helen-pluckrose-fqg73dtd9.

6. Pluckrose and Lindsay, *Cynical Theories.*

7. Writing in 2018, Greg Lukianoff and Jonathan Haidt described a shift occurring on university campuses that began in 2013 and took off in 2015–17 in what they call "The Tumultuous Years." *The Coddling of the American Mind: How Good Intentions and Bad Ideas Are Setting Up a Generation for Failure* (New York: Penguin, 2018), 11. Since then, Haidt has often cited 2015 as the significant year for the turn to identitarianism. As he wrote in a post on X, "The 2015 turn to identitarianism has been a disaster for universities (and for the country). When identity becomes the primary analytical lens and identities are ranked in value, conflict, confusion, and dishonesty are sure to follow." Jonathan Haidt (@JonHaidt), post on X, January 5, 2024, 7:57 a.m., twitter.com/JonHaidt/status/1743255423023489483.

8. As of November 2023, the National Association of Scholars has tracked nearly three hundred cases of academic cancellation in the United States and Canada. It writes, "Academic cancellation usually goes something like this: 1) a professor, administrator, or student says or writes something considered heretical by progressives; 2) outcry ensues among the faculty and student body, who demand institutional discipline; 3) administrators cave to the mob and punish the "culprit." In most cases, it really is that simple." David Acevedo, "Tracking Cancel Culture in Higher Education," National Association of Scholars, November 6, 2023, www.nas.org/blogs/article/tracking-cancel-culture-in-higher-education.

9. For a summary of the Halloween controversy at Yale University involving Nicholas and Erika Christakis, see "Halloween Costume Controversy," Foundation for Individual Rights and Expression (FIRE), www.thefire.org/research-learn/halloween-costume-controversy; for a news article on the controversy over Jordan Peterson's comments about pronouns, see Jessica Murphy, "Toronto Professor Jordan Peterson Takes on Gender-Neutral Pronouns," *BBC News*, November 4, 2016, www.bbc.com/news/world-us-canada-37875695; for an interview with Bret Weinstein in which he discusses events surrounding the Day of Absence programming at Evergreen State College, see Nico Perrino, "Bret Weinstein, Professor in Exile," So to Speak podcast, March 8, 2018, www.thefire.org/news/so-speak-podcast-bret-weinstein-professor-exile; for more on the campaign against Camille Paglia at the University of the Arts, see Conor Friedersdorf, "Camille Paglia Can't Say That," *Atlantic*, May 1, 2019, www.theatlantic.com/ideas/archive/2019/05/camille-paglia-uarts-left-deplatform/587125/; for a summary of the treatment of and charges against Robert Sullivan and his wife Stephanie Robinson at Harvard University, see Shera S. Avi-Yonah and Aidan F. Ryan, "Harvard Law Prof Who Agreed to Represent Harvey Weinstein Ousted as Faculty Dean," FIRE, May 13, 2019, www.thefire.org/news/harvard-law-prof-who-agreed-represent-harvey-weinstein-ousted-faculty-dean.

10. See CNN, "Ellen's Usain Bolt Tweet Deemed Racist," *CNN.com*, August 17, 2016, edition.cnn.com/2016/08/16/entertainment/ellen-degeneres-usain-bolt-tweet/index.html; Alex Culbertson, "Oscars to Have No Host After Kevin Hart Homophobic Tweets," *Sky News*, January 10, 2019, news.sky.com/story/oscars-to-have-no-host-after-kevin-hart-homophobic-tweets-11603296; Hannah Jane Parkinson, "Matt Damon, Stop #Damonsplaining—You Don't Understand Sexual Harassment," *Guardian*, December 19, 2017, www.theguardian.com/commentisfree/2017/dec/19/matt-damon-sexual-harassment; and Gwen Aviles, "J. K. Rowling Faces Backlash after Tweeting Support for 'Transphobic' Researcher," *NBC News*, December 19, 2019, www.nbcnews.com/feature/nbc-out/j-k-rowling-faces-backlash-after-tweeting-support-transphobic-researcher-n1104971.

11. While each of the individual cases referenced in this and the preceding paragraph received significant media coverage and social media attention, often along with video recordings, audio recordings, or images of events in question, less attention was paid to "cancellations" occurring among those without star power and in narrower contexts that lacked the public interest of universities. Those stories are equally important to understanding the nature of cancel culture and the ways in which it has disrupted niche communities. See, for example, episode 37 of the Quillette Podcast titled "Kathrine Jebsen Moore on How Knitting Was Captured by the Social Justice Cult," June 14, 2019, quillette.com/2019/06/14/quillette-podcast-37-kathrine-jebsen-moore-on-how-knitting-was-captured-by-the-social-justice-cult/; Katy Waldman, "In Y.A., Where Is the Line Between Criticism and Cancel Culture?," *New Yorker*, March 21, 2019, www.newyorker.com/books/under-review/in-ya-where-is-the-line-between-criticism-and-cancel-culture.

12. The press Counterweight received at its launch led to even greater waves of people reaching out for assistance. See, for example, Celia Walden, "Why I Started an Anti-Woke Helpline," *Telegraph*, February 17, 2021, available at archive.ph/Fq4TL; Olga Khazan, "A Support Group for the Unwoke," *Atlantic*, September 27, 2021, www.theatlantic.com/politics/archive/2021/09/counterweight-cancel-culture-support-ground/620203/.

13. Frank le Duc, "Campaigner Attacks Council for Promoting 'Racially Divisive' Lessons in Schools," *Brighton and Hove News*, January 10, 2022, www.brightonandhovenews.org/2022/01/10/campaigner-attacks-council-for-promoting-racally-divisive-lessons-in-schools/.

14. Counterweight submitted a report on the issue in humanitarian aid and charities to the UK Parliament. Counterweight, evidence submitted to International Development Committee, "Racism in the Aid Sector," UK Parliament, June 23, 2022, committees.parliament.uk/writtenevidence/26440/pdf/.

15. Noah Carl, "Threats to Free Speech at University, and How to Deal with Them—Part 1," *Areo Magazine*, December 10, 2019, areomagazine.com/2019/12/10/threats-to-free-speech-at-university-and-how-to-deal-with-them-part-1/; Stacy Hawkins, "Sometimes Diversity Trumps Academic Freedom," *Chronicle of High Education*, February 28, 2023, www.chronicle.com/article/sometimes-diversity-trumps-academic-freedom.

16. An example of a Critical Social Justice book intended for toddlers and kindergarteners that teachers have used to teach about skin color and racism is *Our Skin: A First Conversation about Race* by Megan Madison and Jessica Ralli, with illustrations by Isabel Roxas (New York: Rise, 2021). You can find a video of one of the authors reading it here: "Our Skin: A First Conversation About Race -

Read Aloud with the Author," YouTube video, uploaded by Brightly Storytime, May 30, 2022, www.youtube.com/watch?v=z4tx0z_vRuE&t.

17. The gender unicorn was created as a response to the genderbread person designed by It's Pronounced Metrosexual (www.itspronouncedmetrosexual.com) for being insufficiently inclusive. See the discussion in the "Changes from the Genderbread Person" section at "Gender Unicorn," Trans Student Educational Resources, 2015, transstudent.org/gender/. A printer-friendly version of It's Pronounced Metrosexual's genderbread person has been downloaded more than 2.7 million times across more than a hundred countries according to the designer who runs and manages the site. Sam Killermann, "The Genderbread Person," November 2011, www.samkillermann.com/work/genderbread-person/.

18. Timothy Meinch, "Shame and the Rise of the Social Media Outrage Machine," *Discover Magazine*, February 13, 2021, www.discovermagazine.com/the-sciences/shame-and-the-rise-of-the-social-media-outrage-machine; Joe Pinsker, "Trump's Presidency Is Over, So Are Many Relationships," *Atlantic*, March 31, 2021, www.theatlantic.com/family/archive/2021/03/trump-friend-family-relationships/618457/.

19. Geoffrey Miller, "The Neurodiversity Case for Free Speech," *Quillette*, July 18, 2017, quillette.com/2017/07/18/neurodiversity-case-free-speech/.

Chapter 1

1. See, for example, Sarah Hagi, "Cancel Culture Is Not Real—At Least Not in the Way People Think," *Time*, November 21, 2019, time.com/5735403/cancel-culture-is-not-real/.

2. Even those outlets that regularly featured pieces arguing cancel culture is a "scam" have since started publishing pieces acknowledging that cancel culture is not only real but also bound to collapse, given its lack of rules and nuance. See, for example, the contrast between this summer of 2020 piece by Michael Hobbes, "Don't Fall for the 'Cancel Culture' Scam," *Huffington Post*, July 10, 2020, www.huffpost.com/entry/cancel-culture-harpers-jk-rowling-scam_n_5f-0887b4c5b67a80bc06c95e, and the series of pieces published in the fall of 2023 under the following description: "HuffPost explores the phenomenon of cancel culture. This eight-part series covers the evolution of public scorn and accountability, the nuances that aren't talked about nearly enough and why this social experiment so quickly collapsed on itself." "Cancel Culture Unraveled," www.huffpost.com/entertainment/topic/cancel-culture-unraveled.

3. Arguably the first significant work to examine how this phenomenon affects targeted individuals is Jon Ronson, *So You've Been Publicly Shamed* (New York: Riverhead Books, 2015), even though the term "cancel culture" wasn't yet in popular use. A more recent book offers case studies of those who have been subject to public abuse and harassment for things they said or believe. Katherine Brodsky, *No Apologies: How to Find and Free Your Voice in the Age of Outrage—Lessons for the Silenced Majority* (Durham, NC: Pitchstone Publishing, 2024).

4. Even the Editorial Board of the *New York Times* has begun to sound the alarm about the dangers of cancel culture and how it contributes to a "destructive loop" that inhibits society's ability to manage conflict and increases the risk of political violence. See Editorial Board, "America Has a Free Speech Problem," *New York Times*, March 18, 2022, www.nytimes.com/2022/03/18/opinion/cancel-culture-free-speech-poll.html.

5. This term originates with Özlem Sensoy and Robin J. DiAngelo in *Is Everyone Really Equal?: An Introduction to Key Concepts in Social Justice Education* (New York City: Teachers College Press, 2017). However, this particular usage of the term "Critical" has a much longer intellectual history within the realm of political approaches to social justice. I have summarized this history elsewhere. See, for example, my essay "We Need Liberal Social Justice, Not Critical Social Justice," *Symposium* (Substack), April 15, 2021, symposium.substack.com/p/we-need-liberal-social-justice-not.

6. See Michel Foucault, *The Will to Knowledge* (London: Penguin, 1998) and Michel Foucault, *The History of Sexuality* (London: Penguin Books, 2020).

7. These are all real cases that Counterweight worked on.

8. Paulo Freire, *Pedagogy of the Oppressed*, 50th anniv. ed. (New York: Bloomsbury, 2018).

9. For a discussion of this concept, see the entry by Dylan Gray and Colin Bernatzky, "Red Pilled (or Pilling)," in *The Wiley-Blackwell Encyclopedia of Social and Political Movements*, eds. D.A. Snow, D. Porta, B. Klandermans, and D. McAdam (September 27, 2022), doi.org/10.1002/9780470674871.wbespm621.

10. Alison Bailey, "Tracking Privilege-Preserving Epistemic Pushback in Feminist and Critical Race Philosophy Classes," *Hypatia: A Journal of Feminist*

Philosophy 32, no. 4 (2017): 877, doi.org/10.1111/hypa.12354.

11. Ibid., 877.

12. Kiaras Gharabaghi and Ben Anderson-Nathe, "The Need for Critical Scholarship," *Child and Youth Services* 38, no. 2, (2017): 95–97, doi.org/10.1080/0145935X.2017.1327692.

13. Isaac Herschel Gottesman's *The Critical Turn in Education: From Marxist Critique to Poststructuralist Feminism to Critical Theories of Race* (New York: Routledge, 2016) is a very useful book for understanding the "critical" methodology, how it differs from liberal approaches, and how it has moved away from class analysis and into identity-based theories.

14. See Pluckrose and Lindsay, *Cynical Theories.*

15. Allison Wiltz, "Why Being Woke Is More Than Being Kind to Others," *Medium*, April 23, 2023, readcultured.com/why-being-woke-is-more-than-being-kind-to-others-e0140486688c.

16. Sensoy and DiAngelo, *Is Everyone Really Equal?*, xx.

17. Ibid., xx.

18. To get an understanding of how widely approaches to overcoming prejudice and discrimination can differ, one can look at the sheer variety of black intellectuals who address issues of race and racism. They include the Marxist Cedric J. Robinson, *Black Marxism: The Making of the Black Radical Tradition* (Chapel Hill, NC: University of North Carolina Press, 2020); the liberal Thomas Chatterton Williams, "Black and Blue and Blond: Where Does Race Fit in the Construction of Modern Identity?," *Virginia Quarterly Review* 91, no. 1 (2015): 80–87, muse.jhu.edu/article/567018/summary; the libertarian Thomas Sowell, *A Conflict of Visions: Ideological Origins of Political Struggles* (New York: Basic Books, 2007); and the conservative Shelby Steele, *White Guilt: How Blacks and Whites Together Destroyed the Promise of the Civil Rights Era* (New York: Harper Perennial, 2007).

19. Robin J. DiAngelo, *White Fragility: Why It's so Hard for White People to Talk about Racism* (Boston: Beacon Press, 2020).

20. Ibram X. Kendi, *How to Be an Antiracist* (London: Vintage, 2021).

21. Frank Moone, "The Pathology of Masculinity," *Medium*, December 23, 2022, medium.com/writers-blokke/the-pathology-of-masculinity-87318b15550b.

22. Amanda Montañez, "Visualizing Sex as a Spectrum," *Scientific American* (blog), August 29, 2017, blogs.scientificamerican.com/sa-visual/visualizing-sex-as-a-spectrum/.

23. Jane Clare Jones, "'You Are Killing Me': On Hate Speech and Feminist Silencing," *Trouble and Strife*, 2015, www.troubleandstrife.org/new-articles/you-are-killing-me/.

24. Lisa Feldman Barrett, "When Is Speech Violence?," *New York Times*, July 15, 2017, www.nytimes.com/2017/07/14/opinion/sunday/when-is-speech-violence.html.

25. Ijeoma Opara, "It's Time to Decolonize the Decolonization Movement," *Speaking of Medicine and Health*, July 29, 2021, speakingofmedicine.plos.org/2021/07/29/its-time-to-decolonize-the-decolonization-movement/.

Chapter 2

1. See, for example, Robin DiAngelo, in an interview with Soledad O'Brien, "Matter of Fact Listening Tour: The Hard Truth About Bias," YouTube video, uploaded by Matter of Fact, October 8, 2020, youtu.be/JQ0Prpk-cBGs?si=H7rcWKTenGbZNbFT&t=1278.

2. See, for example, this quote from Robin DiAngelo:

> Racial bias does not prevent us from interacting calmly and respectfully with racialized people when decorum demands it, especially when so much of racial bias is implicit rather than consciously held. But even avowed white nationalists can and do tolerate proximity to Black people. Still, implicit forms of bias do surface, often in ways that are unnoticed by the perpetrator. The research on implicit bias is clear; we notice and ascribe meaning and value to racial difference and act accordingly.

Robin DiAngelo, *Nice Racism: How Progressive White People Perpetuate Racial Harm* (Boston: Beacon Press, 2022), 62–63.

3. Nancy Tuana, "The Speculum of Ignorance: The Women's Health Movement and Epistemologies of Ignorance," *Hypatia* 21, no. 3 (2006): 1–19, doi.org/10.1111/j.1527-2001.2006.tb01110.x.

4. The origins of the term "woke" are much more complex than this and more rooted in material reality. It emerged in African American vernacular around the 1930s, although it is hard to date vernacular phrases precisely, and it could be considerably older. The oldest known recorded mention of "stay woke" is by blues musician Lead Belly in an outro to his 1938 protest song "Scottsboro Boys." The blues musician warned his listeners to "stay woke out there" following the false rape accusations against nine black teenagers who had simply refused to leave a train. In this context, the term was a warning to stay alert in an environment in which black people could so easily become victims of false accusations and violence should they antagonize white people by showing insufficient deference. However, the language of "awakening" was also being used by the activist Marcus Garvey as well as within religious organizations (both Christian and Muslim) opposing racism and the labor movement during this same period. What it was precisely that users of the term warned each other to be awake to changed with laws and social norms. As the term evolved, it was used particularly in the context of the black radical tradition and later in Critical Social Justice discourse, where it gained its postmodern element of re-ferring largely to dominant discourses. For a discussion of the origin of the term "woke," see "How Has the Meaning of the Word 'Woke' Evolved?," *Economist*, July 30, 2021, www.economist.com/the-economist-explains/2021/07/30/how-has-the-meaning-of-the-word-woke-evolved. The recording of Lead Belly discussing and singing "Scottsboro Boys" is available at "Lead Belly—'Scotts-boro Boys,'" YouTube video, uploaded by Smithsonian Folkways Recordings, July 2, 2015, www.youtube.com/watch?v=VrXfkPViFIE&embeds_referring_euri=https%3A%2F%2Fwww.vox.com%2F&source_ve_path=OTY3MTQ&-feature=emb_imp_woyt.

5. See Heather Bruce, Robin DiAngelo, Gyda Swaney (Salish), and Amie Thurber, "Between Principles and Practice: Tensions in Anti-Racist Educa-tion—2014 Race & Pedagogy National Conference," Vimeo video, uploaded by Collins Memorial Library, July 26, 2022, vimeo.com/116986053.

6. Jerry Coyne, "The Smithsonian Institution Purveys Critical Race Theo-ry," *Why Evolution Is True*, July 16, 2020, whyevolutionistrue.com/2020/07/16/the-smithsonian-institution-purveys-critical-race-theory/.

7. DiAngelo, *White Fragility*, 119.

8. Ibid., 64

9. Bryan Goodman, "Black Women Often Ignored by Social Justice Movements," press release, American Psychological Association, July 13, 2020, www.apa.org/news/press/releases/2020/07/black-women-social-justice.

10. Ibid.

11. This is the thesis of DiAngelo's *Nice Racism.*

12. Kendi, *How to Be an Antiracist,* 129.

13. DiAngelo, *White Fragility,* 4.

14. Kendi, *How to Be an Antiracist,* 128.

15. Ibid., 140.

16. Ibid., 140.

17. Today's Critical Social Justice antiracists draw less on the work of Martin Luther King Jr. and more on the work of early Critical Race Theorists and its immediate antecedents, including Harvard law professor Derrick A. Bell, who argued, for example, that civil rights law was not aimed to help black people and thus rejected liberal approaches for ending racism, which he saw as permanent and intractable. See Derrick Bell, *And We Are Not Saved: The Elusive Quest for Racial Justice* (New York: Basic Books, 1989).

18. See, for example, Meera Nanda, "We Are All Hybrids Now: The Dangerous Epistemology of Post-Colonial Populism," *Journal of Peasant Studies* 28, no. 2 (2001): 162–186, doi.org/10.1080/03066150108438770; Esther D. Rothblum, Sondra Solovay, and Marilyn Wann, *The Fat Studies Reader* (New York: New York University Press, 2009); and John Coveney and Sue Booth, *Critical Dietetics and Critical Nutrition Studies* (Cham, Switzerland: Springer, 2019).

19. Steven Pinker, *The Blank Slate: The Modern Denial of Human Nature* (London: Penguin, 2019).

20. See, for example, Caroline Lowbridge, "The Lesbians Who Feel Pressured to Have Sex and Relationships with Trans Women," *BBC News,* October 26, 2021; Riley J. Dennis, "Your Dating 'Preferences' Are Discriminatory," *Internet Archive,* video, added June 11, 2017, archive.org/details/videoplayback_20170611.

21. See the fat studies and disability studies chapter in Pluckrose and Lindsay, *Cynical Theories.*

22. Mallory Yu, "Opinion: Harry Potter's Magic Fades When His Creator Tweets," *NPR*, June 10, 2020, www.npr.org/2020/06/10/873472683/harry-potters-magic-fades-when-his-creator-tweets.

23. Roxy Simons, "Here's Everything the Harry Potter Cast Has Said about J.K. Rowling's Transgender Comments," *Newsweek*, December 31, 2021, www.newsweek.com/harry-potter-cast-who-spoke-out-against-j-k-rowling-transgender-remarks-1664256.

24. It is often helpful to cite Frederick Douglass's "Plea for Freedom of Speech in Boston," in which the black intellectual, escaped slave, and abolitionist said:

> Liberty is meaningless where the right to utter one's thoughts and opinions has ceased to exist. That, of all rights, is the dread of tyrants. It is the right which they first of all strike down. They know its power. Thrones, dominions, principalities, and powers, founded in injustice and wrong, are sure to tremble, if men are allowed to reason of righteousness, temperance, and of a judgment to come in their presence. Slavery cannot tolerate free speech. Five years of its exercise would banish the auction block and break every chain in the South.

The full text of the speech, which was delivered on December 9, 1860, is available at Frederick Douglass and Kurt T. Lash, "Frederick Douglass's 'Plea for Freedom of Speech in Boston,'" *Law and Liberty*, August 21, 2019, lawliberty.org/frederick-douglass-plea-for-freedom-of-speech-in-boston/.

25. Greg Lukianoff and Jonathan Haidt, *The Coddling of the American Mind: How Good Intentions and Bad Ideas Are Setting up a Generation for Failure* (United Kingdom: Penguin Books, 2019); Bradley Campbell and Jason Manning, *The Rise of Victimhood Culture: Microaggressions, Safe Spaces, and the New Culture Wars* (New York: Palgrave Macmillan, 2018).

26. Jolivétte Andrew, *Research Justice: Methodologies for Social Change* (Bristol: Policy Press, 2015).

27. José Medina, *The Epistemology of Resistance: Gender and Racial Oppression, Epistemic Injustice, and Resistant Imaginations* (New York: Oxford University Press, 2013).

28. Roger Mortimore and Glenn Gottfried, "A Review of Survey Research on Muslims in Britain," Ipsos, March 21, 2018, www.ipsos.com/en-uk/review-survey-research-muslims-britain-0.

29. Barbara Applebaum, *Being White, Being Good: White Complicity, White Moral Responsibility, and Social Justice Pedagogy* (Lanham: Lexington Books, 2011); DiAngelo, *White Fragility*.

30. The most thorough and current argument for how to understand the principle of color-blindness and live by it is offered by Hughes, *The End of Race Politics*.

31. Kendi, *How to Be an Antiracist*, 128–9; DiAngelo, *White Fragility*, 4.

32. John Eligon, "The 'Some of My Best Friends Are Black' Defense," *New York Times*, February 16, 201 9, www.nytimes.com/2019/02/16/sunday-review/ralph-northam-blackface-friends.html.

33. See the chapter "The Good/Bad Binary" in DiAngelo, *White Fragility* and p. 4.

34. Derald Wing Sue et al., "Racial Microaggressions in Everyday Life: Implications for Clinical Practice," *American Psychologist* 62, no. 4 (2007): 271–286, doi.org/10.1037/0003-066x.62.4.271.

35. For the thread, see Vagina Museum (@vagina_museum), "If you're still with us and feeling inspired by this discussion, the good news is that it's actually quite easy to adapt your language and be more inclusive!," post on X, July 15, 2021, 10:44 a.m., twitter.com/vagina_museum/status/1415683742924824578.

36. DiAngelo, *White Fragility*, 9.

37. Philomena Harrison, "Sitting with Discomfort: Experiencing the Power of Racism and Working to Imagine Ways Forward?," *Critical and Radical Social Work* 10, no. 2 (July 1, 2022): 178–91, doi.org/10.1332/20498602 1x16533768386813.

38. Larry Diamond et al., "Opinion: Americans Increasingly Believe Violence Is Justified If the Other Side Wins," *Politico*, September 10, 2020, www.politico.com/news/magazine/2020/10/01/political-violence-424157.

Chapter 3

1. Sensoy and DiAngelo, *Is Everyone Really Equal?*, 44.

2. DiAngelo, *White Fragility*, 142.

3. Layla Saad, *Me and White Supremacy: How to Recognise Your Privilege, Combat Racism and Change the World* (London: Quercus, 2022), 19.

4. Anthony G. Greenwald et al., "Measuring Individual Differences in Implicit Cognition: The Implicit Association Test," *Journal of Personality and Social Psychology* 74, no. 6 (June 1998): 1464–1480, doi: 10.1037//0022-3514.74.6.1464.

5. Joel Schwarz, "Roots of Unconscious Prejudice Affect 90 to 95 Percent of People, Psychologists Demonstrate at Press Conference," *UW News*, September 29, 1998, www.washington.edu/news/1998/09/29/roots-of-unconscious-prejudice-affect-90-to-95-percent-of-people-psychologists-demonstrate-at-press-conference/.

6. More than fifty papers critical of the IAT and implicit bias are accessible at OSF, osf.io/74whk.

7. Anthony G. Greenwald et al., "Statistically Small Effects of the Implicit Association Test Can Have Societally Large Effects," *Journal of Personality and Social Psychology*, 108, no. 4 (April 2015): 553–61, doi: 10.1037/pspa0000016.

8. Sara E. Gorman and Jack M. Gorman, *Denying to the Grave: Why We Ignore the Facts that Will Save Us* (Oxford: Oxford University Press, 2016).

9. As Haidt writes,

> For millions of years, our ancestors' survival depended upon their ability to get small groups to include them and trust them, so if there is any innate drive here, it should be a drive to get others to think well of us. Based on his review of the research, Leary suggested that self-esteem is more like an internal gauge, a "sociometer" that continuously measures your value as a relationship partner. Whenever the sociometer needle drops, it triggers an alarm and changes our behavior.

Jonathan Haidt, *The Righteous Mind* (New York: Penguin Books, 2013), Kindle, 77.

10. DiAngelo, *Nice Racism*, 149.

11. Lee Jussim et al., "IAT Scores, Racial Gaps, and Scientific Gaps," to appear in *The Future of Research on Implicit Bias*, ed. Jon A. Krosnick et al. (New York: Cambridge University Press, forthcoming), osf.io/mpdx5.

12. Carrie Clark, "Unconscious Bias Training: Social Lubricant or Snake Oil?," briefing, Free Speech Union, September 2020, freespeechunion.org/unconscious-bias-training-social-lubricant-or-snake-oil.

13. Susan Chequer and Michael G. Quinn, "More Error Than Attitude in Implicit Association Tests (IATS), a CFA-MTMM Analysis of Measurement Error," *PsyArXiv*. May 1, 2021, doi:10.31234/osf.io/afyz2.

14. Ibid.

15. Anthony Greenwald and Mahzarin Banaji, *Blindspot: Hidden Biases of Good People* (New York: Delacorte Press, 2013).

16. Greenwald et al., "Statistically Small Effects of the Implicit Association Test."

17. Olivia Goodhill, "The World Is Relying on a Flawed Psychological Test to Fight Racism," *Quartz*, December 3, 2017, qz.com/1144504/the-world-is-relying-on-a-flawed-psychological-test-to-fight-racism#:.

18. Jesse Singal, "Psychology's Favorite Tool for Measuring Racism Isn't Up to the Job," *Cut*, January 11, 2017, www.thecut.com/2017/01/psychologys-racism-measuring-tool-isnt-up-to-the-job.html.

19. Jesse Singal, "The Creators of the Implicit Association Test Should Get Their Story Straight," *New York*, Intelligencer, December 5, 2017, nymag.com/intelligencer/2017/12/iat-behavior-problem.html.

20. Lee Jussim, "12 Reasons to Be Skeptical of Common Claims about Implicit Bias," *Psychology Today*, Rabble Rouser blog, March 28, 2022, www.psychologytoday.com/gb/blog/rabble-rouser/202203/12-reasons-be-skeptical-common-claims-about-implicit-bias.

21. Singal, "Psychology's Favorite Tool for Measuring Racism."

22. German Lopez, "For Years, This Popular Test Measured Anyone's Racial Bias—But It Might Not Work after All," *Vox*, March 7, 2017, www.vox.com/identities/2017/3/7/14637626/implicit-association-test-racism.

23. Lee Jussim et al., "Do IAT Scores Explain Racial Gaps?," paper prepared for the *21st Sydney Symposium of Social Psychology: Applications of Social Psychology*, convened by Joseph P. Forgas et al., Visegrad, Hungary, July 8–12, 2019, www.sydneysymposium.unsw.edu.au/2019/chapters/JussimSSSP2019.pdf.

24. Elizabeth Levy Paluck and Donald P. Green, "Prejudice Reduction: What Works? A Review and Assessment of Research and Practice," *Annual Review of Psychology* 60 (2009): 339–67, doi: 10.1146/annurev.psych.60.110707.163607.

25. Frank Dobbin and Alexandra Kalev, "Why Diversity Programs Fail," *Harvard Business Review*, July–August 2016, hbr.org/2016/07/why-diversity-programs-fail.

26. Patrick Forscher et al., "A Meta-Analysis of Procedures to Change Implicit Measures," *Journal of Personality and Social Psychology* (June 2019), doi: 10.1037/pspa0000160.

27. Tomas Chamorro-Premuzic, "Science Explains Why Unconscious Bias Training Won't Reduce Workplace Racism: Here's What Will," *Fast Company*, June 12, 2020, www.fastcompany.com/90515678/science-explains-why-unconscious-bias-training-wont-reduce-workplace-racism-heres-what-will.

28. Dobbin and Kalev, "Why Diversity Programs Fail."

29. Behavioural Insights Team, "Unconscious Bias and Diversity Training—What the Evidence Says," December 2020, assets.publishing.service.gov.uk/government/uploads/system/uploads/attachment_data/file/944431/2012-14_UBT_BIT_report.pdf.

30. Adam Hahn et al., "Awareness of Implicit Attitudes," *Journal of Experimental Psychology: General* 143, no. 3 (June 2014): 1369–92, doi: 10.1037/a003502.

31. Kristen Liesch, "The Problem with Unconscious Bias Training," Tidal Equality, www.tidalequality.com/blog/dont-do-unconscious-bias-training. See also the relevant study that Liesch cites: Adam D. Galinsky and Gordon B. Moskowitz, "Perspective-Taking: Decreasing Stereotype Expression, Stereotype Accessibility, and In-group Favoritism," *Journal of Personality and Social Psychology* 78, no. 4 (May 2000): 708–24, doi: 10.1037//0022-3514.78.4.708.

32. Michelle Penelope King, "Unconscious Bias Training Does Not Work, Here's How To Fix It," *Forbes*, November 10, 2020, www.forbes.com/sites/michelleking/2020/11/10/unconcious-bias-training-does-not-work-heres-how-to-fix-it/?sh=4f4535df63f0. See also the relevant study that King cites: Michelle M. Duguid and Melissa C. Thomas-Hunt, "Condoning Stereotyping? How

Awareness of Stereotyping Prevalence Impacts Expression of Stereotypes," *Journal of Applied Psychology* 100, no. 2 (March 2015: 343–59, doi: 10.1037/a0037908.

33. Liesch, "The Problem with Unconscious Bias Training."

34. Frank Dobbin and Alexandra Kalev, "Why Doesn't Diversity Training Work?," *Anthropology Now* 10, no. 2 (September 2018): 48–55, doi: 10.1080/19428200.2018.1493182.

35. Paula Caligiuri, "Is Unconscious Bias Training Making Matters Worse?," *HR Daily Advisor*, February 10, 2022, hrdailyadvisor.blr.com/2022/02/10/is-conscious-bias-training-making-matters-worse.

36. Caligiuri, "Is Unconscious Bias Training Making Matters Worse?"

37. Jacquie D. Vorauer, "Completing the Implicit Association Test Reduces Positive Intergroup Interaction Behavior," *Psychological Science* 23, no. 10 (October 2012): 1168–75, doi: 10.1177/0956797612440457.

38. Rohini Anand and Mary-Frances Winters, "A Retrospective View of Corporate Diversity Training from 1964 to the Present," *Academy of Management Learning and Education* 7, no. 3 (September 2008): 356–372, www.jstor.org/stable/40214554.

39. Joanne Lipman, "How Diversity Training Infuriates Men and Fails Women," *Time*, January 25, 2018, time.com/5118035/diversity-training-infuriates-men-fails-women.

40. Tessa L. Dover, Brenda Major, and Cheryl R. Kaiser, "Diversity Policies Rarely Make Companies Fairer, and They Feel Threatening to White Men," *Harvard Business Review*, January 4, 2016, hbr.org/2016/01/diversity-policies-dont-help-women-or-minorities-and-they-make-white-men-feel-threatened.

41. Dobbin and Kalev, "Why Doesn't Diversity Training Work?," 51–52.

42. Lipman, "How Diversity Training Infuriates Men and Fails Women."

Chapter 4

1. These organizations are by no means the only ones to actively promote Critical Social Justice ideology, but they are among the more conspicuous ones. For an essay on how Critical Race Theory informs the thinking and actions of Black Lives Matter, see Angela Onwuachi-Willig, "The CRT of Black Lives Matter," *Saint Louis University Law Journal* 663 (Summer 2022), scholarship.law. bu.edu/faculty_scholarship/3225. The Critical Social Justice lens employed by many organizations and individuals associated with the Black Lives Matter movement can be seen in their initial response to the October 7, 2023, attack on Israel by Hamas. See, for example, Matthew Impelli, "Black Lives Matter Org Praises Hamas, Sparks Backlash," *Newsweek*, October 10, 2023, www. newsweek.com/black-lives-matter-praises-hamas-sparks-backlash-1833630; Jason L. Riley, "Black Lives Matter and the World's Oldest Hatred," *Wall Street Journal*, October 31, 2023, www.wsj.com/articles/black-lives-matter-and-the-worlds-oldest-hatred-anti-semitism-0e0c324e. Both the Southern Poverty Law Center (SPLC) and the American Civil Liberties Union (ACLU) have abandoned many of the liberal principles for which they were once known and embraced Critical Social Justice ideology in whole or in part. See, for example, the educational resources that the SPLC offers through its Learning for Justice program (www.learningforjustice.org/classroom-resources), including its guide for teachers titled *Let's Talk*, which is heavily grounded in Critical Social Justice ideology. *Let's Talk: Facilitating Critical Conversations with Students*, 2nd ed. (Montgomery, AL: SPLC, 2022), www.learningforjustice.org/sites/default/files/2022-09/LFJ-Lets-Talk-September-2022-09062022.pdf. Notably, the most popular video on the SPLC's Learning for Justice YouTube channel is titled "Intersectionality 101," uploaded May 18, 2016, www.youtube.com/watch?v=w6dnj2IyYjE (last accessed February 1, 2024). Regarding the ACLU's shift toward Critical Social Justice ideology, see, for example, its claim that the sex binary is a "myth." Chase Strangio and Gabriel Arkles, "Four Myths About Trans Athletes, Debunked," ACLU.org, www.aclu.org/news/lgbtq-rights/four-myths-about-trans-athletes-debunked; Fraser Myers, "Why Can't the ACLU Say the Word 'Woman'?," *Spiked*, May 12, 2022, www.spiked-online.com/2022/05/12/why-cant-the-aclu-say-the-word-woman/. For more on how the missions of the SPLC and ACLU have changed, see, respectively, David Montgomery, "The State of Hate," *Washington Post Magazine*, November 8, 2018, www.washingtonpost.com/news/magazine/wp/2018/11/08/feature/is-the-southern-poverty-law-center-judging-hate-fairly; Michael Powell, "Once a Bastion of Free Speech, the A.C.L.U. Faces an Identity Crisis," *New York Times*, June 6, 2021, www.nytimes.com/2021/06/06/us/aclu-free-speech.html. For an examination of the ideological nature of the World Professional Association for Transgender Health (WPATH) recommendations, see James

Esses, "WPATH's New Guidelines Promote Ideology over Science," *Reality's Last Stand*, October 3, 2022, www.realityslaststand.com/p/wpaths-new-guidelines-promote-ideology.

2. The first part of this book should enable you to do that. A more in-depth look can be found in Pluckrose and Lindsay, *Cynical Theories*. For an even greater understanding of the theories, it is valuable to read for yourself many of the primary sources from the scholars who advocate them. Many of these sources are cited both here and in *Cynical Theories*.

3. Eric London, "The 'Grievance Studies' Hoax Exposes Postmodernist Charlatans," *World Socialist Web Site*, October 13, 2018, www.wsws.org/en/articles/2018/10/13/pers-o13.html.

4. Glenn Loury, "Black Self-Making," *Glenn Loury* (Substack), July 5, 2021, glennloury.substack.com/p/black-self-making?s=r.

5. Jesse Marczyk, "When It's Not about Race per Se," *Psychology Today*, Pop Psych blog, November 18, 2016, www.psychologytoday.com/gb/blog/pop-psych/201611/when-its-not-about-race-se; David Pietraszewski et al., "Constituents of Political Cognition: Race, Party Politics, and the Alliance Detection System," *Cognition* 140 (2015): pp. 24-39, doi.org/10.1016/j.cognition.2015.03.007.

6. Thomas F. Pettigrew and Linda R. Tropp, "A Meta-Analytic Test of Intergroup Contact Theory," *Journal of Personality and Social Psychology* 90, no. 5 (2006): 751–83, doi: 10.1037/0022-3514.90.5.751.

7. Thomas Chatterton Williams, *Self-Portrait in Black and White: Unlearning Race* (London: John Murray, 2021); Thomas Sowell, *Discrimination and Disparities* (London: Basic Books, 2019); Steele, *White Guilt*; McWhorter, *Woke Racism*.

8. See, for example, the creation of the Council on Academic Freedom at Harvard (sites.harvard.edu/cafh/). As Harvard law professor Mark Ramseyer wrote in an email to a university list,

> Harvard is a vastly less tolerant place than it was when I arrived in 1998. The intolerance is a function of an increasingly large fraction of our colleagues. And we—the rest of us on the Harvard faculty—let it happen. The cancelling, the punishments, the DEI bureaucracy, the DEI statements, the endless list that we could all recite—all this happened on our

watch. We saw it happen, but we did nothing. We were too busy. We were scared to speak up. We—we on the faculty—let Harvard become what it is. The Harvard that we have is the result of our own collective moral failure. The alumni who are furious are not trying to turn Harvard into something we do not want. They are trying to rescue Harvard from what we let it become. We as a faculty failed. That is why the alumni are speaking up. That is why we formed the Council on Academic Freedom in the first place.

As quoted by Carole Hooven (@hoovlet) in a post on X, December 18, 2023, 2:15 p.m., twitter.com/hoovlet/status/1736827574527934572.

9. Stephen Hawkins et al., *Hidden Tribes: A Study of America's Polarized Landscape* (New York: More in Common, 2018), hiddentribes.us/.

10. Sylvia R Karasu, "What Is Preference Falsification?," *Psychology Today* (Sussex Publishers, April 27, 2021), www.psychologytoday.com/gb/blog/the-gravity-weight/202104/what-is-preference-falsification.

Chapter 5

1. For example, *Critical Race Theory: An Introduction*, explicitly numbers "critique of liberalism" in its core tenets, saying: "[C]ritical race scholars are discontented with liberalism as a framework for addressing America's racial problems. Many liberals believe in color blindness and neutral principles of constitutional law. They believe in equality, especially equal treatment for all persons, regardless of their different histories or current situations." Richard Delgado, Jean Stefancic, and Angela Harris, *Critical Race Theory: An Introduction*, 3rd ed. (New York: New York University Press, 2017), Kindle, 26. This is deemed unsatisfactory because of the belief in unconscious bias, as the authors go on to explain: "But if racism is embedded in our thought processes and social structures as deeply as many crits believe, then the 'ordinary business' of society—the routines, practices, and institutions that we rely on to do the world's work—will keep minorities in subordinate positions. Only aggressive, color-conscious efforts to change the way things are will do much to ameliorate misery" (p. 27).

2. See, for example, Chrstian Spencer, "Former Leader of Black Lives Matter Slams the Organization for Stances on Black Families and Education," *Hill*, June 2, 2021, thehill.com/changing-america/respect/equality/556552-former-leader-of-black-lives-matter-slams-the-organization/.

3. John Sailer, "Diversity, Equity, and Inclusion Is Tearing Academia Apart," *Unherd*, August 10, 2022, unherd.com/thepost/diversity-equity-and-inclusion-is-tearing-academia-apart/.

4. Office for Faculty Equity and Welfare, "Sample Rubric for Assessing Candidate Contributions to Diversity, Equity, Inclusion, and Belonging," University of California, Berkeley, ofew.berkeley.edu/recruitment/contributions-diversity/rubric-assessing-candidate-contributions-diversity-equity.

5. "Assistant/Associate/Full Professor of Biology," Liberty University job posting in the *Chronicle of Higher Education*, January 7, 2023, jobs.chronicle.com/job/37430397/assistant-associate-full-professor-of-biology/.

6. "Doctrinal Position," Liberty University, www.liberty.edu/about/doctrinal-statement (last accessed February 1, 2024).

7. See, for example, Kristen Mack and John Palfrey, "Capitalizing Black and White: Grammatical Justice and Equity," MacArthur Foundation, August 26, 2020, www.macfound.org/press/perspectives/capitalizing-black-and-white-grammatical-justice-and-equity.

8. For more on this point of view, see Rachel S. Ferguson, "Juneteenth Is as American as Apple Pie," *Discourse*, June 16, 2023, www.discoursemagazine.com/p/juneteenth-is-as-american-as-apple-pie.

Chapter 6

1. Jennifer Wolak, "Conflict Avoidance and Gender Gaps in Political Engagement," *Political Behavior* 44, no. 1 (July 2020): 133–156, doi.org/10.1007/s11109-020-09614-5; Andreas Friedl et al., "Gender Differences in Social Risk Taking," *Journal of Economic Psychology* 77 (2020): 102182, doi.org/10.1016/j.joep.2019.06.005.

2. Timur Kuran, *Private Truths, Public Lies: The Social Consequences of Preference Falsification* (Cambridge, MA: Harvard University Press, 1997).

3. His concerns were completely valid. See, for example, "University of California Berkeley: University Finally Turns over 'Diversity Statements' Used in

Faculty Hiring Years after FIRE Requested the Public Records," FIRE, www.the-fire.org/cases/university-california-berkeley-university-finally-turns-over-di-versity-statements-used; Jerry Coyne, "Berkeley, DEI, and FIRE," *Why Evolution Is True*, June 20, 2023, whyevolutionistrue.com/2023/06/20/berkeley-dei-and-fire/; "University of North Carolina at Chapel Hill: School of Medicine Conditions Tenure and Promotion on DEI Commitments," FIRE, www.thefire.org/cases/university-north-carolina-chapel-hill-school-medicine-conditions-ten-ure-and-promotion-dei.

4. Bradley Campbell and Jason Manning offer a good explanation of the differing cultural responses to perceived slights in *The Rise of Victimhood Culture.*

5. "Dear Smith College: I Have a Few Requests," YouTube video, uploaded by Jody Shaw, October 28, 2020, video, www.youtube.com/watch?v=blqp-CMChBpI&ab_channel=JodiShaw. See also Bari Weiss, "Whistleblower at Smith College Resigns over Racism," *Free Press*, February 20, 2021, www.thefp.com/p/whistleblower-at-smith-college-resigns.

6. Aaron Terr, "FIRE Calls on Bridgewater State University to Uphold Academic Freedom by Rejecting Proposed Changes to Research-Approval Body," FIRE, July 20, 2021, www.thefire.org/news/fire-calls-bridgewater-state-univer-sity-uphold-academic-freedom-rejecting-proposed-changes.

7. Aaron Terr, in a letter on behalf of FIRE to Bridgewater State University president Frederick W. Clark Jr. dated July 16, 2021, www.thefire.org/re-search-learn/fire-letter-bridgewater-state-university-july-16-2021.

Chapter 7

1. "There is no in-between safe space of 'not racist.' The claim of 'not racist' neutrality is a mask for racism." Kendi, *How to Be an Antiracist*, 9; "All white people are invested in and collude with racism." DiAngelo, *White Fragility*, 11.

2. Marguerite Ward and Rachel Premack, "What Is a Microaggression? 14 Things People Think Are Fine to Say at Work—but Are Actually Racist, Sexist, or Offensive," *Business Insider*, March 2, 2021, www.businessinsider.com/microaggression-unconscious-bias-at-work-2018-6?r=US&IR=T#youre-so-ar-ticulate-1.

3. Elisa van Dam, "Unpacking 'Microaggression'—It's about Impact,

Not Intent," Simmons University Institute for Inclusive Leadership, May 27, 2021, www.inclusiveleadership.com/research-insights/unpacking-microaggression-its-about-impact-not-intent/.

4. Franz Kafka, *The Essential Kafka: The Trial, the Castle, Metamorphosis, Letter to My Father and Other Stories* (Ware: Wordsworth Editions, 2014). The term "Kafka Trap" comes from the 1925 novel *The Trial* by Franz Kafka but refers to a situation in which denial of an accusation is seen as evidence of the truth of the accusation. For example:

> Accuser: "You have been socialized into holding unconscious white supremacist beliefs and require training to dismantle them."

> Defender: "I already despise and actively oppose white supremacist beliefs."

> Accuser: "This is evidence of how unconscious you are of your white supremacist beliefs and how much you need the training."

5. Benjamin Fearnow, "Rashad Turner, Ex-BLM Leader, Calls Out Group, Says It Doesn't Care about Black Families," *Newsweek*, June 1, 2021, www.newsweek.com/rashad-turner-ex-blm-leader-calls-out-group-says-it-doesnt-care-about-black-families-1596611.

Conclusion

1. Curtis Bunn, "Hamstrung by 'Golden Handcuffs': Diversity Roles Disappear 3 Years after George Floyd's Murder Inspired Them," *NBC News*, February 27, 2023, www.nbcnews.com/news/nbcblk/diversity-roles-disappear-three-years-george-floyd-protests-inspired-rcna72026.

2. Jennifer Elias, "Tech Companies Like Google and Meta Made Cuts to DEI Programs in 2023 after Big Promises in Prior Years," *CNBC*, December 22, 2023, www.cnbc.com/2023/12/22/google-meta-other-tech-giants-cut-dei-programs-in-2023.html.

3. Juliana Menasce Horowitz et al., "Support for the Black Lives Matter Movement Has Dropped Considerably from Its Peak in 2020," Pew Research Center, June 14, 2023, www.pewresearch.org/social-trends/2023/06/14/support-for-the-black-lives-matter-movement-has-dropped-considerably-from-its-peak-in-2020/.

4. Musa al-Gharbi, "The 'Great Awokening' Is Winding Down," originally published by *Compact Magazine*, February 8, 2023, musaalgharbi.com/2023/02/08/great-awokening-ending/.

5. Adam William Chalmers and Robyn Klingler-Vidra, "Post-Woke: Corporate America Has Reduced Woke Communications since 2020," *Global Policy*, January 23, 2024, www.globalpolicyjournal.com/blog/23/01/2024/post-woke-corporate-america-has-reduced-woke-communications-2020.

6. Helen Pluckrose, "Can We Please Not Throw LGBT Rights Away?," *The Overflowings of a Liberal Brain* (Substack), September 9, 2023, helenpluckrose.substack.com/p/can-we-please-not-throw-lgbt-rights.

7. Muni Abdi, "Language Is Important: Why We Are Moving Away from the Terms 'Allyship' and 'Privilege' in Our Work," MA Consultancy Ltd., ma-consultancy.co.uk/blog/language-is-important-why-we-will-no-longer-use-allyship-and-privilege-in-our-work.

8. Tre Ventour, "Telling It Like It Is: Decolonisation Is Not Diversity," Diverse Educators, April 1, 2021, www.diverseeducators.co.uk/telling-it-like-it-is-decolonisation-is-not-diversity/.

9. Ashitha Nagesh, "What Exactly Is a 'Karen' and Where Did the Meme Come From?," *BBC News*, July 30, 2020, www.bbc.co.uk/news/world-53588201.

10. Haley D. O'Shaughnessy, "Homonationalism and the Death of the Radical Queer," *Inquiries Journal/Student Pulse* 7, no. 3 (2015), www.inquiriesjournal.com/articles/1003/homonationalism-and-the-death-of-the-radical-queer.

11. "The Lesbians Who Feel Pressured to Have Sex and Relationships with Trans Women," *BBC*, October 26, 2021, www.bbc.com/news/uk-england-57853385.

12. One US survey found that a clear majority of parents were in favor of education about racial history and racism, but much more divided about whether contemporary critical theories of race should be the way to do that. Evan Rhinesmith and J. Cameron Anglum, "Do Parents Want Schools to Be Able to Teach about Racism?," *Education Week*, March 2, 2022, www.edweek.org/teaching-learning/opinion-do-parents-want-schools-to-be-able-to-teach-about-racism/2022/03. A UK bipartisan report revealed the level of unscientific and radical views about gender identity within both education and policy in schools and raised safeguarding concerns. Lottie Moore, *Asleep at the Wheel: An*

Examination of Gender and Safeguarding in Schools (London, Policy Exchange, 2023), available at policyexchange.org.uk/publication/asleep-at-the-wheel/.

13. Bianca Betancourt, "Adele Says It's 'Not Her Job' to Validate Public Perception about Her Body," *Harper's Bazaar*, November 14, 2021, www.harpersbazaar.com/celebrity/latest/a38247581/adele-talks-public-criticism-of-her-body/; Zachary Kussin, "Dieters Say They're Being Shamed for Losing Weight," *New York Post*, July 7, 2021, nypost.com/2021/07/12/diet-backlash-leaves-some-feeling-ashamed-about-weight-loss/.

14. Steven Pinker, "A Five-Point Plan to Save Harvard from Itself," *Boston Globe*, December 11, 2023, www.bostonglobe.com/2023/12/11/opinion/steven-pinker-how-to-save-universities-harvard-claudine-gay/.

15. According to FIRE, Harvard is the worst college in the United States for free speech, placing dead last and receiving the lowest score possible in its 2024 rankings. "2024 College Free Speech Rankings," rankings.thefire.org/. As one example of the school's "abysmal" free speech environment, lecturer and evolutionary biologist Carole Hooven was caught in a "DEI web" at Harvard after stating "banal facts about human biology" that ultimately led her to leave the university. You can read her first-person account at Carole Hooven, "Why I Left Harvard," *Free Press*, January 16, 2024, www.thefp.com/p/carole-hooven-why-i-left-harvard. This made Gay's congressional testimony regarding university policy toward calls for the genocide of Jews all the more striking. As she argued there, "It depends on the context." She later apologized for her remarks. Miles J. Herszenhorn and Claire Yuan, "'I Am Sorry': Harvard President Gay Addresses Backlash over Congressional Testimony on Antisemitism," *Harvard Crimson*, December 8, 2023, www.thecrimson.com/article/2023/12/8/gay-apology-congressional-remarks/.

16. Her involvement in the disciplining of Harvard economist Roland Fryer is especially notable. Winkfield Twyman Jr., "Claudine Gay Made a Career of Attacking Black Scholars. Don't Defend Her for Being Black," *Newsweek*, December 27, 2023, www.newsweek.com/claudine-gay-made-career-attacking-black-scholars-dont-defend-her-being-black-opinion-1855912; Glenn Loury, with John McWhorter, "The Exquisite Irony of Claudine Gay's Downfall," *Glenn Loury* (Substack), January 9, 2024, glennloury.substack.com/p/the-exquisite-irony-of-claudine-gays. Also see the mini-documentary directed by Rob Montz, "How Claudine Gay Canceled Harvard's Best Black Professor," You-

Tube video, uploaded by Blue Kid Productions, March 9, 2022, www.youtube.com/watch?v=m8xWOlk3WIw.

17. Mallory Newall et al., "Americans Divided on Whether 'Woke' Is a Compliment or Insult," Ipsos, March 8, 2023, www.ipsos.com/en-us/americans-divided-whether-woke-compliment-or-insult#:~:text=Two%20in%20five%20(40%25),take%20it%20as%20a%20compliment.

18. "Woke vs. Anti-Woke? Culture War Divisions and Politics," Policy Institute, King's College London, October 2023, www.kcl.ac.uk/policy-institute/assets/woke-vs-anti-woke-culture-war-divisions-and-politics.pdf.

19. Andrea Cavallier, "How Netflix's Woke Reversal Saved It from Going Broke," *Daily Mail*, March 15, 2023, www.dailymail.co.uk/news/article-11863745/How-Netflix-clawed-way-financial-ruin-going-anti-woke.html.

20. Scott Whitlock and Yael Halon, "Disney CEO Bob Iger Tells Employees He Wants to 'Quiet' Down Culture Wars, 'Respect' the Audience," *Fox Business*, November 29, 2022, www.foxbusiness.com/media/disney-ceo-bob-iger-tells-employees-wants-quiet-culture-wars-respect-audience.

21. Jeffrey M. Jones, "More Say Birth Gender Should Dictate Sports Participation," Gallup, June 12, 2023, news.gallup.com/poll/507023/say-birth-gender-dictate-sports-participation.aspx.

22. al-Gharbi, "The 'Great Awokening' Is Winding Down."

23. Pamela Paul, "As Kids, They Thought They Were Trans: Now, They No Longer Do," *New York Times*, February 2, 2024, www.nytimes.com/2024/02/02/opinion/transgender-children-gender-dysphoria.html.

24. Sean Stephens, "Introducing FIRE's Campus Deplatforming Database," FIRE, February 8, 2024, www.thefire.org/news/introducing-fires-campus-deplatforming-database.

25. Tyler Cown, "Update on the New York Times Word Frequency Chart," Marginal Revolution, February 25, 2023, marginalrevolution.com/marginalrevolution/2023/02/update-on-the-new-york-times-word-frequency-chart.html.

26. Slavoj Žižek, "Wokeness Is Here to Say," *Compact Magazine*, February 22, 2023, compactmag.com/article/wokeness-is-here-to-stay.

27. Chalmers and Klingler-Vidra, "Post-Woke."

28. Helen Pluckrose and James Lindsay, "Identity Politics Does Not Continue the Work of the Civil Rights Movements," *Areo Magazine*, September 25, 2018, areomagazine.com/2018/09/25/identity-politics-does-not-continue-the-work-of-the-civil-rights-movements/.

29. Pluckrose, "Can We Please Not Throw LGBT Rights Away?"

30. Adam B. Coleman, "The Anti-Woke Right's Race-Conscious Problem," *Speaking Wrong at the Right Time* (Substack), August 24, 2023, www.adamb-coleman.com/p/the-anti-woke-rights-race-conscious.

31. Jeffrey M. Jones, "Fewer in U.S. Say Same-Sex Relations Morally Acceptable," Gallup, June 16, 2023, news.gallup.com/poll/507230/fewer-say-sex-relations-morally-acceptable.aspx.

32. Alexander von Sternberg, "The Backlash against Sexual Freedom and How to Fix It," *Queer Majority*, July 21, 2023, www.queermajority.com/essays-all/the-backlash-against-sexual-freedom.

33. William Turton, "How Charlie Kirk Plans to Discredit Martin Luther King Jr. and the Civil Rights Act," *Wired*, January 12, 2024, www.wired.com/story/charlie-kirk-tpusa-mlk-civil-rights-act/; "Caucus Clash! + The Myth of MLK | Vince Everett Ellison," Rumble video, streamed by the Charlie Kirk Show, January 15, 2024, rumble.com/v475jn9-caucus-clash-the-myth-of-mlk-vince-everett-ellison-live-1.15.24.html.

34. Isaac Arnsdorf, "Republicans Opposition to LGBTQ Rights Erupts in Backlash to Pride Month," *Washington Post*, June 30, 2023, www.washingtonpost.com/politics/2023/06/30/republicans-pride-month-lgbtq/.

35. Jasmine Aguilera, "What Will Happen to Same-Sex Marriage around the Country If *Obergefell* Falls," *Time*, December 14, 2022, time.com/6240497/same-sex-marriage-rights-us-obergefell/.

36. Pluckrose, "Can We Please Not Throw LGBT Rights Away?"

37. See, in particular, the arguments and activism of Christopher F. Rufo. Christopher F. Rufo, "D.E.I. Programs Are Getting in the Way of Liberal Education," *New York Times*, July 27, 2023, www.nytimes.com/2023/07/27/opinion/christopher-rufo-diversity-desantis-florida-university.html; "Weekend Listen: Debating 'Book Bans' with Yascha Mounk," *Christopher F. Rufo* (Substack), May 28, 2023, christopherrufo.com/p/weekend-listen-debating-book-bans.

38. Corky Siemaszko, "Texas Lawmaker Says 850 Books Ranging from

Race to Sexuality Could Cause 'Discomfort,'" *NBC News*, October 27, 2021, www.nbcnews.com/news/us-news/texas-lawmaker-says-850-books-ranging-race-sexuality-cause-discomfort-rcna3953; Brian Lopez, "Texas House Committee to Investigate School Districts' Books on Race and Sexuality," *Texas Tribune*, October 26, 2021, www.texastribune.org/2021/10/26/texas-school-books-race-sexuality/. The full list is available at static.texastribune.org/media/files/94fee7ff93eff9609f141433e41f8ae1/krausebooklist.pdf.

39. Lukianoff and Schlott, *The Canceling of the American Mind*, 149–155.

40. "Transcript of Arif Ahmed's speech at King's College London," Office for Students, October 10, 2023, www.officeforstudents.org.uk/news-blog-and-events/press-and-media/transcript-of-arif-ahmeds-speech-at-kings-college-london/.

41. Lukianoff and Schlott, *The Canceling of the American Mind*, 143–144.

42. See Nadra Nittle, "Even Dictionaries Aren't Safe from Censorship in This Florida School District," *19th*, January 12, 2024, 19thnews.org/2024/01/florida-escambia-county-book-bans-censorship-dictionaries/; Reshma Kirpalani and Hannah Natanson, "The Lives Upended by Florida's School Book Wars," *Washington Post*, December 21, 2023, www.washingtonpost.com/education/2023/12/21/florida-school-book-bans-escambia-county/; Lisa Tolin, "More Than 1,600 Books Banned in Escambia County, Florida," Pen America, January 9, 2024, pen.org/escambia-county-florida-banned-books-list/.

43. See the discussion about bias in US public schools here: Neal McCluskey, "Are Public School Libraries Accomplishing Their Mission?," Cato Institute, Policy Analysis no. 962, October 17, 2023, www.cato.org/policy-analysis/are-public-school-libraries-accomplishing-their-mission; Paul Best, "How to Combat the Biased School Library Book Selection Process," *Real Clear Education*, January 30, 2024, www.realcleareducation.com/articles/2024/01/30/how_to_combat_the_biased_school_library_book_selection_process_1008498.html.

44. Lukianoff and Schlott, 145.

45. Darryl I. MacKenzie et al., *Occupancy Estimation and Modeling: Inferring Patterns and Dynamics of Species Occurrence*, 2nd ed. (Academic Press, 2018).

46. Leah Henderson, "On the Mutual Exclusivity of Competing Hypotheses" (preprint), 2022, philsci-archive.pitt.edu/20800/.

47. Dobbin and Kalev, "Why Doesn't Diversity Training Work?"

48. Christine Hauser, "Teacher Is Fired for Reading Book on Gender Identity in Class," *New York Times*, April 18, 2023, www.nytimes.com/2023/08/18/us/georgia-teacher-fired-gender-book.html#:~:text=The%20teacher%20in%20Georgia%20was,the%20colors%20blue%20and%20pink; Associated Press, "Georgia Teacher Fired for Reading a Book to Students about Gender Identity," *NBC News*, April 18, 2023, www.nbcnews.com/nbc-out/out-news/georgia-teacher-fired-reading-gender-identity-book-class-rcna100598.

49. Associated Press, "Georgia Teacher Fired for Reading a Book."

50. As the political analyst Ross Douthat wrote,

> In the Trump years we saw that in an atmosphere of political emergency, when fear of populism or authoritarianism organized every left-of-center thought, many liberals struggled to resist demands of ideological fealty made by movements to their left. Now the emergency mentality has retreated, and resistance and skepticism are easier. But what if it comes back, whether under a Trump restoration or in some other form? In that scenario, today's entrenchment of ideological conformity surely bodes well for tomorrow's would-be enforcers. If liberals accept loyalty oaths under calm conditions, what will they accept in an emergency? Probably too much—in which case the next peak of wokeness will be higher, the next revolution more complete.

Ross Douthat, "Is 'Peak Woke' behind Us or Ahead?," *New York Times*, September 16, 2023, www.nytimes.com/2023/09/16/opinion/peak-woke-anti-racism-canceled.html.

Glossary

1. Steven Asarch, "YouTuber Contrapoints Labeled 'TRUSCUM' by Nonbinary Community after Inclusion of Buck Angel in Latest Video," *Newsweek,* October 21, 2019, www.newsweek.com/youtuber-contrapoints-attacked-after-including-controversial-buck-angel-video-1466757.

2. A particularly good example of this comes from the leading white anti-racist theorist, Robin DiAngelo, who, in her book *Nice Racism,* argues that white people receiving "feedback" on their racism from black people should not be defensive but accept it before going on to defend herself against the criticisms of her work by the black linguist John McWhorter (pp. 126–127). To be fair, DiAngelo does acknowledge that black people have diverse viewpoints and that it is not possible to accept them all, saying, "Do I think all feedback I am given from BIPOC people is 100 percent correct and should be followed? How could I? On a daily basis I receive conflicting feedback from BIPOC people and would be immobilized if I tried to follow all of it"(p. 165). However, by discussing the choices she has to make in deciding which black people to ally herself with, DiAngelo exemplifies the ways in which such allyship is with ideological groups and not racial ones. Robin Diangelo, *Nice Racism*.

3. Kendi, *How to Be an Antiracist*, 9–20.

4. Souleymane Bachir Diagne, "Négritude," *Stanford Encyclopedia of Philosophy*, May 23, 2018, plato.stanford.edu/entries/negritude/.

5. Delgado, Stefancic, and Harris, *Critical Race Theory*, 26.

6. Helen Pluckrose, "Demystifying Critical Race Theory so We Can Get to the Point," Counterweight, July 2, 2021.

7. Kagendo Mutua and Beth Blue Swadener, *Decolonizing Research in Cross-Cultural Contexts: Critical Personal Narratives* (Albany, NY: SUNY Press, 2011).

8. Dan Goodley, *Dis-Ability Studies: Theorising Disablism and Ableism* (New York: Routledge, 2014).

9. Richard Kahlenberg, "Affirmative Action Should Be Based on Class, Not Race," *Economist*, September 4, 2018, www.economist.com/open-future/2018/09/04/affirmative-action-should-be-based-on-class-not-race.

10. DiAngelo, *White Fragility*.

11. Tomberry, "Oppression Olympics," *Know Your Meme*, June 28, 2022, knowyourmeme.com/memes/oppression-olympics.

12. See the document titled "Examples of Microaggressions" at www.imperial.ac.uk/media/imperial-college/faculty-of-engineering/public/Resource---Examples-of-Microaggressions.pdf (last accessed July 18, 2022), which is adapted in part from Derald Wing Sue, *Microaggressions in Everyday Life: Race, Gender and Sexual Orientation* (Hoboken, NJ: Wiley & Sons, 2010).

13. I. E. Smith, "Minority vs. Minoritized: Why the Noun Just Doesn't

Cut It," *Odyssey Online*, September 2, 2016, www.theodysseyonline.com/minority-vs-minoritize.

14. Kate Manne, *Down Girl: The Logic of Misogyny* (New York: Oxford University Press, 2018).

15. Jessi Elana Aaron, "'Lame,' 'Stand Up' and Other Words We Use to Insult the Disabled without Even Knowing It," *Washington Post*, May 13, 2015, www.washingtonpost.com/posteverything/wp/2015/05/13/lame-stand-up-and-other-words-we-use-to-insult-the-disabled-without-even-knowing-it/.

16. "White Saviorism: Examples, Impact, and Overcoming It," *Healthline*, July 14, 2021, www.healthline.com/health/white-saviorism#examples.

17. Ellen K. Pao, "We Need to Talk about What It Means to Be 'White-Adjacent' in Tech," *Medium*, May 15, 2021, medium.com/projectinclude/we-need-to-talk-about-what-it-means-to-be-white-adjacent-in-tech-f91fbcce7a42.

18. Anna Lindner, "Defining Whiteness: Perspectives on Privilege," *Gnovis*, 18, no. 2 (Spring 2018): 43–58, hdl.handle.net/10822/1050459.

19. Aja Romano, "A History of 'Wokeness': Stay Woke," *Vox*, October 9, 2020, www.vox.com/culture/21437879/stay-woke-wokeness-history-origin-evolution-controversy.

20. See, for example, "Why 'Womxn' Isn't Exactly the Inclusive Term You Think It Is," *Girlboss*, girlboss.com/blogs/read/womxn-meaning. Meanwhile, some argue that pronouncing "womxn" as "women" or "woman" is not inclusive of blind people, who cannot see the "x." See "Why Womxn with an 'X'?," Womxn's Center for Success, University of California, Irvine, womxnscenter.uci.edu/why-womxn-with-a-x/.

21. Luis Noe-Bustamante, Lauren Mora, and Mark Hugo Lopez, "About One-in-Four U.S. Hispanics Have Heard of Latinx, but Just 3% Use It," Pew Research Center, August 11, 2020, www.pewresearch.org/hispanic/2020/08/11/about-one-in-four-u-s-hispanics-have-heard-of-latinx-but-just-3-use-it/.

Appendix

1. Erec Smith, *A Critique of Anti-Racism in Rhetoric and Composition: The Semblance of Empowerment* (Lanham: Lexington Books, 2020); Shelby Steele, *Shame: How America's Past Sins Have Polarized Our Country* (New York: Basic Books, 2015).

2. Joshua Rhett Miller, "BLM Site Removes Page on 'Nuclear Family Structure' amid NFL Vet's Criticism," *New York Post*, September 24, 2020, ny-post.com/2020/09/24/blm-removes-website-language-blasting-nuclear-family-structure/.

3. See the GoFundMe fundraiser "UKBLM Fund," created by UKBLM on June 2, 2020, www.gofundme.com/f/ukblm-fund.

4. "#DEFUNDTHEPOLICE - Black Lives Matter," Black Lives Matter, blacklivesmatter.com/defundthepolice/.

5. Juliana Menasce Horowitz, "Support for Black Lives Matter Declined after George Floyd Protests, but Has Remained Unchanged Since," Pew Research Center, September 27, 2021, www.pewresearch.org/fact-tank/2021/09/27/support-for-black-lives-matter-declined-after-george-floyd-protests-but-has-remained-unchanged-since/; Lydia Saad, "Black Americans Want Police to Retain Local Presence," Gallup, August 5, 2020, news.gallup.com/poll/316571/black-americans-police-retain-local-presence.aspx.

6. Ashley Jardina, *White Identity Politics* (Cambridge: Cambridge University Press, 2019).

7. Debra Soh discusses the various views among sexologists in her book *End of Gender: Debunking the Myths about Sex and Identity in Our Society* (New York: Threshold Editions, 2020). The leaked files from WPATH provide further cause for grave concern about the medical transition of children and vulnerable adults. This includes links between transgender hormone therapy and cancer and an awareness among professionals who prescribe such treatments that children and even some adults do not always understand the long-term implications of medicalization. Daniel Martin, "Doctors Admit Link between Transgender Hormone Therapy and Cancer in Leaked Emails," *Telegraph*, March 5, 2024, www.telegraph.co.uk/news/2024/03/05/wpath-tansgender-hormone-therapy-cancer-links-leaked-emails/.

Index

About the Author

Helen Pluckrose is a liberal political and cultural writer and was one of the founders of Counterweight. A participant in the Grievance Studies Affair probe that highlighted problems in Critical Social Justice scholarship, she is the coauthor of *Cynical Theories* and *Social (In)justice*. She lives in England and can be found on X @HPluckrose.